"Richthofen is dead.

"All airmen will be pleased to hear that he has been put out of action, but there will be none amongst them who will not regret the death of such a courageous nobleman . . . every member of the Royal Flying Corps would have been proud to shake his hand had he fallen into captivity alive . . ."

from *The Aeroplane,* April, 1918

On the morning of April 21, 1918, a red Fokker triplane was seen to pass low over the trenches in hot pursuit of a British Sopwith Camel. Seconds later, the red triplane banked up on one wing and then glided down to crash behind the Allied lines. Within minutes Aussie soldiers were scavenging the wreck, and by nightfall the word was out: Baron Manfred von Richthofen, the greatest German ace of the war, was dead.

Based on more than fifteen years of research and the eyewitness reports of scores of airmen and ground soldiers, author Dale M. Titler recreates the most dramatic single event of the 1914-1918 air war—*The Day The Red Baron Died.*

DON'T MISS THESE BALLANTINE
WAR BOOKS

The Day The Red Baron Died

Dale Titler

BALLANTINE BOOKS • NEW YORK

An Intext Publisher

SBN 345-02939-9-150

First printing: August 1970
Second printing: November 1972

Cover art by Ivan Barnett

Printed in the United States of America

BALLANTINE BOOKS, INC.
101 Fifth Avenue, New York, N.Y. 10003

Acknowledgements

Grateful recognition is made to the following individuals and institutions:

To my wife, Helen Ruth, who for many years has patiently endured the ghost of a long-dead German flying officer in our home.

To Robert Buie, former Gunner of the 53rd Battery, for his detailed account of the action that made possible the downing of Richthofen, and for the use of supporting documents and photographs.

Oliver C. LeBoutillier, former Captain, 209 Squadron, R.A.F., for his eyewitness account of von Richthofen's fall, and for providing the key, through the revelation of previously undisclosed data, to clarify much of the Richthofen Riddle.

David Greswolde Lewis, former Lieutenant, Number 3 Camel Squadron, R.A.F., now retired Undersecretary, Administration, Department of Native Affairs, Salisbury, for his exciting account in the chapter: "Today You; Tomorrow Me."

H. E. Hart, former Sergeant and Battery Clerk of the 53rd Battery, later its official historian, for his informative account of the activities during and following the decisive encounter.

Special recognition is deserved by three gentlemen whose unselfish labor provided historical accuracy, color, and details so necessary for the recording of this chronicle:

Major-General Leslie E. Beavis (retired), C.B., C.B.E., D.S.O., former Commander of the 53rd Battery, Australian Field Artillery.

General der Flieger a.D. Karl Bodenschatz, former adjutant of Jagdgeschwader Number 1 in its brightest hours and its darkest day.

Air Chief Marshal Sir Robert M. Foster, K.C.B., C.B., C.B.E., D.F.C., former 209 Squadron pilot, RAF, and participant in von Richthofen's final air engagement. R. L. C. Hunt, P. Frith, R. McDiarmid, T. G. Lovell, J. D. Work, D. L. Fraser, E. C. Tibbits, K. McKay, J. V. Rake, R. Ross, E. P. L. deBomford, H. D. Billings, R. Barker and T. Faunt, all of whom were able to document details of the final action and the events that followed the crash. T. C. Pendlebury, for supplying valuable research information, and R. J. Falconer, A. H. Smith, N. H. Ramsden, Guy Round, G. E. Golding, J. M. Prentice, J. Willats, A. G. Franklyn and E. C. Banks for supporting data.

Major-General Basil Morris (Retired) and Major-General J. H. Cannan (Retired) formerly of the Australian Imperial Force, for the use of their valued comments regarding the event.

Frank R. McGuire, for his valued advice and clarifications, and for permission to use data that appeared in his articles: *Who Killed von Richthofen?* (*Cross and Cockade*, Summer 1963), and *The Richthofen Controversy, Part I*, 1918-1962 (*Cross and Cockade*, Spring 1967).

Mrs. Herman Brown, for English translations of German letters and publications, and A. Koster, M.D., former Captain of Infantry, German Imperial Army, for his eyewitness accounts of the shooting down of D. G. Lewis, R. Raymond-Barker, and Manfred von Richthofen.

Mrs. George Bridge, and Mr. Stephen St. Martin, for the use of photographs of 209 Squadron personnel.

To Dennis Connell, and to Frank, whose devotion to this subject and whose tireless efforts behind the scenes is deserving of my sincere thanks, and to Lieutenant-Colonel K. S. Brown (Retired), former Director of the Air Force Museum, for assistance in research.

The United States Weather Bureau; Mr. John P. Webber, Head of Library, for photostats of the British, French and American weather maps for April 20, 21 and 22, 1918. Mr. Huron Marmon, U.S. Weather Bureau Forecaster, and Mr. Walter Campbell, Weather Technician, U.S. Army, for an analysis of the meteorological conditions prevailing at the time of von Richthofen's fall. Doctors Doyle E. Sharpe and William Bullock, Jr., former flight surgeons, USAF Medical Corps, for medical clarification of the effects of the wounds sustained by von Richthofen.

The Australian War Memorial, its present director, W. R. Lancaster, Canberra; its former director, J. McGrath, and their patient staff who supplied official reports, photographs and comments as well as permission to quote reprints from Dr. C. E. W. Bean's *Official History of the A.I.F. in France*. The Imperial War Museum, London; A. J. Charge and J. A. Golding, for the use of photographs and documentary data. The Royal Canadian Military Institute, Toronto; W. A. Stewart, Librarian, for information and assistance.

Mr. Edgar Meos and Mr. Jerry Sloniger for details on the later activities of Wolfram von Richthofen.

These publishers: The Robert McBride Company, for permission to quote from Richthofen's *The Red Battle Flyer*. Grosset and Dunlap, for excerpts reprinted from *The Fighters* by Thomas R. Funderburk. Copyright © 1965, 1966 by Thomas R. Funderburk, by permission of the publisher, Grosset and Dunlap, Inc. Ryerson Press, for excerpts from *Pilots of the Purple Twilight* by Philip Godsell, published by Ryerson Press, Toronto. Holt, Rinehart and Winston for excerpts from *They Fought for the Sky* by Quentin Reynolds, copyright © 1957. The *Ottawa Journal*, for excerpts from a Canadian Press news agency dispatch from Toronto printed in the *Ottawa Journal* of December 1, 1925. The Sydney *Daily Mirror* for permission to quote from a historical article that appeared in the April 27, 1953, issue of the *Daily Mirror* Newspaper, Sydney, Australia. *Mirror Newspapers Limited*, Sydney, for permission to quote from a letter written by J. M. Prentice, ex-Lieutenant, 39th Battalion, First A.I.F. The *Newcastle Sun,* Newcastle, New South Wales, for permission to quote from a letter written by a former German spy who commented on the death of von Richthofen. The *Toronto Star Syndicate*, for permission to use several excerpts concerning A. R. Brown and W. R. May. *Reveille Magazine,* Anzac Memorial, Hyde Park, Sydney, for excerpts from A. R. Brown's letter to the editor. The *Chicago Tribune* News Service, The *Carleton Place Canadian* and the *Edmonton Journal*, for background data. Knorr, Hirth Verlag, Munich, for the use of photographs from Bodenschatz's *Jagdstaffel In Flandern Himmel*, 1940. *Truth and Sportsman Magazine,* Sydney, the *Melbourne Herald*, the *Sydney Evening News* and the *Murwillumbah Daily News* for materials from their files and publications. *A. Weichert Verlag*, Hanover, and *Verlag Ullstein*, Frankfurt, for the use of photographs and quotations from books by Udet and Richthofen.

From *The Aeroplane*, April, 1918:

Richthofen is dead.

All airmen will be pleased to hear that he has been put out of action, but there will be none amongst them who will not regret the death of such a courageous nobleman. Several days ago, a banquet was held in honour of one of our aces. In answering the speech made in his honour, he toasted Richthofen, and there was no one who refused to join. Both airmen are now dead. Anybody would have been proud to have killed Richthofen in action, but every member of the Royal Flying Corps would also have been proud to shake his hand had he fallen into captivity alive.

His death is bound to have a gravely depressing effect on the German Flying Service for obviously the younger and less brave will argue that if a von Richthofen cannot survive their chances must be small. Equally his death is an encouragement to every young French and British pilot who can no longer imagine that every skillful German pilot that attacks them is von Richthofen himself.

Manfred von Richthofen is dead. He was a brave man, a clean fighter and an aristocrat. May he rest in peace.

Very best congratulations to No. 209 Squadron and Captain Brown on bringing down the redoubtable von Richthofen.

General J. M. Salmond

To: 5th Australian Division—Major General T. J. Hobbs

No. 3801 Gunner R. Buie

    53rd Battery, Australian Field Artillery

Please convey to 53rd Battery 5th Australian Division my best thanks and congratulations on having brought down the celebrated German aviator RICHTHOFEN.

General H. S. Rawlinson

Contents

ABOUT
THIS TESTIMONY

About This Testimony

A documentary account of the fall of Germany's great warbird—as told by those who witnessed it.

With the accounts of:

Robert Buie   former Gunner, 53rd Battery, 14th Battalion, Australian Field Artillery

H. E. Hart   former Sergeant, Battery Clerk and Official Historian of the 53rd Battery, A.I.F.

David Greswolde Lewis   former Lieutenant, Number 3 Camel Squadron, R.A.F.

Oliver Colin LeBoutillier   American volunteer, former Captain and Flight Leader of 209 Squadron, R.A.F.

This book is about a singular event in air-war history, a battleground on the Western front, and a sudden death that was destined to spark half a century of controversy.

But mostly, this book is about a misty Sunday morning in April of 1918, the day Manfred von Richthofen was shot and killed. For 52 years sensationalists have filled the undocumented gaps of this day with lurid and dramatic imaginings. For all it was worth, they moulded the war drama of a national tragedy and highlighted the mystery and contention. In time, the facts of this gallant nobleman's violent finish became so enmeshed in fiction that the early war records and eyewitness accounts were submerged in a sea of fabrications.

In the first section, *Days Before*, I have included two chapters of background. *Postscripts*, the final section, tells of the later activities of the men whose accounts are contained here. These asides should place the events of April 21st in perspective.

It was in 1939, when an air war in Spain was ending, and a new one was beginning in Poland, that I became interested in the controversial death of Baron von Richthofen. World War I had already been thoroughly documented, its chaos recorded and its histories told. The valiant deeds of every battle were known. But somehow, perhaps because of faulty reporting, inexplicable military machinations, or the personal wishes of men in power, the death of von Richthofen would not remain a part of the past. Like a restless ghost this episode returned again and again to hover at the side of the war historians. Neither Jones nor Bean, official RAF and Australian war historians, could agree, after an extensive collection of data, as to how the great ace met his death.

I began to collect notes, pictures, maps and data of the event, and slowly, the question of what had transpired whetted my curiosity as to who—in fact—vanquished Germany's Red Knight of the Sky. Soon there were several notebooks; one marked *Richthofen-General*, one labeled, *Australian Accounts*, another, *The Air Battle*, and still another, *After The Crash*. One had the heading: *Medical Evidence*. It was interesting (and at times bewildering) to read the varied reports of what allegedly happened before, during, and after the ace's fall. Australian recorders claim Richthofen was shot down by a ground gunner; the English historians insisted that the flier was killed during the air fight.

Early in the compilation, I discovered that the accuracy of certain official records was open to serious question. Some official and quasi-official reports on the death blow bristled with inconsistencies, even as to the nature and extent of the wound that killed the famous fighter. Here was the clear truth that in the heat and hell of combat the eyes can play tricks, vision and sound can be deceptive, time may be compressed in the mind of one man; lengthened for another, and the myriad emotions experienced in the thick of battle may well color those narratives later put down calmly on paper.

Six years ago, when my interest in the argument reached its height, I established contact with a number of men who observed this moment in air-war history. The result was a formidable file of correspondence from former ground troopers and combat pilots, among them O. C. LeBoutillier—whom I personally interviewed at length—an American volunteer who served with 209 Squadron of the R.A.F. Another who personally related what he saw was H. E. Hart of the 53rd Battery, Australian Field Artillery. Slowly, item by item, the pieces formed a different picture, and into it I wove the testimonies of these men, sometimes as narrative, sometimes in their precise phrasing. A few eyewitnesses were able to describe the situation so well that I reported the entire conversations.

My only misgiving after completing this work is that I may be regarded as an authority on the subject. On the contrary, the only authorities are those who took part in the action. The men who knew and flew with Richthofen; the men who were gathered around the 53rd Battery when the famous all-red *dreidecker* became a target. Those airmen who viewed the chase from overhead. The Australians who pulled Richthofen's body from his smashed machine, laid it gently on the ground, identified it and reported the facts within minutes. The diggers and medics who examined the Baron's body beside the wreckage, later at the 53rd's dugout, and still later on a crude table in a spare tent hangar of the Australian Flying Corps. The men who prepared it for burial and conducted the funeral services on the 22nd. Here are the only experts, and in the light of their accumulated testimonies, the opinions of those who were not present do not carry much credence.

We shall never know all of the facts of this singular skirmish. Still, enough has now been gathered to reach the long-overdue conclusion and put aside all doubt as to how the famous Rittmeister was killed—and by whom.

In treating those remaining areas of disagreement, I decided to present the accounts according to (1) the relationship of an event with what occurred immediately before or after it, and (2) the weight of the evidence that supported one version. I confess that I took liberties in describing the actions and thoughts of certain officers and men. I did this only when the actions and thoughts could be based on what the individual actually knew or did at the time. If this is journalism, I trust it is of the honest variety.

Much of what has been written about the Baron's last rendezvous ignored the rich source of research material waiting in Australia. Unfortunately, too many writers were content to fan the flames of controversy in reviving the tired old puzzle for sensation's sake.

To be perfectly candid, what happened on that crisp Spring morning in 1918 was a rather simple act of war. An experienced—and tired—fighter pilot violated his own tactical concept, and paid the price.

Dale M. Titler
Gulfport, Mississippi
April 21, 1970

THE 20th
OF APRIL

CHAPTER ONE
Cappy

On spring days like this one, the young Rittmeister usually lounged in the adjutant's office, heavy with its scent of peat smoke and damp wool. They would sip chicory braced with cognac and listen to the rain. And talk. But on this gray-leaden Saturday afternoon the Commander decided to continue his self-imposed exile and clear away overdue details.

The rain made a steady drumming sound on the barracks roof; its patter against the windows mingled with the sounds of the gently creaking field stove. Usually he had no difficulty in composing his thoughts for paper. He had drawn the field desk near for comfort, but the words would not come. There seemed to be no respite from the melancholy that engulfed him. His old head wound had pained him earlier, but that had passed.

It was his coming leave—and Cappy. He had not been quite the same person since Jagdgeschwader I moved here where all his Staffels were on one base. From his headquarters he commanded a fair view of the field and hangar row. The place was five kilometers from a desolated village, near the bank of the Somme where the river flows due west. It was large for an operational airfield; a place of circus marquees and low wooden barracks, huts, wagon-mounted fuel drums and gaudy— uncommonly gaudy—flying machines. When their engines whirled, popped, and roared, the air became fetid with the sickeningly sweet aroma of castor oil. And there was always the mud. Soupy, brown-black French earth flecked with white calcium.

In the dim half-light of every dawn the tents loomed spectrally, faint etchings against a gray backdrop. Shadowy mechanics disappeared into the black mouths of the circus tents and reappeared with squat, oil-streaked triplanes. It was a place where the Fatherland's finest war machines—the highly maneuverable and deadly Fokker Dr.Is—were prosaically readied for war in the sky. Yet it was a place not so near to the front; larks could still pause in their morning flight to huddle on the wires of the telephone shack.

His pen scratched erratically and paused. Once again some motion on the far road caught his eye. Infantry. The guns and troops passed less frequently now, but with more urgency. A crawling, square lorry rocked in the ruts behind a plodding horse-drawn munitions wagon. The back of the animal glistened in the mist and when it tossed its tired head the young man in the warm room remembered the chestnut mare his father had once given him. *Santuzza.* It was in the autumn of 1912, when he had earned his epaulettes.

Half a mile behind the creeping lorry trudged a company of dirty infantry. He watched them for a moment because he still could not concentrate on air tactics. If he would not think about his leave . . . It would begin on Monday, when he and Joachim Wolff would depart for the Black Forest to hunt quail as the guests of Herr Voss, father of his late Staffelführer, Werner Voss. He looked forward to his favorite pastime, to seeing the German countryside again, especially in April, when the budding woods were beautiful with birches and junipers and chestnuts. And the villages with their familiar half-timbered dwellings. The barns, and the orchards with their white-washed tree trunks. How different they were from the rustic untidiness of the French farms. They planned to fly there in the old Albatros C. III, but if foul weather prevailed, they had train reservations and the tickets were even now on the adjutant's desk.

He hoped they could fly. Fly relaxed and free over the

peaceful meadows spread with the first flowers, and through calm skies, blue and clean. Through white clouds where there were no lurking English scouts. Now his pen began to scratch again, and he wrote without pausing.

Like a dark wedge, the wet company of field-gray infantry passed westward along the worn road. The column approached what had been a cluster of white-washed houses with thatched roofs. Once they were surrounded with wheat fields that gleamed in the slanting light of a summer afternoon. Once there was a smooth meadow on the outskirts where cows had grazed, where the farmland nestled beside the wood, its earth freshly turned for spring planting.

The miserable heap of ruins no longer had any semblance of that farm village. The waves of bloody, mire-streaked men and horse artillery that surged through the square a few days before had converted the cluster of dwellings to a heap of rubble in the span of a morning. The windows of the scarred houses were holes. Chimneys had scattered their bricks with abandon. Beams and shingles lay in splintered heaps, buried in crushed masonry. Here a shutter hung awkwardly by a hinge, there a door was shattered. The square had been wrenched with violence. On the far side one roof was standing; but it was only a framework of lattice devoid of shingles. Nor had the big guns overlooked what was once a row of gentle hemlocks along the main road into the village.

A wall. It belonged to a house that now spilled on the cobblestone street. Everywhere were ruined and demolished structures, remnants of houses, and jagged tree trunks.

On the outskirts the company found the muddy banks of the water-filled ditches cluttered with tangles of splintered trees and trash. The nearby woods were devastated and the trees were uprooted. Everywhere the artillery bursts had plowed the ground.

An occasional tree stood alone on the battlefield,

naked, fractured, and seeming much out of place. In shell holes and low places the faint odor of sulphur lingered. Underfoot were the tools of war that had been scattered and abandoned in General Sir Hubert Gough's desperate counter charge that failed to stem the German wave. Ammunition boxes, burned-out tanks, a shell-smashed lorry, crushed mess kits and dead, torn pack animals that had been dragged off the road. Gas masks lay where they had been dropped by tin-hatted Anzacs and Tommies.

As he advanced, the German foot soldier was at last able to learn how deficient in power he really was. Compared with British provisions and equipment he was—except for weapons—a threadbare and hungry fighting man. In the enemy's abandoned food stores he found an affluence of bacon, beef, cheese, wines, and sweets. Even the British horses had an ample ration of oats. The German's daily fare was plain, and the family he left at home was also ill fed. Taken prisoner, he bolted his food down as would any half-starved man. The British found their prisoners to be very young or men of fifty and over. Some youngsters said they were only 17 but looked 15. Many had never shaved.

The young recruits of the trudging company had been strangely morose for the last three miles. An hour earlier they had their first look at the war—a pathetic huddle of wet French refugees stumbling along the roadside. The children, wide-eyed, clutched their parents' hands or clung to their mothers' skirts as the soldiers moved past. A few whimpered and the older girls led the little ones, stumbling forward. They kept looking back at the fading column. One or two held muddy threadbare dolls, and all were deathly silent when the troops passed. The old bearded peasants glowered and kept silent.

The infantrymen had found their way easier on the hard cobblestone street of the French village. The ruins were behind them now, and once again they sloshed ankle-deep in mire, each great bobbing head dark against the milky gray overcast. Rain dripped from the stocks of their reversed rifles; their helmets gleamed softly in the half-light of the late afternoon. Low grumblings mingled with the muted sounds of boots on soupy earth as the men softly cursed the slippery path and the rain that drizzled on them. Somewhere a dog howled.

The downpour slackened after they had passed through the ruins, but now a chill wind came and pushed the wetness into their soaked ponchos and the damp wool of their battle dress. The wind was stronger now, and they leaned into it. It was a miserable corduroy road that led to the front, made by steel-rimmed wagons drawn by tired, boneyard nags and narrow-wheeled lorries. The soldiers plodded, heads down, gaunt faces expressionless, and listening to the monotonous sucking sounds of their boots. Under their ponchos the mess tins made muffled rattles and every man in the company thought of warm food.

A bearded one growled and hitched his Mauser higher on his broad back. He was thinking of sleeping in the wet reserve trenches this night. He knew the front and he enjoyed scaring the recruits. He told them that tomorrow they would be privileged to play hide and seek with the daisy cutters.

The sallow-faced recruits, who had been silent, were having thoughts of the lines ahead. As they cocked their ears to each distant rumble the tension built within them. They had the look of boys playing at soldier. Their boots were too big and their patched uniforms hung on narrow, stooped shoulders. Downy features were almost lost under their helmets.

The low babble in the column dropped to guarded whispers. The company commander, an esthetic-faced youngster, trotted up the line astride a mare that had known better days. In his steel helmet the officer resembled the knights who must have traveled this very road a time long past. His mount splashed little fountains of mud on the near file, and the troops shielded their faces and cringed as the animal clomped abreast of them. A chorus of low protests rippled through the ranks in the wake of their mounted leader.

The formation rounded a gentle curve in the road and

left the main path for a smaller road across the fields. A dripping copse of young poplars that had somehow evaded destruction fell away to reveal a cluster of brown circus tents. Three stubby triplanes were parked in a neat row before the gaping mouth of the nearest tent, their wings rocking gently in the fresh breeze. Mechanics were rolling others from the darkened openings. The gay coloring of the machines—yellows, blues, and reds—clashed sharply with their dismal surroundings.

On the opposite side of the road, in a cluster, wooden barracks and a few umbrella tents were arranged in no particular order. The brown-gray buildings looked warm and cozy and dry with the smoke wisping from their stovepipe chimneys.

A stoop-shouldered rookie grinned at the buildings. "Now there's the outfit for us, comrades. Talk about the comforts of home—those fellows have it. Warm beds, dry blankets, clean underwear every week . . ."

"And frauleins."

"—and real pig," the youth continued. "None of this ground fish for sausage and burnt roots for coffee."

". . . real liver-sausage and good liquor in the mess every night . . ."

The bearded veteran stared at the machines. "My cousin was an observer in one of those flimsy things. He smashed down burning at Verdun. Fell into a village that looked like the one we just passed—what was it?"

"Cappy," the lance-corporal said.

"Fried to a crisp," the older man went on. "Scraped them up with a spade and buried them in a rations box."

A downy faced boy-soldier shivered under his poncho. "Sometimes the engines stop."

"Huh," grunted grizzle-beard. "Or the French 75s pluck you out of the sky—*poof* . . . or the English shoot you in back with their little scout machines." He shook his head and wiped the back of his broad peasant hand across his whiskers. "I'll take my chances in the line. I won't have far to fall."

One recruit hitched his 98 on his shoulder like an old hand and agreed matter-of-factly, "You couldn't get me up in one of them. I don't need a full belly and a warm bed that badly."

A few laughed. Their lance-corporal glanced up quickly, but the Leutnant was 300 yards ahead. He had slowed his mount to a walk.

One private whistled low. "Look at the colors of those machines!"

The veteran's eyes narrowed. "There's only one flying squadron with machines like that. I saw them in action over—"

"Quiet!" the lance-corporal snapped. The men glanced forward. Their commander had reined his mount before a moustached officer in a dress cap and poncho who was waiting for the column to pass. The horseman saluted smartly and spoke to the ground officer.

" . . . and a few front hogs returning from leave," they overheard as they squished past. "But mostly recruits going into action for the first time. If the weather continues to clear, I can have them in the reserve trenches by nightfall."

The moustached officer nodded. It was not usual for troops to be allowed to cut across the airfield, but it was shorter, and the front waited.

"Who commands these Fliegers?" the horseman asked.

"Rittmeister von Richthofen," the officer replied. "I am Oberleutnant Bodenschatz, Geschwader adjutant . . ."

The troop passed out of earshot and the emaciated rookie with the smooth features whispered hoarsely, *"Did you hear that! This is von Richthofen's Fliegers. He has shot down over 75 of the enemy—more than any pilot in the war!*

"I know," nodded grizzly-beard. "As I said, I saw him in action last month—over Lechelle. Quite a show."

"Look at the scarlet machine," marveled the stoop-shouldered one.

"That's the one I saw. The Baron's personal bird."

"It looks like it was dipped in blood."

The bearded one stifled a chuckle. "Probably was," he said, with a sly wink to the lance-corporal.

Twenty-eight-year-old Karl Bodenschatz, polished and immaculate except for his spattered boots, passed his eyes over the departing company. In his gaze there was no contempt for the foot soldier. He could find no humor in the sight of bent men struggling under their packs on a slippery road. There was only sympathy—and something of sadness in his eyes. Forty-eight years later the warmth remained when he wrote: "They always asked about Richthofen. Relations with the ground soldiers were friendly ... the troops were very thankful for air support."

Bodenschatz was a former infantry officer. He had seen the war in all its naked brutality. This company would reach the front at dusk—the worst time for the new men. If the enemy made a night attack they would be especially confused. The rain had already soaked their blankets and seeped through their tunics. They were cold and they would never be dry as long as they were in the parapets. Their uniforms would stay gritty with dried mud, their rifles would be caked, and when they went over the top, no man's land would run everything together in the brown-yellow pools of water in the shell holes. There would be torn red flesh and streams of blood from the sick, wounded and dead. It would trickle into the whirlpools of water ... and some of them would be pounded into the earth with it. Bodenschatz reflected that his lot could be worse than that of an administrative officer of a chaser group—then he continued on his way to the commander's quarters.

In the warm hut, the Rittmeister lifted his pale blue eyes and gazed out the window. He tapped his pen absently on the desk. Through the moisture-fogged glass he recognized the approaching figure that sloshed stiffly through the mud. Every step spun flakes of wet earth from the toes of the adjutant's boots as he stepped gingerly over the water-filled ruts.

Beyond the adjutant, the commander saw ragged

gray-blue patches between scattered breaks in the overcast. A few dark clouds rolled low in the distance, but the drizzle had slackened and a breeze was tearing at the wisps of low scud to the southwest. Manfred von Richthofen realized that for the past half hour he had been so absorbed in his work that he failed to notice the clearing skies.

Bodenschatz's boots sounded on the step; there was a single apologetic rap and the door opened, admitting a cold, damp gust with the man. He stepped into the room quietly, for the Rittmeister frequently napped in the afternoon, but when he saw his commander at the desk, he smiled and closed the door with a clatter. His face was ruddy from the brisk walk and his poncho dripped water in thin rivulets.

Richthofen looked up and acknowledged the handsome officer. Bodenschatz informed the Rittmeister that the weather service was reporting clearing skies in their sector. *Flugmeldedienst* indicated enemy air activity at Treux and Albert. He had posted a patrol; there was still time.

Von Richthofen nodded and laid the pen in its holder. He felt a quiet comradeship toward this man whom he had invited to become his adjutant almost a year earlier, and to whom he could confidently entrust any of his military matters—short of leading his Jastas into combat. Bodenschatz was not a pilot.

Richthofen half-turned in his chair and slowly drew a gold watch from his trousers pocket. It was a few minutes before 6 PM. He pursed his lips in thought, nodded again and agreed there was still time to find an Englishman. He stood up slowly and stretched his athletic form into a backward arc. A thin smile played on his face and he squinted his pale eyes. He ventured that no doubt the cubs were restless . . . not a good day's hunting for almost a week. Bodenschatz nodded and said that several were already on the alert line. Jasta 11. He asked how many he should post for patrol.

Richthofen reflected for a moment, hands on hips. He

was not tall, but he had the solid quality of a man who would be obeyed. Not a martinet, he could justify every order if he had to. But he was never asked.

His smile widened, and this was unusual for Richthofen's smiles were rare—and mysterious. He told Bodenschatz that as many as wished could go . . . that they must keep their hand in the business or they'd forget how to bag a Lord.

Bodenschatz asked if that included the fledgling— their newest member. The Baron did not reply immediately. He listened to the chill wind slap the window pane and rattle the door. Then he shook his head and decided Wolfram could await better conditions for his first hunt. He knew the air was rough aloft and the newcomer would have trouble holding the formation. Tomorrow would be better. He told Bodenschatz he would be at the planes in a quarter of an hour.

The adjutant nodded, departed and closed the door behind him. Again the icy draft swept against the ace and he shivered, despite his heavy woolen sweater and his nearness to the pinging field stove.

Bodenschatz headed back to the line where small clusters of pilots and mechanics were already gathering in small groups near their machines. The tense waiting was over and the pilots, now ready to fly, were relaxed. Their loud voices and laughter carried across the wet ground, but more than bright sounds were needed to chase the still-dismal atmosphere of gloom the foul weather held over the place. Moritz, the Danish hound, J.G.I's mascot and the Baron's pet, had been strangely morose for several days.

Every pilot in the four Staffels had considered the possibility of their leader's death in combat, but Bodenschatz had never heard one man of J.G.I express the opinion that it would happen. If the pilots weighed this possibility in their minds it was based on pure statistics, much as one would play at pinocle. They knew there were few who could survive the day-in, day-out rush of air fighting for almost two and one half years.

Sounds from the adjoining cubicle told Richthofen that his personal orderly, Corporal Menzke, was gathering his flying gear. The 25-year-old man whom Field Marshal von Ludendorff thought equal to a division of German infantry paused quietly in his small room. His square shoulders betrayed a weariness uncommon to his straight-backed Prussian stance. Three years of bitter war were behind him, three years of almost daily action or flying, moving squadrons en masse in wagons—often with an hour's notice—and starting anew on a strange airfield, to fly and fight again. Three years, two fronts, 25 decorations, and now, on April 20, 1918, the war had at last brought the hard, blond nobleman to Cappy—with the great German offensive stalled.

Richthofen passed a hand through his short-cropped hair. He was weary of the strain, still, the ghosts that haunted his cockpit after his wound and fall no longer caused him concern over the next flight being his last one. He had no premonitions that from this field on foreign soil he would fly to the end of the road. He only knew, with a silent but unwilling acceptance, that he was now caught up in the beginning of his beloved nation's defeat. He had known this for a long time; since October of 1917 when, on convalescent leave at Schweidnitz, he quietly confided to the woman nearest his heart: "Mama, I do not believe Germany will win this war." Manfred remembered that the Baroness, seeing the dead seriousness in her eldest son's eyes, said nothing.

March 21st was Der Tag. The Day. A deafening artillery bombardment opened the holocaust in the predawn, thick with a fog that had deafened every sound and isolated every man to the extent of his own visibility. For five hours, to a depth of 20 miles, the British Third and Fifth Armies dug in under a violent outburst of terrible power; a rain of shrapnel and high explosives. Lewisite and Mustard shells were lobbed as far as the line of British heavy guns. Then came the infantry. Fifty-six bayonet-wielding divisions in an unstoppable gray wave moved silently under a mantle of low-hanging fog and smoke, grim and eager in their Fatherland's last great bid for victory.

The British tried desperately to hold their ground, but the Tommies, drunk with lack of sleep, feeble from loss of men, guns and communication, stumbled backward from the very first. Then they retreated in panic.

When it began, J.G.I was at Lechelle, but on April 2nd, in the wake of the victorious surge of infantry, Richthofen's four Jagdstaffels were ordered to forward airfields. He personally took command of Staffel 11—his favorite—and moved with them to Harbonnières. No sooner were they operational than rain and clouds brought air activity almost to a standstill.

Finally, on April 6th, Richthofen led a patrol and shot down a Sopwith Camel over Villiers-Brettoneaux. On this day he also welcomed his cousin, Wolfram von Richthofen, to Jasta 11. There were now three Richthofens in J.G.I (Manfred's younger brother Lothar was in Düsseldorf Hospital recovering from head injuries sustained when he crash-landed on March 13th), and there was no question that rank had its privileges. The Rittmeister gave express orders that fledgling Wolfram was to be thoroughly indoctrinated in handling the Dr.-I before his first sortie.

The following day, the 7th, the Commander bagged an S.E.5 over Hangard and a Spad over Villiers-Brettoneaux to bring his victory score to the fantastic total of 78. Then rain and poor visibility curtailed fighter patrols for two weeks. It was early on the 8th that orders arrived from the army directing J.G.1 north to the plain of the Lys River, where a battle was raging. Cappy was selected as a more permanent base of operations. Once more the circus tents were collapsed, folded, and packed in good wagons with quartermaster supplies. Within the day the order was countermanded. Then, amid frustration and confusion, the field telephone rang again. Move.

By the 10th, Jasta 11 was flying patrols from Cappy. The Rittmeister assessed their new location. The facilities were isolated, and the nearest town, Peronne, was 12 miles to the east. Its war-ravaged appearance was even more depressing than nearby Cappy. And there were the refugees—the pathetic flotsam of war. The fleeing groups were going somewhere, carrying their goods on their grief-bent figures. The more fortunate trundled their belongings on a wheelbarrow, or at best a dog cart. They trudged, faces filled with despair and resignation. Richthofen noted that the hopeless columns of the homeless were the same in Russia, Belgium, and France. The shell-pocked surroundings, rain, gray oppressive skies, unseasonable cold and crumbling ruins added a grotesque note. With Allied resistance stiffening by the hour, he could not understand why he was moved from the most crucial fighting area. In this setting of total destruction and eerie desolation, Richthofen sloshed impatiently in the Somme mud and petitioned the skies to clear.

The four squadrons, Staffels 11, 10, 6 and 4, were connected by telephone to the *Flugmeldedienst*—the Air Warning Service. With the central station J.G.I had direct connection to the front line, anti-aircraft batteries, artillery battalions and company commanders. From these places the squadrons at Cappy constantly received reports that Bodenschatz collected and gave to von Richthofen, who selected targets and patrol sectors.

The weather remained unsettled and showery; "airman's weather," marked with later than usual drinking hours and much daytime rest. On April 19th the offensive was completely stalled. It rained steadily from predawn until late evening, and in a short, semiformal ceremony in his quarters, Richthofen congratulated Leutnant Loewenhardt on his appointment as Staffelführer of Jasta 10. On such depressing afternoons he withdrew from his normal activites to seek comfort alone in his quarters.

Jasta 27, near Erchin to the northeast, was commanded by a stocky Staffelführer with a fast-growing score of enemy planes. This Oberleutnant was—like Richthofen— a disciplinarian. He tolerated no foolishness in the business of air fighting. The commander of J.G.I was of course acquainted with him; the preceding October this man's name had appeared on a roster of the most successful pilots with 10 or more victories. His name was Hermann Goering.

On this day, along the Somme front, a lance-corporal in the 16th Bavarian Reserve Infantry Regiment was celebrating his 29th birthday. A shy, moushtached soldier who was studious and sensitive, he had been twice wounded and twice decorated for bravery. His trials were not yet over, for before the Armistice he would be gassed and temporarily blinded. The corporal had seen Richthofen in action overhead, and heard of his exploits, but Richthofen would never hear of this inconspicuous little headquarters runner who was lost in the grey herd, who used the war to confirm his belief in its heroic virtues and authoritarianism. His name was Adolph Hitler.

Menzke, the orderly, carried the flying garb into the room; a leather jacket, fur boots, and a dark brown, one-piece fleece-lined flying suit. The corporal placed the jacket and coveralls over a chair and departed with the other garments to meet his commander at the plane. Richthofen donned the coveralls and jacket and pulled on his black leather boots. He took a folded map marked with the patrol sector and walked toward the line of Fokkers. He noted that the wind marker was snapped briskly by the moist gusts.

At the line he was greeted by Leutnant Joachim Wolff and Leutnant Karjus, who opened their huddle to admit him. A respectful silence came over the group. Bodenschatz was near the door of the telephone shack, talking with Leutnant Krefft, the technical officer. Wolfram hovered on the outside of the group, still hopeful that his famous cousin would change his mind and allow him to accompany the *Kette*. He wanted to ask, but propriety stayed him.

The Rittmeister had a new triplane for this patrol. Like his other planes it was a rich dark red, except for the square black crosses with their thin white border, and its all-white rudder. On its fuselage was the number 425/17. In all, 320 of the feisty fighters were manufactured, and Anthony Fokker, an acquaintance of the Baron, had outdone himself in this highly agile flying gun platform. Here was a match for the spunky Sopwith Camel, for in the hands of an experienced pilot, the Dr.-I had a maneuvering edge.

More fliers gathered, bundled in fur and leather. They turned their backs to the wind while Menzke, like a medieval page, set about to gird the Kaiser's most illustrious knight for battle. In the quiet years he would spend as a family retainer on the grand old Richthofen estate, Menzke would remember these last days. He strapped the Heinecke harness around the ace's middle, then straightened. Richthofen handed the batman his garrison cap and Menzke gave the Rittmeister his goggles and leather helmet. Richthofen slipped them on over his fair head and, taking his map, turned and spread it on the center plane of his machine. The men crowded around.

"If the air is rough," he announced crisply, "keep the formation loose." He turned to Oberleutnant Lischke, a ground officer. "What's the latest along the front?"

Lischke elbowed forward. "Fighters west of Albert, Herr Rittmeister, heading south-southeast at about 2,500 meters—500 meters above the clouds. Some observation machines near Corbie at 2,000 meters, in the clouds. Scattered activity farther south."

Richthofen scanned the map and nodded. "We'll fly at 3,000 meters and patrol from Aubercourt to Grandcourt, then turn home."

The pilots scattered eagerly to their machines. Richthofen swung easily into the Dr.I's small cockpit, and a mechanic buckled the safety harness to the crude—and not too dependable—parachute. It was a new innovation for pilots, although balloon observers on both sides used them almost from the beginning of the war.

The straps adjusted, Richthofen nodded to his personal mechanic, Holzapfel, who had just squirted raw gasoline in the intake port of each cylinder with an oil can.

Then, with his assistant, they turned the propeller several times.

Holzapfel called: "Free! Ready to go!"

The Rittmeister acknowledged by moving the switch that controlled the magneto. The two mechanics swung the mahogany propeller in unison and the well-tuned rotary popped to a blattering roar. On both sides the other machines barked to life. The ground vibrated under their combined rumblings.

Richthofen adjusted the fuel and air valves carefully for maximum RPM. He scanned the few instruments, then looked right and left. His pilots were watching him, ready. He raised his left hand in signal then pressed the coupé button on the control stick with his thumb. It momentarily killed the engine, a signal for Holzapfel to pull the wheel chocks. The line of 15 gaudy triplanes, Richthofen in the lead, shaped itself into a forward moving V and roared down the field.

The air above the clouds was cold and turbulent. Lieutenant Lewis huddled in his flight dress and watched his squadron commander's Camel bob and rock in the rough currents. Since their takeoff from Candas, their flight had climbed in a south-southeasterly direction toward the lines. Albert slipped under his left wing just as they reached the broken, wispy clouds.

As with J.G.I, foul weather had grounded Number 3 Camel Squadron for the greater part of the day. No German air activity was expected, a factor Captain Bell considered before scheduling fledgling Lewis for this, his first patrol across the lines. Douglas Bell nosed the six-plane formation through the clouds, skirted the seemingly dense banks, and skimmed through the misty peaks of ragged stratus. In the higher levels a layer shifted in lazy languor. Now, through the lower breaks, the newcomer saw the line's southwestward curve at Le Hamel. They were passing into German-held ground, but from 10,000 feet the surface details were beginning to run together. Where the Somme made its sharp bend at

Corbie, Lewis could make out a range of hills, distant and indistinct.

Lewis was the youngest—and the greenest—member of the squadron. A Rhodesian colonial, he came to England a few months earlier and now, instead of a baptism of fire, he was about to experience an inferno. Within minutes, young Lewis would see his squadron commander, Major R. Raymond-Barker in the Camel scant yards ahead of him, plunge to the ground under Richthofen's guns, an orange whorl of flame, a silently tumbling bundle of burning linen and spruce. Seconds later, he would himself become the next—and final—target of the celebrated airman.

Higher, at the apex of his *Kette*, Richthofen swept his restive eyes across the sky. Against the cloud floor that moved in oily sluggishness, he singled out the line of dots that slowly became six flying machines. They had crossed the lines. He signaled for a slow turn to cut their retreat, but the the British fighters veered toward him, head-on. This was no surprise to Richthofen; such courageous tactics had earned his respect and admiration.

In less than a minute the onrush began. The Camels loomed ahead and closed at a surprising speed, Vickers guns winking. They flashed past in the peculiar side-sliding motion of aircraft passing in an angled path. Thus began the final combat that Richthofen would record.

CHAPTER TWO

"Today You: Tomorrow Me"

*Forty-eight years after his fall, D. G. Lewis
tells of his brief and almost fatal encounter
with the Kaiser's "Red Devil."*

After reaching England I was posted to the Inns of Court
Officers Training Corps to be trained for a commission in
the Royal Welsh Fusiliers, but when volunteers were
asked for by the Royal Flying Corps, I offered my
services and was sent to Reading.

Here I attended the School of Military Aeronautics,
where I took courses in engines, wireless telegraphy
map reading, gunnery, and other subjects necessary in
aerial war. Upon completion I was ordered to Number
98 Training Squadron at Rochford, just outside the town
of Southend in which we were billeted.

I was trained to fly on an Avro (a 504 I think). It was
a biplane with a Monosoupape engine. As the name indicated, it had a single valve, which was the exhaust
and the air inlet, the petrol intake ports being in the
bottom of each of the nine cylinders imbedded in the
crank case.

Following my flight training, I graduated to Sopwith
Camels and was posted to Number 78 Squadron, Home
Defence, located at Hornchurch in Essex. The function
of the Home Defense Squadron was to protect London
from the night air raids that earlier were carried out by
Zeppelins and later by Gothas. Most of my fellow
officers named their Camels after their girlfriends, but as

I had no girlfriend at the time I named my machine "Rhodesia" after my country of origin. Serving with me was Douglas Bell, a close friend who later became my flight commander in France. He was to gain 20 aerial victories and be awarded the Military Cross.

I spent nine months in Number 78 Home Defence Squadron and was engaged in operating at night against enemy machines, which were bombing London and England and, although I saw enemy machines, I was unable to bring them to combat.

With approximately 20 flying hours to my credit, I arrived in France and was posted to Number 3 Squadron. I was issued with a brand new Camel, which was painted in combat colors of a dirty greenish khaki. It is not easy to forget my squadron details, for I was in the *third* flight, in the *Third* Squadron, in the *Thirteenth* Wing, of the *Third* Brigade, of the *Third* Army. Those who are superstitious might make something of that.

My squadron was located a mile or so from Candas—on the Doullens-Amiens Road—which was frequently bombed at night. Our aerodrome was only a few miles behind the lines. We could hear the thundering of the guns, while in the darkness their flashes appeared to be right around us. On occasions at night, Captain Bell and I used to slip up to our front line trenches to visit a friend of his, Major Bishop, of a New Zealand Regiment. The New Zealanders were usually found to be sitting on the trench parapets completely unperturbed by the shells from the German Artillery traveling over their heads to our positions behind. I was thankful *not* to be an infantryman.

The sum total of my service in France was a month, during which time I flew over the Front making myself familiar with the ground, landmarks and lines below. I had yet to experience my first aerial engagement. My Flight Commander (C Flight) was, as I mentioned earlier, my former flying companion, Douglas Bell.

Poor flying weather had prevailed all day of the 20th of April, but at 5:15 the weather had cleared sufficiently to permit of a decision to carry out the patrol. The two flights of planes, twelve in all, were made ready by the mechanics and the engines started prior to take-off. It was not expected that there would be much aerial activity over the German lines. This impression was only too soon to be dispelled.

Our Commanding Officer, Major R. Raymond-Barker, M.C., expressed a desire to accompany the two flights prepared for the late patrol. This was unusual as it was not customary for administrative officers to take part in offensive sorties and, although an experienced pilot with seven victories, he usually did not accompany patrols.

I did not know Major Raymond-Barker well since, as a squadron pilot, I had very little to do with him, all my dealings having been with Bell, who told me that he liked Raymond-Barker very much and that he was a good commanding officer.

It was about 6 P.M. when I took off with the two six-plane flights, Bell leading, and headed, climbing steadily, across the lines. From the outset our patrol had an unlucky start, for the area was still stormy and the air was boisterous from the earlier atmospheric disturbances. The entire front was overhung with clouds that were low and heavy over the German positions.

Captain Bell, aware that the German anti-aircraft guns probably had the exact range of the cloud layer and not wishing to make the patrol an easy target, led us through to the clearer air above. Once in the clouds, we lost touch with our other flight and on emerging on top of the cloud layer at 10,000 feet, we continued without them, six strong, still heading deeper into German-held territory.

We were arranged in an arrow formation, Captain Bell leading with Major Raymond-Barker and myself on his right, the two other machines, one on his left and one on my right, then each slightly behind the one in front. The sixth machine brought up the rear. I am unable to remember the names of my other companions in our flight.

Four miles behind the enemy lines we sighted a German formation of 15 Fokker triplanes some miles away, flying at right angles to our direction of flight and above us. They flew in one block. Captain Bell had instructed me before our take-off to keep as close as possible to him and not leave the safety of the formation. I do not think he expected to contact the enemy on that day. His instructions, of course, turned out to be impossible to obey.

Captain Bell was one of the most courageous men I have ever met and from his action that day, I do not think he had any intention, whatever the odds, of returning to the safety of the territory we occupied. Had he entertained that idea he had ample time to turn toward our lines when we first sighted the enemy in the distance. The German formation, however, may have thought that this was our plan, for they manuevered to cut off our escape from behind and swung into a favorable position for the attack.

Although outnumbered three to one, Bell frustrated their strategy by deliberately turning to meet them head-on. Thus the engagement began—the two opposing flights rushing toward one another at a closing speed of over 180 miles per hour with machine guns firing away.

As soon as we had shot past the enemy formation and turned to select an opponent, I knew we had met Richthofen's famed Circus. The planes were painted all colors of the rainbow, each to personally identify the pilot. One was painted like a draughtboard with black and white squares. Another was all sky blue. One looked like a dragon's head and large eyes were painted on the engine cowling. Others had lines in various colors running along the fuselages or across them; machines painted black and red, dark blue, gray. There was a yellow-nosed one, too.

Richthofen, of course, led the formation in his Fokker triplane painted a brilliant pillar-box red. Its black crosses were edged with white.

The melee had hardly begun and I barely had time to single out an enemy machine, when I saw Major Raymond-Barker's Camel explode on my left. An incendiary bullet must have entered his petrol tank. Then I found myself on the tail of a bright blue triplane which was crossing my path directly ahead of me at the same level. I brought my guns to bear on it and was just about to try to finish it off when I heard the *rat-tat-tat* of machine guns close behind me, the bullets cracking loud in my ears. Fragments of my machine flew past my face as bullets splintered the cabane center section struts in front of and inches above my head. I forgot all about the man in the blue triplane and took evasive action immediately, twisting and turning to shake my attacker from my tail. As the Camels were wonderfully maneuverable planes, for the moment I was safe. I risked a glance over my shoulder and saw that my adversary was flying the familiar all-red triplane—the renowned Richthofen himself!

My first thought was that I should have to be very good and very lucky to escape his attentions so I thought more of keeping out of his line of fire than competing with him.

In engaging the blue machine below me, I had lost altitude, a big mistake in fighting triplanes—or for that matter any enemy machine—and when Richthofen started firing on me, Captain Bell, who must have had a watchful eye open for my safety, chased him off my tail as I sought to escape the machine-gun bursts. Bell's act was told me afterward and I imagine he "shook" Richthofen with his robust attack, for the red triplane lost height and sight of me for a few seconds and I found myself in a good attacking position. The Baron had slipped below me, and performing a slight turn, I was in a favorable position to attack him. My heart leaped in those brief moments and I was excited by the thought: *I may bring him down!*

As Richthofen slipped into my sights at a fairly close range, I opened fire and my tracers appeared to strike several parts of his machine, although I could not be certain of this as I did not see splinters or fragments fly off his triplane. My Vickers guns were belt fed and fired

.303-caliber bullets, with tracer bullets in the proportion of one in 20.

My concern over my own unprotected rear prevailed, however, and in looking out for the possibility of another enemy machine approaching from behind, I failed to maintain a concentrated fire. In a trice Richthofen slipped away from me by performing a steep right-hand climbing turn and I found myself again his target. Again I lost no time in trying to avoid his fire, but he was too experienced for me and seemed to anticipate my every maneuver. He managed to approach quite close—between 50 and 25 yards off my tail—before he began firing.

He delivered a vicious burst with telling effect. Why I was not killed outright I do not know, for my compass, mounted on the dash panel directly in front of my face, suddenly disintegrated before my eyes, spraying liquid over my face and scattering splinters and glass fragments throughout the cockpit. One of Richthofen's bullets struck my goggles where the elastic joined the frame of the glass on the side of my head, and they disappeared over the side. I often wonder if they were found on the ground somewhere in France. Another bullet passed through the sleeve of my coat and still another through my trousers at the knee, yet none touched my body.

This last burst put me out of the fight, for another one of the Baron's incendiary bullets set one of my petrol tanks alight. I was not sure which tank—main or emergency—had caught alight, but suspected that the flames, which sought to devour me, had emanated from petrol. Both tanks were located a few inches behind the plywood backrest of the cockpit. As it turned out, only the small, seven-gallon gravity tank was alight, which fortunately did not explode as had one of Major Raymond-Barker's a few minutes earlier. I switched the engine off as I had always been taught to do when fire was about or threatened and the next thing I realized, I was falling, striving for control of the burning Camel, but never quite getting it. We had no parachutes in those days, so I could not abandon the aircraft.

The fire, fanned by the slipstream, periodically grew larger and hotter and, on occasions during my descent in the dive, appeared to overtake the machine and come billowing up from my feet and over my body, creating intense heat for a few seconds, then subsiding and repeating the behavior all the way down until the petrol was exhausted. I expect that if I had not this respite I would have vacated my seat for the coolness of the wing outside the cockpit. I remained in my seat for the whole of the descent.

The wings continued to give some lift and restriction to the fall, but repeated attempts to bring the machine to an even keel were unsuccessful as the elevator response was very sluggish. By now the small petrol tank had burned itself out, and as I approached the ground I made one last attempt to flatten out for a landing. I miscalculated and acted far too late, with the result that I struck the ground at an angle, and at a speed of about 60 miles an hour. With so much to think of during my fall, I had not released my safety belt prior to the crash and perhaps it was just as well that I had not, for it broke upon impact and I was thrown 20 yards clear of the wreckage. Fortunately again, the main tank did not explode, otherwise I would not be giving this account.

I had crashed about four miles northeast of Villiers-Brettoneaux.

Half stunned, I picked myself up and looked around. I had no broken bones, but my body had numerous bruises, burns, and small cuts. Fifty yards away Major Raymond-Barker's Camel was blazing fiercely, and I staggered and stumbled to it in a shocked state to see if I could pull him out. I should have realized that I could do nothing for him, for he must have been killed in the air. I was beaten back by the flames and in any event, it was too late.

I went back to my own machine, and after examining it for awhile I understood why I could not control it. From a point next to the three-ply wood at my cockpit, along the fuselage, back to and including the tailfin, the fabric had been burnt away, leaving only a few strips of material remaining on both the tailplane and elevators. I considered completing the job by exploding the main tank with my Very pistol, but finally decided against it.

Looking up to see the progress of the fight, I saw the remaining planes of my flight saved from annihilation by the timely arrival of a squadron of S.E.5s. Richthofen separated from his flight and came down to within a hundred feet of me and waved. I returned the wave.

Richthofen also waved to some German troops nearby and I walked a few hundred yards to a trench in which stood some armed German soldiers who had been watching me. Since I was uncertain of my future, I raised my hands, but did not maintain that attitude for long as I considered they would appreciate the fact that as my hands had been raised once, my intention was to surrender. A few soldiers escorted me to a dugout and into the presence of an infantry captain who spoke broken English. The first question he asked me was whether or not I was armed. As my reply was in the negative the matter was dropped, signifying that he accepted an officer's word, so I was not searched. Of course I was unarmed.

The captain then ordered one of his orderlies to bandage my face, which had been burned rather badly. Afterwards he presented me with a drink of schnapps, presumably since he saw his young captive was nervous and injured.

A short time later I was turned over to an escort—two unmounted Uhlans—and we walked toward Peronne, which was approximately 22 miles distant. British artillery shelled the road, and soon it became quite intense. For some reason or other my escort left me to continue the journey alone. Eventually I took cover in a ditch by the road until the bombardment had subsided and when I resumed my journey I was rejoined by my escort. After awhile we met German Infantry going in the opposite direction, presumably into the trenches. The mounted officer in charge spoke to my escort, and upon learning that I had just been shot down by von Richthofen, he cantered down the line to tell them this. They all evinced an interest in me as I passed into captivity.

Although I walked a considerable distance, I am not certain at this stage that I did not arrive in Peronne by motor transport. It seems silly to have to admit it, but I cannot remember that detail. I was in the hospital there for one night and was relieved of my sidcot flying suit and my fleece-lined thigh boots. These were possibly used later by a German pilot, though of course the orderly may have appropriated them for his own use.

Very soon after my capture I was handed a card to be filled in by myself, stating whether I was ill, wounded, etc., and it was sent to England through Switzerland. I could not, however, communicate with my squadron but was glad nevertheless for the opportunity to send the message. Captain Bell had reported that I had gone down in flames and that there was little hope of my survival and he wrote to my parents accordingly.

The next day I was moved to Cambrai Hospital by train. I remember that the countryside was littered with damaged tanks—the aftermath of General Gough's aborted advance. I remained at Cambrai, where my burns were treated for several weeks. The medical treatment was excellent, but the sanitary conditions were bad. This hospital, incidentally, was the one to which Richthofen was taken when he was shot down and sustained a head wound.

After undergoing treatment at Cambrai, I was taken to Karlsruhe for interrogation by German Intelligence, and lived for a period in a hotel which had been commandeered by the German authorities whilst the interrogation continued. There were a number of British prisoners here. Although the examination was rigorous, I was neither ill treated nor bullied. The officer who questioned me was able to answer most of the questions to which I refused a reply. When I objected to telling him the name of my commanding officer, he was able to inform me of his name, and I, of course, saw it was pointless denying the fact. After much questioning he told me that he had asked me the questions merely to confirm what he already knew. Leaving Karlsruhe by train under guard, I was taken to Graudenz prison camp. I recall an interesting incident which occurred enroute to Graudenz. We stopped at a railway station and I was taken into a restaurant. I was directed to a table at the far end of the room, and noticed that some German flying officers in my proximity rose from their tables and bowed to me. I acknowledged the salutes. They must have heard that I was shot down by Richthofen and this was their way of paying respect to a fellow pilot. To be honest, I am not sure that this was so, but at the time I strongly felt that this was the reason.

I very much regret that I am completely unable to say when I first heard of Richthofen's death and it would not be correct to hazard a guess.

As officers, we were not required to perform labor, so I had no duties. If the Germans exercised firm treatment of us during our captivity, it was completely our own fault. In the absence of bad behavior our treatment by the Germans in charge of us was very good. A great deal of course, depended on the character of the commandant. In some camps the prisoners were treated with inexcusable strictness.

The Germans could do no better than give us two meals a day, and there was no doubt that the blockade was having its effect on their food supply situation. Each meal consisted of a soup which was none too thick. No breakfast was provided, but we got a kind of ersatz coffee in the morning, the first meal being given us at 12 o'clock.

It was not until September 1918 that my Red Cross food parcels caught up with me. Prisoners who had been captured earlier were receiving theirs regularly and were comparatively well off for food. Our bread ration was distributed on Sundays. It was a heavy loaf of a kind of brown bread and was expected to last until the next Sunday. I was very young at the time and very hungry, so my loaf was finished by Tuesday. Some of the wise prisoners divided their rations into sections to last the week. I did not, so during the time I was without Red Cross parcels I suffered a certain amount of distress, but when once I started getting mine I was adequately catered for. Toward the end of the war we were actually feeding the German children who came round the camp walls. Later we received nice white loaves of bread from Denmark and then things really began to look up.

Quite a number of escapes were organized and various means of getting away were used. With a motley assortment of tools, tunnels were dug, but with the type of tools we had these tunnels took months to complete. One night 14 prisoners escaped by way of a tunnel, but all were recaptured within a fortnight and given punishment of solitary confinement for a short period. I was not prepared to try to escape since I knew nothing of the German language and both Holland and Switzerland (both neutral) were a considerable distance away, and the reception one would get in Russia was uncertain though I believe some people did take that direction. One man made a lone escape by using a board to slide down the power lines which entered our camp. Unfortunately he died of blood poisoning following a scratch received from some barbed wire.

When the Armistice was declared, the prison gates were thrown open and we could, had we wished, have walked out of the camp and made our way back to England. But we received word that arrangements were being made for our repatriation and that we should remain in camp. On December 2, 1918, we were dispatched in batches to Danzig, where we boarded a Russian hospital ship operated by the British. We docked at Leith, Scotland. The only reason I can imagine for our late repatriation is that it required over a month for the necessary preparations to be made.

The number of officers and men who encountered Richthofen is fast diminishing. I was 19 at the time of my meeting with him—the youngest pilot in each of my squadrons. Details of the Baron's death did not reach me until after I was home, but I always understood that

Richthofen was shot down by Roy Brown. I never saw or spoke with Brown or May, but corresponded with Brown. He mentioned nothing of his encounter with the Baron as I had merely asked him if he intended to take part in the impending war and his reply was in the negative, and when the 1939-1945 war broke out we both decided not to take part for various reasons.

In 1953, while in England, I saw a number of American Sabre Jets. I wish I had had one when I met the Baron!

Von Richthofen's combat report gives the impression that I must have been killed in the air and yet it was he who came down to view the remains of my machine. I cannot understand or reconcile his report with his behavior. Otherwise, I have no criticism of his combat report, which is substantially in accordance with events which took place that day, thousands of feet above France. I was very lucky not to have received one of his 50 bullets in my person, but they certainly did their best to break up my machine.

In all, the air fight was a clear example of the philosophy of some of the more experienced pilots to this type of warfare; with my own fall one day, the Baron's the next. There are some things about the encounter which cannot be forgotten.

On occasion, when I mentally relive those long perilous minutes when Richthofen sent me, burning, into the German lines, I realize there is no denying the fact that it was a miracle I escaped with my life.

(80th victory)
20. 4. 1918　　　6:43 P.M.
Northeast from Villiers-Brettoneaux
Englishman
Fokker Dr. I 425/17 painted red
Burned

Three minutes after I shot the first one down burning, I attacked out of the same group a second Camel. The opponent went intentionally into a diving turn, recovered and repeated the maneuver several times. Then I closed in at the next following engagement and shot him on fire with approximately 50 rounds. The fuselage burned up in the air. The rest of the aircraft fell northeast from Villiers-Brettoneaux.

v. R.
Rittmeister and Geschwaderkommandeur

DAYS BEFORE

CHAPTER THREE

No Bugles; No Bombardments

Fame was his. He could have had gaiety and the attentions of any admirer he chose, but he preferred to hunt alone in the shadowy forest, enjoy the companionship of his dog, Moritz—and practice the art of soldiering.

If you would see clearly the day of April 21, 1918, you must first understand the unique personality of Germany's shy, handsome *Red Knight of the Air*. Much of what happened to Richthofen on this day had its beginnings in the months and years before. A pattern of action became a steel trap that brought the German Air Service to its darkest hour.

After each war in our century, air tacticians recapitulate the great sky battles. Eventually the conversation turns to the mysterious psychology of that most paradoxical of all soldiers—the fighter ace.

What made him tick? Why was he deadly? How did one pilot accumulate a score of victories while his squadron mates bagged only a few?

Invariably, the name of Richthofen is mentioned. How is it, someone will ponder, that his name still grips the attention of all manner of people? Thousands of brave men fell in the First Great War and have been forgotten, but the name *Richthofen* refuses to die. Why is the same interest not shown in other aces: Bishop, Fonck, Udet, Rickenbacker?

Richthofen was totally different.

"He was about average height, stocky, dark blond with blue eyes," recalls former Lt. Karl August von Schoenbeck of Richthofen's J.G.I. "A voice of middle range, his manner of speech clipped, clear and concise. He had a noble way of speech and never swore or used foul language of any kind. There was always a discussion after a flight and during these dissections he was calm and self-controlled and spoke with much humor, no matter how dangerous the action might have been. One could not help but feel and be touched daily by his extraordinary energy and will power. He shone with calm in the most critical moments which quite naturally exercised the most salutary influence on all of us."

Although withdrawn in his relations with others, and never articulate, Richthofen maintained firm discipline among his pilots. He set examples and expected them to be followed. Typically aggressive in the air, he was convinced the defensive air fighter seldom won victories. "The greatest thing in air fighting," he told his men, "is that the decisive factor does not lie in trick flying, but in the personal ability and energy of the aviator." He watched each replacement for signs of circumspection, and if this undesirable trait was evident, the newcomer was sent packing to another squadron.

"If von Richthofen liked a man it was for purely material reasons," commented Ernst Udet some years later in assessing Richthofen's objective dedication. "His estimate of a man was formed by what the man achieved for the cause, and whether he happened to be a good fellow or not was a secondary consideration. But once you had proved your worth, he supported you by every means in his power and with his whole personality. If you were a failure he dropped you without a second's hesitation, without the flicker of an eyelid."

The Commander himself darted quickly into the fray, attacked before the others, and while his pilots jockeyed for positions, the enemy machine he singled out well in advance of the rush was plunging toward the trenches. To his pilots he preached, "The aggressive spirit, the offensive, is the chief thing everywhere in war—and the air is no exception. In my opinion, the aggressive spirit is everything. . ." To Richthofen, the principle of *attack* was elementary; he did not discover its importance in a book on military strategy. It was the simple difference between the hunter and the hunted, and whether stalking manmade birds in the rushing sky or flushing woodcock from the stillness of the forest floor, Richthofen preferred to be the hunter.

Doubtless this ace of aces had 20-20 vision, but it was not his acuteness of sight that marked his success; it was his restless awareness—and the simple fact that he knew precisely *what to look for*. He saw the speck on the horizon that went unnoticed by his comrades; it was he who pointed to the almost unseen flicker of motion against the distant towering cloud mass—the slight movement that told him the enemy was in the same sky. Richthofen once wrote: "The commanding officer is responsible that neither he nor any of his pilots are surprised by the enemy. If he cannot see to that, he is no good as a leader."

With this leadership went teamwork and tactics. Immelmann and Boelcke had sought for a way to use the fighter planes en masse to win air battles; Richthofen, disciplined to a painstaking Prussian thoroughness, perfected the lethal plan. He passed Boelcke's principles on to his men, one of which was: "Turn to meet the enemy, rather than try to escape." At daily meetings he discussed tactics with his Staffelführers and insisted that every pilot adopt them—regardless.

"Each time we came back von Richthofen told us what we had done right and where we had made mistakes," von Schoenbeck said. "Thus I noticed, to my great astonishment, that he never lost sight of us even when fighting for his life.

"We knew we could depend on him like a rock. If things were going badly, if we were ever in a hole, he'd notice it and pull us out. It gave the Jasta a great feeling of safety."

To replacements about to receive their baptism of fire, Richthofen said: "Don't waste your bullets on enemy machines. Always go straight for the man. In the case of a two-seater, shoot the gunner first and the pilot afterward." He told them the surest way to put the enemy out of action was to "send him down burning." He eschewed the naïve courage of other famous combat pilots; he flew with his brains. He knew, for example, that firing on an inexperienced enemy pilot who was slightly out of range would likely unnerve him and cause him to zigzag frantically. The turning and twisting motions slowed the enemy plane and brought the novice within easy range for a well-aimed machine-gun burst. This calculating, mathematical certainty grew with the Baron's flying skill and he learned to use the airplane as a simple and natural extension of his own tactical principles. It became a weapon to be strapped on with a safety harness. He was at home in it. Except that his airmanship, by itself, was never outstanding. Richthofen had no illusions as to this shortcoming, and it is strange but true, that this man who became the highest-scoring ace of the war was an airman of modest flying ability. Once, when the ace brought home a guest on leave, the friend confided to the Baroness that her son's skill in the air did not match his courage, his marksmanship—or his ability to command.

Marksmanship, by itself, never made an ace. But once blended with his other qualities, this deadly talent put the keen edge to an inimitable fighting combination. When Richthofen seized every advantage, closed the gap, and in crowded quarters cut loose a withering fusillade with deadly accuracy, he was a combat pilot without peer. He used the "chaser plane" in the manner for which it was precisely designed—as a flying gun platform.

The Rittmeister knew his tactical style proved well and good in high-altitude combat. To his men he preached: do not become so absorbed in killing the enemy that you fail to divide your attention among other attackers; do not become trapped low behind the enemy's lines and become prey to ground fire.

One day, the survivors of J.G.I would reflect on these wise maxims, and ponder why their leader forgot them.

Manfred von Richthofen was born in Breslau, May 2, 1892, the first-born son of Major Albrecht and Kunigunde von Richthofen. The Major retired before the War to Schweidnitz, a small Silesian town in the Weistritz Valley. Sheltered by two wooded mountain ranges, the serene lower lands abounded with game, and young Manfred spent happy, carefree hours stalking prey in the shadows of the dense forests. Though a strong and wiry lad, he did not grow as tall as his brothers Lothar and Bolko, nor his sister Ilse. Always active on horseback with his guns and dogs, he—more often than they—gave his parents some anxious moments. But they refused to pamper young Manfred, and this freedom, tempered with private tutoring until age nine, moulded him through the formative years. There were signs in early boyhood that Manfred would be a rugged individualist. He harbored a quiet dislike for discipline, although he never questioned the decisions of his parents nor complained to them.

"As a boy of eleven," he later wrote, "I entered the Cadet Corps. I was not eager to become a cadet, but my father wished it. So my wishes were not consulted."

His was an indigenous sense of duty; as much a part of him as was his unquestioning obedience to authority. Manfred's personality traits were at once clear to all. He was absolutely honest; he was determined to excel in whatever he chose to do.

"I did not care very much for the training I received at Wahlstatt," he admitted. "I was never good at learning things. I did just enough to pass. In my opinion it would have been wrong to do more than was just sufficient, so I worked as little as possible. Consequently, my teachers did not think very much of me.

"On the other hand, I was very fond of sport. I particularly liked gymnastics, football and other outdoor activities. I could do all kinds of tricks on the horizontal bar—for which I received prizes from the commander.

"I had a tremendous liking for all risky foolery. One day, with my friend Frankenberg, I climbed the famous steeple of Wahlstatt by way of the lightning conductor and tied my handkerchief to the top. I remember exactly how difficult it was to balance on the gutters. Ten years later, when I visited my little brother at Wahlstatt, I saw the handkerchief still tied high in the air."

Manfred was 12 when he climbed Wahlstatt tower. Years later he said that all of his combat flying failed to equal the sensation he felt on the day he looked down on the streets far below.

At the senior school in Lichterfelde—through which many of the Fatherland's future aces would soon pass— he completed his cadet training and entered the Army on Easter, 1911. To his joy he was placed in the regiment of his choice, the First Uhlans, *Emperor Alexander III.* "I had a colossal liking for serving with my regiment," he wrote. "It is the finest thing for a young soldier to be a cavalryman." But this young soldier was destined to lead, not follow, and at the War Academy in Berlin he was commissioned a Leutnant of Cavalry in the autumn of 1912.

In the summer of 1914 talk of war was common at Ostrovo, Manfred's frontier station. The young officers had packed and repacked their service trunks so often it became tiresome. No one believed war would come.

"We were sitting with the men of the detached squadron 10 kilometers from the Russian frontier, in the officer's club," Richthofen reported, "eating oysters, drinking champagne and gambling a little. We were very merry; no one thought of war.

"The next day we were ordered to the field."

The command was received with mingled disbelief and sobriety. Leutnant Richthofen was quietly elated and looked forward to the first cavalry engagement. He did not know the horse soldier would soon pass forever and a new weapon, the "aeroplane," would become the Army's eyes. So, for yet awhile he could glory in the color and traditions of the cavalry, and imagine the files of mounted men poised for battle with their lances high and tipped with streaming standards.

At midnight of the day after the war began, the Leutnant led his file of Uhlans across the Russian frontier. He met no opposition and at daybreak the group invaded the village of Kieltze. Although new at the business of military occupation, Richthofen convinced the villagers that he was firmly in charge of the situation and would tolerate no foolishness.

"Everything happened without seeing anything of the enemy or rather without being seen by him. The question now was what should I do in order not to be noticed by the villagers? My first idea was to lock up the "pope." We fetched him from his house, to his great surprise. I locked him up among the bells in the church tower, took away the ladder and left him sitting there. I assured him that he would be executed if the population should show any hostile inclinations. A sentinel on the tower observed the neighborhood.

"I had to send reports every day by dispatch-riders. Very soon my small troop was converted entirely into dispatch-riders and dissolved, so that finally, as the only one remaining, I had to bring in my own report.

"Up to the fifth night everything had been quiet. Then my sentinel suddenly came rushing to the church tower near where the horses had been stabled. He called out: "The Cossacks are here!" The night was black as pitch. It rained a little. No stars were visible and one couldn't see a meter ahead.

"As a precaution we had already breached the wall 'round the churchyard. Through the breach we led the horses into the open. It was so dark we were perfectly safe after having advanced 50 meters. Then the sentinel and I, carbines in hand, went to the place where he said he saw the Cossacks.

"Gliding along the churchyard wall I came to the street. There I felt a queer sensation. The streets swarmed with Cossacks! I looked over the wall where the rascals put their horses. Most of them had lanterns and acted very incautiously and were loud. I estimated there were 20 or 30 of them. One had left his horse and gone to the pope, whom I'd released the day before.

"Immediately it flashed through my mind: *"Of course— we are betrayed!"* We had to be doubly careful. I could not risk a fight because we had only two carbines. So I decided to play police and robbers. After resting a few hours, our visitors rode away.

"The next day I thought it wise to change quarters. On the seventh day I was back at my garrison. Everyone stared at me as if I were a ghost. The stares were not because of my unshaven face, but because of the rumor that Wedel and I had fallen at Kalish. The place where it was supposed to have happened, the time and all the circumstances of my death had been reported with such a wealth of detail that it had spread throughout Silesia. My mother had already received visits of condolence."

Manfred's Russian campaign was a short-lived one, for the Uhlans were ordered to Belgium. Advancing on Arlon, he saw the first airplane used in war. The impression stuck. "I was entirely ignorant about the duties of our flying men," he later admitted, "and got tremendously excited whenever I saw an aviator."

On patrol Richthofen was ordered to find the strength of the enemy in the Virton forest. Here the German Fifth and the French Third Armies were about to clash, and with 15 Uhlans he confidently penetrated the dense, shaded wood. When his troop drew no fire he probed deeper. All was strangely quiet. He signaled a halt, dismounted and examined the ground. There were signs that a considerable body of cavalry had recently passed this way. Richthofen remounted and cautioned his men to be ready for trouble.

"In my mind's eye I saw myself at the head of my little troop, sabering a hostile squadron, and was quite intoxicated with expectation. The eyes of my Uhlans sparkled. We followed the spoor at a rapid trot. After a sharp ride of an hour through the most beautiful mountainside, the wood became thinner. We approached the exit and I was certain we would meet the enemy. Therefore, caution! To the right of our narrow path was a steep, rocky wall many meters high. To the left was a narrow rivulet and at the far side a meadow was surrounded with barbed wire. Suddenly the traces of the horse's hooves disappeared over the bridge and into the bushes. My leading man stopped because the exit was blocked by a barricade!

"Immediately I realized I had fallen into a trap. To my left I saw a movement among the bushes and noticed dismounted hostile cavalry. I estimated there were fully a hundred rifles. My path ahead was cut by the barricade. To the right were steep rocks. To the left the barbed wire around the meadow prevented me from attacking as I intended. Nothing could be done except retreat . . . a second later we heard the first shot, followed by intensive rifle fire from the wood. The range was 50 to 100 meters.

"I had instructed my men to join me immediately when they saw me lift my hand. I knew we had to retreat so I lifted my arm and beckoned my men to follow. They misunderstood my signal and the cavalrymen behind me thought I was in danger and came rushing up at high speed to help me escape. Since we were on a narrow forest path one can imagine the confusion that followed. The horses of the two lead men rushed away in panic because the noise of every shot was intensified tenfold by the narrowness of the hollow. The last I saw of them they were leaping the barricade. I never saw them again; no doubt they were made prisoners. I turned my horse and gave him the spurs—probably for the first time in his life. I had the greatest difficulty making my Uhlans understand that they should not advance any farther, but should turn and get away.

"The enemy had surprised us beautifully. They had probably observed us from the very beginning and had intended to trap us unawares, as is the character of the French."

Leutnant Richthofen's pride was injured, but he refused to excuse his blunder. He was as stern and demanding toward himself as he was toward his men.

Soon afterward he received new orders. He was assigned to the entrenchments before the cluster of forts around Verdun, where there was no need for cavalry. Here he saw the war grind to a bloody stalemate and the maddening boredom of rearline duty drove him to seek action. But he failed at every turn and with each passing day he felt more like a human mole. In a state of dejection he wrote to his mother: "Unfortunately we Uhlans have been attached to the infantry. I say 'unfortunately' because I'm certain that Lothar has already been in the big cavalry charges that we will never have here." That his younger brother would distinguish himself first was one of Manfred's gravest concerns. The fortunes of war!

He approached the lines only on rare occasions. With preparations under way a mile distant for a decisive battle of the war, he was forced to sit idly by and listen to the rumbling of the German heavy guns and the answering French 75s and 155s. It was maddening. He loathed the trenches and the barbed wire, the endless trails of mud and inactivity along the entire eight-mile front. The steep Meuse hills on all sides seemed to close in on him.

With much time to think, he began to reflect on the future of the horse soldier. It did not look promising. Like other restless fighting men his eyes turned skyward to the German and Allied air machines that droned idly over the battlefield. He envied them; at least they could see the tide of combat.

> "I am a restless spirit so my activity before Verdun was boresome. At first I was in the trenches at a place where nothing happened. Then I became a dispatch-bearer and hoped to have some adventures. But here I was mistaken. The fighting men immediately degraded me a base-hog and although I was not really at the base, I was not allowed to advance farther than within 1,500 meters of the front trenches. Here, below the ground, I had a heated, bombproof room. Now and then I had to go into the front-line trenches and that meant great physical exertion for I had to trudge uphill and downhill, crisscross through unending trenches and mire holes until I arrived at a place where the men were firing. After visiting them, my own position seemed a very stupid one. At that time the digging business was beginning and it became clear to cavalrymen what it is to dig endless approaches and trenches.

At night nothing stirred. Richthofen was listless and wretched. During the day, the intoxicating magnetism of flying and fighting in the air grew within him. Then, suddenly, it appeared that the trench monotony would be broken.

"One fine day our division became busy. We intended a small attack and I was delighted, for at last I would be able to do something as a connecting link! But it was another disappointment! I was given a different job! Now I had enough of it!"

Deep in thought, nursing his bitter disappointment, Richthofen paused to lean against his dugout door. Overhead a German Aviatik droned over the great rounded hump that was Fort Douaumont. The Leutnant nodded once to himself, stooped and entered his bomb-proof. He seated himself on his bunk and reached for pen and paper.

"I wrote a letter to my commanding general and at first my superiors wanted to snarl at me—but they fulfilled my wish. I joined the Flying Service at the end of May, 1915. My greatest wish was fulfilled!"

Manfred gathered his kit, slapped his favorite mount an affectionate farewell and said his goodbyes. From this day forward there would be no bugles and no bombard-ments. If he held any reservations as to the wisdom of his decision, he gave no outward sign. A few weeks earlier he shunned the flying service because he thought it would mean three action-filled months away from the hostilities. Like most of his comrades, he was certain the war would be over before he could finish air training. But now he was desperate for a change; it seemed to be the only way to get into the fray.

The first war planes were not fighting units. They were slow, lumbering two-seaters attached to the Army for reconnaissance work. Formation flying and individu-al air-to-air combat was yet to come, but now aerial photography and artillery spotting demanded as many trained observers as pilots. This was Richthofen's assign-ment. At Number 7 Air Replacement Section, Cologne, he was scheduled for four weeks of classes and 15 flying hours in navigation and map usage. Upon his arrival he was ordered to prepare for his first flight the next morning. This was his "test flight" designed to reveal his reactions, tendencies toward airsickness and squeamishness, and fear of high altitude and maneuvering. But from the very first, the man who was to become the most effective killing force in the yet-to-be-born *Luftstreitkräfte*—Air Force—thrived on the exciting new sensations. He wrote:

"The next morning at seven o'clock I was to fly for the first time as an observer! I was very excited, for I had no idea what it would be like. Everyone I asked told me a different story. That night I went to bed earlier than usual to be thoroughly refreshed the next morning. We drove to the flying ground and I got into the flying machine for the first time. The blast from the propeller was a great nuisance and I found it impossible to make myself understood by the pilot. Everything was carried away by the wind. If I took a piece of paper it disappeared. My safety helmet slid off. My muffler dropped off. My jacket was not tightly buttoned and in short I was uncomfortable. Before I knew what was happening, the pilot went ahead at full speed and the machine started rolling. We went faster and faster. I clutched the sides of the cockpit. Suddenly, the shaking stopped, the machine was in the air and the earth dropped away from me.

"I had been told the name of the place to which we were to fly and I was to direct the pilot. At first we flew straight ahead, then the pilot turned to the right, then left. I had lost all sense of direction over our own aerodrome! I hadn't the slightest notion where I was!

"I looked cautiously over the side at the country. The men looked ridiculously small and the houses seemed to have come out of a child's toy box. Everything seemed pretty. Cologne was in the background; the cathedral looked like a toy. It was a glorious feeling to be so high above the earth, to be master of the air. I didn't care a bit where I was, and when the pilot thought it was time to go down I was disappointed.

"I wanted to start immediately on another flight . . . I counted the hours to the time we would start again."

First Leutnant Zeumer was Richthofen's pilot. He was a small, frail man who was dying of tuberculosis. One of the first military aviators, he had a masterful hand on the controls of an Albatros B. II observation plane. But neither officer was impressed with the other; each was distant and reserved. Because of his crippling malady, Zeumer found it difficult to keep pace with his energetic observer.

In the summer of 1915 the largest army ever assembled under one man pushed forward as General von Mackensen began his historic advance from Gorlice to Brest-Litovsk. Richthofen's first assignment after completing his training was on the Russian front, and when the famous German sportsman, Count Holck, joined the squadron, Manfred transferred to the racing champion's aircraft. They hit it off splendidly. Richthofen wrote: "We went on many beautiful reconnoitering flights—I don't know how many—into Russia. Although Holck was young I never felt insecure with him. On the contrary he was always a support to me in critical moments. When I looked around and saw his determined face I had twice the courage as before."

Together they watched Mackensen's armies gain thousands of square miles a day, saw his sweeping onslaught with 15,000 artillery pieces, and joyously thumped one another's back when the Russians retreated in mass disorder.

Their last flight together nearly caused their deaths. It was early in August and they were flying toward Brest-Litovsk. Deep in Russia the plane approached the burning town of Wicznice. To observe the enemy columns they had to fly either through or around a pillar of dense smoke arising from the smouldering ruins. Richthofen tells of the folly that caused them to tumble 3,000 feet toward the flaming town with a smoke-choked engine.

"A gigantic smoke column went up to 6,000 feet and prevented us from continuing our flight because we flew at an altitude of only 4,500 feet in order to see better. For a moment Holck reflected. I asked him what he intended to do and advised him to fly around the smoke cloud which would have involved a roundabout way of five minutes. Holck did not intend to do this. On the contrary, the greater the danger the more the thing attracted him. Therefore, straight through! I enjoyed it too, to be with such a daring fellow, but our daring nearly cost us dear, for as soon as the tail-end of the machine disappeared into the smoke, the airplane began to reel. I couldn't see a thing because the smoke made my eyes water. The air was much warmer, and below me I could see nothing but a huge sea of fire. Suddenly the machine lost its balance and fell, turning round and round. I managed to hang on, otherwise I would have been thrown from the cockpit. The first thing I did was to look at Holck. Immediately I regained my courage, for his face showed an iron confidence. My only thought was: "It is stupid, after all, to die a hero's death so unnecessarily."

"Later, I asked Holck what he had been thinking at that moment. He said he never experienced so unpleasant a feeling.

"We fell to 1,500 feet above the burning town. Either through Holck's skill or by a Higher Will, perhaps both, we suddenly dropped out of the smoke cloud. Our good Albatros found itself again and once more we flew level.

"We had enough of it and instead of going to a new base we decided to return to our old quarter as quickly as possible. We were still above the Russians and only at 1,500 feet. Five minutes later I heard Holck shout behind me: *'The motor is giving out!'*

"Holck did not have as much knowledge of motors as he had of horseflesh, and I had not the slightest idea of mechanics. One thing was certain: we would have to land among the Russians if the motor went on strike. So one peril followed another.

"I was convinced that the Russians below were still marching with energy; I could see them quite clearly from our low altitude. Besides, it wasn't necessary to see them, for they shot at us with machine guns with the utmost diligence. The firing sounded like chestnuts roasting near a fire.

"Then the motor was hit and stopped dead. We went lower and lower and just managed to glide over a forest and land at an abandoned artillery position. I told Holck that the evening before I reported that this very site was still held by the Russians. We jumped from the plane and ran for the woods for cover. All I had was a pistol and six cartridges. Holck had nothing.

"When we reached the woods I turned, and with my glasses watched a soldier run toward our plane. I got a chill when I saw he wore a cap instead of a spiked helmet. I was certain he was a Russian but when the man came near, Holck shouted for joy. He recognized the man as a grenadier of the Prussian Guards. They had stormed this position at daybreak."

Separate assignments for Richthofen and Holck ended the warm companionship of the two noblemen and they reluctantly parted. In Brussels Manfred again met Zeumer; they were to be together again in a top secret unit being formed at Ostend under strictest security. Germany was forming the first long-distance bombing unit with two types of twin-engine biplanes. The *Grossflugzeuge* (large battle planes) intrigued Richthofen at first, but after two flights he disliked their slow, hulking flight. His plane was so unspeakably clumsy that he named it his "apple barge."

"One fine day we started with our large battle plane to delight the English with our bombs. We reached our objective and the first bomb fell. It is very interesting to watch the effect of a bomb; at least you like to see it exploding. Unfortunately my large battle plane had a stupid peculiarity which prevented me from seeing the effect of a bomb drop, for immediately after it was released the machine came between my eye and the target, covering it completely with its wings. This always made me wild because I did not like to be deprived of my amusement. If you hear a *bang* below and see the delightful grayish-white cloud of the explosion where you aimed, you are always well pleased. So I waved to Zeumer to bend a little to one side. While waving I forgot the infamous object on which I was traveling, my "apple barge," had two propellers which turned on either side of my observer seat. I meant to show him where the bomb had hit and *bang!* my finger was struck.

"Having been hit on the hand I did not care to throw

any more bombs. I quickly got rid of the lot and hurried home. My love for the large battle plane, which had not been great in the first place, suffered even more because of my accident. I had to sit quietly for seven days and was barred from flying. Only my beauty was slightly damaged, but after all, I can say with pride that I have been wounded in the war."

By September the veteran observer had become fascinated with the prospect of an aerial tourney. Airmen of both sides were carrying pistols and repeating rifles, and a few had crudely mounted light machine guns. Flying one day with Zeumer he found a Farman pusher over the lines. They made for it and Richthofen, in the forward cockpit, managed to get off four shots before it whizzed past. The Farman observer returned the fire and put several bullet holes through their wings. Zeumer wheeled for another pass, but the Farman declined. This incident whetted Richthofen's desire to bring down a machine; in a short time it became an obsession.

At Ostend there was a single-engine Albatros C. III, a two-seater in which the pilot flew from the front cockpit while the observer sat in the rear. There was a lightweight machine gun for the observer—just what Manfred wanted for the next meeting in the air. With another pilot, Osteroth, Richthofen penetrated three miles into French ground and found another Farman. Instead of approaching it head-on as Zeumer had done, Osteroth pulled alongside the Farman and as the range narrowed, Richthofen opened fire. After two bursts his gun jammed. To their surprise, this other machine also had a machine gun, and Richthofen's untimely jam gave the French observer time to train his weapon on the Albatros floating lazily just a few short yards off his wingtip. Osteroth never wavered as Richthofen worked furiously to clear his gun. Bullets zipped toward them across the short span of sky. Now Richthofen's gun was working again and he returned the fire. For half a minute the planes sailed side by side coolly trading broadsides of lead.

"When I had exhausted my hundred rounds I thought

I could not trust my eyes when my opponent started down in curious spirals," Richthofen said in recounting the action later. "I tapped Osteroth's head to draw his attention. Our opponent fell and fell and dropped at last into a large crater. There he was, his machine standing on its head, the tail pointing to the sky. According to our map he fell three miles behind the front. We brought him down on enemy ground, otherwise I would have one more victory to my credit. But after all, the main thing is to bring him down; it doesn't matter whether one is credited for it or not."

When Richthofen became a "chaser pilot" his personal feelings on victory credits remained unchanged. For his squadron pilots, however, it was firm. He guarded the honor of his men jealously and hotly protested when other staffels claimed victories that rightly belonged to his men. "An officer's first duty is to his men," he explained simply.

Zeumer transferred to single-engine Fokker monoplanes—escorts for Richthofen and Osteroth in their clumsy bomber. October brought a new assignment. As the flying Uhlan boarded a train that was to carry him to his next base, he was unaware that before his journey was ended he would meet the man who was to make the greatest change in his life.

Richthofen found his first attempts to bag human game highly frustrating. Although he had one unconfirmed victory, he knew it was exceptional for an airman to approach close enough to an enemy plane to shoot it down. The sluggish maneuverability and the crude armament of his clumsy bomber made a kill difficult. He pondered much on this problem.

Seated opposite Richthofen in the dining car was the famous Oswalde Boelcke, the man who had shot down four enemy machines singlehandedly. Manfred asked him: "Tell me, how do you do it?" Boelcke laughed politely. "Well, it's quite simple. I fly close to my man, aim well, and then of course he falls down."

Richthofen frowned and shook his head. "I've done

that Herr Oberleutnant, but my opponents don't go down."

Boelcke nodded and smiled wisely. "The reason, Leutnant Richthofen, is because you fly in a large *Grossflugzeug* and I fly a Fokker monoplane."

Richthofen turned the great ace's words over and over in his mind, and before he arrived at his new quarters he was determined to become a pilot—and a chaser pilot at that. Another training course meant more time away from the front, and so when he was once again reunited with Zeumer, he approached the frail airman with the prospect of taking lessons in the squadron's old two-seater. Zeumer agreed, and Richthofen spent every spare moment at the task.

Richthofen admitted to having been a poor academic student, but he was worse as a flying student. He overcontrolled, overcorrected and flailed the controls wildly about the cockpit. The weary biplane took much abuse at his heavy hands. His landings were desperate grabs for terra firma; 25 training flights were needed before Zeumer was willing to approve his student's solo. On an October evening Richthofen mechanically prepared for his first take-off alone. He said later:

"I started the take-off. The aeroplane went at the correct speed and I could not help noticing that I was actually flying. After all, I did not feel uneasy, but rather elated. I did not care for anything. I should not have been frightened no matter what happened. With contempt of death I made a large curve to the left and slowed the machine over a tree, exactly where I had been ordered to. I looked forward to see what would happen next. Now came the most difficult part: the landing. I remembered exactly what movements I had to make. I acted mechanically and the machine moved quite differently from what I expected. I lost my balance, made some wrong movements, stood on my head and succeeded in converting my aeroplane into a battered school bus. I was discouraged when I saw the damage I had done to the machine—which after all wasn't great—and had to suffer from the jokes of others.

Zeumer neglected to explain to his impulsive student that without the weight of the instructor the plane would be much lighter and more sensitive. Richthofen was unprepared for the different control response. He overcorrected, zoomed upward, waited too long to level out, stalled and crashed. A smash-up on the first solo is usually enough of a jar to discourage an average student from further flying attempts, but Richthofen was not an average student. He refused to accept failure. "Two days later I went at flying with a passion and suddenly I could handle it!" On Christmas Day, 1915, he completed his flight training at Döberitz and the following March he joined the Second Battle Squadron before Verdun. As an Albatros pilot he could now look down at the mud and miles of barbed wire he was once forced to endure.

Now his ingenuity joined forces with his determination. He mounted a machine gun on the upper wing of his plane so that it could be fired forward and upward. While his fellow pilots laughed at the crude, makeshift affair, Richthofen went over the front, found a Nieuport and shot it down! It was his turn to laugh, but instead he blandly reported: "I had an aerial fight and have shot down a Nieuport." Again his victim came to earth behind the Allied lines and again he could not be credited officially with the victory.

His daring defied the elements. In 1915, weather reporting for pilots was unheard of. Though storms were generally avoided, their devastating effects on planes were well known. Flimsy machines had been torn to shreds in the vicious vertical air currents, but to Richthofen, a young fledgling with a few hours under his belt, to fly around the storm was the coward's path. The challenge of a new and untried experience was too tempting.

He flew from his base at Mont to nearby Metz and was preparing to return . . .

"When I pulled my machine out of the hangar I saw the first signs of an approaching thunderstorm. Clouds like a gigantic pitch-black wall approached from the north. Old, experienced pilots urged me not to fly. However, I had promised to return and I would have considered myself a coward if I failed to come back because of a mere thunderstorm. Therefore, I meant to try.

"When I took off, the rain began falling and I had to throw away my goggles, otherwise I would not have seen anything. The trouble was that I had to fly over the Moselle Mountains where the thunderstorm was raging. I told myself that I would be lucky to get through. I rapidly approached the black cloud that reached to the earth. Flying at the lowest possible altitude I was absolutely compelled to leap over houses and trees. Soon I was lost. The gale seized my machine as if it were a piece of paper and drove it along. My heart sank for I realized I could not land among the hills. I was compelled to go on.

"I was surrounded by inky blackness. Beneath me trees bent in the gale. Suddenly I saw a wooded height in front of me. I could not turn—but my Albatros managed to take it. I could only fly in a straight line so I had to take every obstacle in front of me. My flight became a jumping competition pure and simple. I had to jump over trees, villages, spires and steeples, for I had to stay a few yards from the ground, or I'd have seen nothing. The lightning played around me. I didn't know then that lightning could not touch flying machines. I was certain of death for it seemed inevitable that the gale would hurl me into a village or forest at any moment. If the motor stopped I would have been done for.

"Then, on the horizon, the darkness became less thick. Over there the thunderstorm had passed. I would be saved if only I could get there! Concentrating all my energy I flew toward the light. Suddenly I left the thundercloud, but the rain was still falling in torrents. Still, I was saved.

"I landed at my aerodrome in pouring rain. Everyone was anxious for me, for Metz had reported my start and told them I had been swallowed up by a thundercloud.

"I vowed to never again fly through a thunderstorm unless the Fatherland should demand it."

Soon afterward, Richthofen realized his wish to fly a single-seater fighter. He shared a Fokker monoplane with a friend, Leutnant Reimann. Richthofen flew it in the morning and Reimann in the afternoon . . . and each was certain the other would smash it. Late one afternoon Reimann fought a Nieuport over Mort and received a bullet in his engine. Spiraling down unsteadily, he crash-landed between the lines and set the plane on fire to prevent it from falling into enemy hands. After nightfall, Reimann slipped back to the German trenches.

Richthofen became the sole pilot of the next Fokker assigned to his unit, but on his third take-off the engine quit without warning. He tried desperately to land in a nearby field, but he handled the emergency clumsily and in a twinkling his beautiful new bird was a twisted heap of scrap. The crash was serious, and mechanics—convinced the pilot was gravely injured or dead—rushed forward with a stretcher. Richthofen crawled out unhurt, stiffly pulled himself erect, and waved them away.

In June of 1916 he was ordered to Russia, where he flew two-seaters with *Kampfgeschwader II*.

There were many fine targets and when he dropped his 300 pounds of bombs he circled to strafe troops and mounted Cossacks. "An aerial attack upsets them completely," he related to his fellow pilots with a devilish flair. "Suddenly the lot of them rush away in all directions of the compass. I wouldn't like to be the commander of a Cossack squadron being fired upon by an airplane."

While the young flying officer was having a grand time in Russia fighting a one-sided air war, the situation on the Western front was not favorable. French and English air scouts now ruled the air with their superior machines. Not only did they outnumber the Germans, they outmaneuvered and outgunned them as well. Allied planes appeared at will over most of the front. They bombed rear supply dumps, freely photographed troop movements and directed artillery fire unmolested. Their fast fighters swept to treetop levels along the German trenches and sprayed the soldiers with machine-gun fire. Morale suffered. A bitter cry went up from the Kaiser's infantrymen during the bloody battle of the Somme.

*Gott strafe England, unsere Artillerie und
unsere Flieger!*
(May God punish England, our Artillery and
our Fliers!)

Back to the Western front went Richthofen, this time
as one of Oswalde Boelcke's select pupils. Boelcke was
developing a new "formation flying" squadron to check
the surging Allied victories. In company with Boelcke
on a morning hunt, flying an Albatros D.II, the Leutnant gained his first singlehanded victory, an F.E.2b of
Number 11 Squadron, R.F.C. He was elated. In the
Boelcke Squadron there were 12 pilots. During six
weeks of operation that autumn, six were killed outright,
one was incapacitated by wounds and two collapsed
from nervous strain. Von Richthofen flew on. Success
followed success and his victories mounted—but not
without cost. On the morning of October 28, 1916, Boelcke, after gaining 40 victories, was killed in a mid-air
collision with one of his own pilots—a close friend. Five
months later Richthofen narrowly escaped death in his
first combat defeat, and to this day no one knows who
put him out of action.

"I was flying with the squadron and noticed an opponent
in another squadron over Lens. I had to fly quite a
distance to get there. It tickles your nerves to fly toward
the enemy, especially when you see him at a distance and
when several minutes must pass before you can start
fighting. I imagine that at such a moment my face turns a
little pale ... I like the feeling: it is a wonderful nerve
stimulant. You see the enemy from afar. You have recognized that his squadron is really an enemy formation. You
count the number of machines and consider whether the
conditions are favorable or not. An important factor is
whether the wind forces you away from or toward our
lines.

"We had five machines. Our opponents were three times
as numerous. The English flew about like midges. It is not
easy to disperse a swarm of machines which fly together in
good order. It is impossible for a single machine to do it
...

"I watched whether one of their fellows would hurry to take leave of his colleagues. There! One of them is stupid enough to depart alone! I can reach him and I say to myself 'That man is lost!' Shouting aloud, I am after him. I am getting very near him. He starts shooting prematurely, which shows he is nervous. So I say to myself: 'Go on shooting—you won't hit me.' He shot with a kind of ammunition that ignites, so I could see his shots passing me and felt as if I were sitting in front of a gigantic watering pot. The sensation was not pleasant.

"At that moment I think I laughed aloud. But soon I got a lesson. When I approached the Englishman quite closely and had come to a distance of about 300 feet, I got ready for firing, aimed, and gave a few trial shots. My machine guns were in order. The decision to fire would come before long and in my mind's eye I saw him dropping.

"My former excitement was gone. In such a position one thinks calmly and collectively and weighs the probability of hitting and being hit. As a rule the fight itself is the least exciting part of the business. If you get excited in air fighting you are sure to make mistakes; you will never get your enemy down. Besides, calmness is a matter of habit. At any rate, in this case I was calm as I approached up to 50 yards of my man. I fired some well-aimed shots and thought I was bound to be successful. That was *my* idea. Suddenly I heard a tremendous *bang!* after I had scarcely fired 10 cartridges. Then something hit my machine again. I realized my machine was hit and at the same time smelled the powerful stench of benzine and saw the engine running slack. The Englishman noticed it too, for he started shooting at me with redoubled energy while I had to stop firing.

"I went right down. Instinctively I switched off the engine. It was high time, for when the benzine tank has been punctured and the infernal liquid is squirting around your legs, there is great danger of fire. Up front is a combustion engine that is red hot. If a single drop of benzine should fall on it the entire machine would be in flames.

"I left a thin white cloud in the air. I knew its meaning from my enemies, for it is the first sign of a coming explosion. I was at 9,000 feet and had to go a long way to get down. By the kindness of Providence my engine stopped running. I have no idea how fast I went down;

the speed was so great I couldn't put my head out of the machine without being pushed back by the rush of air.

"Soon I lost sight of my enemy, but I had time to see what my four comrades were doing as I dropped to the ground. They were still fighting and their machine guns, as well as those of the enemy, could still be heard. Suddenly I noticed a rocket. A signal of the enemy? Evidently a machine is on fire. Which machine? The burning airplane looks like one of our own. *No!* Praise the Lord, it is one of the enemy's. Who could have shot him down? Immediately afterward a second machine drops out and falls to the ground turning, turning, turning exactly as I did, but suddenly it recovers its balance and flies straight toward me. It is an Albatros that no doubt had the same experience as I had.

". . . I found a meadow . . . Everything went as desired. I had ample time to inspect the damage. My machine had been hit several times. The bullet that caused me to give up the fight had gone through both benzine tanks. I did not have a drop left . . ."

The engine, by stopping the other bullets, saved him, but the British gunner had an eagle eye and a steady finger. His name is lost to history, but had one of his tracers ignited the Albatros's fuel tanks, Richthofen's promising career would have been nipped.

From that day forward, Richthofen pulled rein on his impetuous dash, for he realized that eagerness led to overconfidence and carelessness. Still, he failed to completely check this tendency to lower his guard at crucial times. It was his only combat fault, and it led to trouble a number of times—the last time fatally.

The Fatherland could not ask for more in a young fighting pilot. Richthofen himself had no illusions about this struggle; it was war, plain and simple—a matter of kill or be killed. He drove himself hard and expected the same of his men. Having never been pampered, he did not favor nursing young replacements through their first combat. Once a new pilot was sent to his squadron, and after being assigned to a plane he was welcomed by the Rittmeister. As they chatted, the field telephone from the Air Warning Post rang. A British squadron returning from a raid would pass overhead in a few minutes. Richthofen turned to the fledgling and said: "Get into your machine. The British are coming over. Go after them and kill some!" The excited youngster climbed into his waiting plane and took off. Fifteen minutes later he was dead.

Although generous with advice on tactics, and willing to teach what he knew about planning an attack, when the squadrons clashed in the air and the planes scattered for single combat, Richthofen's men were on their own. As a leader, no German officer received more respect with less effort. He did not openly demand attention; his mere presence commanded it. He spoke slowly, with a conviction that he would be listened to, and he looked only at the person to whom he spoke. He administered in true Prussian fashion; his subordinates never questioned his judgment, and everyone knew that those who fell short of his standards would be speedily transferred. He was not standoffish, but neither was he a hail-fellow well-met. He never enjoyed the close bond of fellowship that soldiers in the field come by so naturally. His popularity did not suffer because of this, for his men sensed in this aloofness a way of keeping the dignity of his rank. When his men spoke of him, it was with unquestioning devotion. Possibly he did not know how to make friends; possibly it was a welcome cover for the shortcomings of his personality. His natural shyness made him seem almost afraid of young women; and having been in uniform since age 11, he had not time to learn the social graces or develop warmth. Although he was the most eligible bachelor in all Germany, his mind was filled with the practical matters of conflict; he was never concerned about the mysteries he created. He discouraged speculation as to the "real Richthofen" that lay beneath his austere surface. He was as courteous as he needed to be, but it was a courtesy that discouraged intimacy. Occasionally he joined his men for a drink or a game of pinocle. He drank with moderation and smoked rarely, and after awhile he would leave them and retire to his desk where he faithfully wrote to his mother several times a week. He always retired late, but was first on the line for the early patrol. Off base Richthofen traveled alone. On several occasions he was seen in the Hotel Metropol in Brussels, dining alone. He rarely confided in anyone.

During his 19 months as a fighter pilot and Geschwader Commander, Richthofen permitted himself few—if any—close comrades. He chose them with more care than he chose his pilots. They were the old associates who had been with him in the original *Jasta Boelcke*. He hunted game with Karl Schaefer, who was killed in June of 1917. Kurt Wolff, the only man with whom Richthofen clearly indicated a comradeship, fell three months later. When Karl Allmenroder and Werner Voss died, Manfred von Richthofen was the last of the original Boelcke pilots. Here perhaps was one reason Richthofen did not encourage close friendships; it would not place him in a position where he would feel the loss when it came. He protected his sensitivity.

He was a man of contrasts. In the air his attitude toward the enemy was clear cut. Get him or he will get you. On the ground it was different. Downed airmen were brought to his squadron mess for drinks and an exchange of views. The amiable Englishmen in their knee-length flying coats of burnished leather were pleasant diversions. Higher headquarters had given strict orders against such fraternization with captives, but Richthofen winked at this and permitted his men to "rescue" enemy pilots from the ground troops. Toasts were exchanged, theories expounded as to who would win the war, and backs genially slapped until the evening's ration of schnapps was gone. Then the fallen foeman was packed merrily off to interrogation and prison camp.

Lothar, who joined the squadron in March of 1917, was strikingly different. Jovial, warm, and devil-may-care, he was the absolute opposite of his elder brother. With never a thought to the odds, in his first month of action he gained 20 victories. In 77 days at the front he downed 40 enemy planes.

A month after Boelcke's death, on November 23, 1916,

Richthofen won a notable air combat. His opponent was the "British Immelmann"—Major Lanoe Hawker, holder of the Victoria Cross and the Distinguished Service Cross. They were well matched; Richthofen had ten victories, Hawker nine. South of Bapaume at 10,000 feet they met. Of the two machines, Hawker's DeHavilland pusher was the more maneuverable, but Richthofen's Albatros could outclimb it.

"The impertinent fellow was full of cheek, and when we got down to about 3,000 feet he merrily waved to me as if he would say, 'Well, how do you do?'

". . . I had time to take a good look at my opponent. I looked down into his cockpit and could see every movement of his head. If he had not worn a cap I would have noticed what kind of a face he was making."

The circling planes maneuvered for a favorable position for 35 minutes, losing altitude all the while. Hawker, who had ventured over German-held ground, was running dangerously low on fuel, and he knew the predominate west wind was against him. Richthofen, aware of his own advantage, forced the DH pilot lower and lower in tighter circles, trying to make him land and surrender before he could cross the lines to safety. Hawker knew the outcome would be close; he zigzagged when Richthofen's guns pounded close behind; he flew straight when his fuel indicator reminded him that his tank was almost dry. At these times Richthofen could have shot to kill, but he deliberately aimed wide, still hopeful the pilot could be forced to land.

Hawker suddenly performed several quick loops to shake the persistent Albatros, during which he fired several blistering bursts uncomfortably close to the German aviator. They were now less than 300 feet over Ligny, and at the last moment, with the lines dead ahead, Hawker broke off combat in a desperate dash to reach his lines. Richthofen made a decision. As they passed low over the shelled square, he took deliberate aim and depressed the Spandau triggers. Hawker received a bullet in his head and crashed full-tilt into the upper story of a gutted house. A shower of bricks and debris cascaded through the air, and the biplane dissolved in a ghastly jumble of metal, wood and shredded fabric.

By January of 1917, the Baron's score was 16. He was given command of Jasta 11 at Douai and awarded the *Pour le mérite*, the decoration he coveted. Now he was free to expand the principles set forth by Boelcke. He insisted that his men keep a close watch behind. "Don't be taken unawares," he preached, "and don't underestimate the English. They absolutely challenge us to battle and never refuse a fight." Richthofen admired this in an enemy. He respected the offensive dash of the Allied fliers who dared to penetrate well behind the German lines to find their opponents. Because the German Air Service was nearly always generally outnumbered, it ordered its tactical patrols to follow a more practical plan—a defensive one—and not venture into the Allied camp. Too, the prevailing wind was westerly, and for this reason many more Allied airmen were captured on German-held ground than vice versa.

April of 1917 was the month America entered the war. "Bloody April" it was called by the Royal Flying Corps. Richthofen was promoted to Rittmeister, and his victory score exceeded that of his old master, Boelcke. He was the Fatherland's leading ace. The tide had turned dramatically since those bitter, gloomy days of 1916 when Allied planes had all but swept the skies of German airmen. Now there was a four-to-one victory ratio in favor of the Kaiser's *Fliegers*. Superior aircraft design, skilled engineering and an all-out production program put scores of new German fighting machines in the skies months before the new British models appeared in quantity. The slow, lumbering B.E.s and F.E.s were outmaneuvered, outnumbered and outgunned by sleek and deadly Halberstadt and Albatros scouts in the hands of youngsters with far less flying experience. The Maltese Cross ruled the air over the Western front while the Allied air tactical philosophy remained unchanged. Daily the British doggedly "carried on" and flew their missions in the face of almost certain death. Richthofen wrote: "...they are always ready to fight, regardless of their position, and so they fall like flies." Eight days in April Richthofen scored single victories. On three days he scored triples. On the 29th of April he scored four times and brought his total to the unheard of figure of 52 enemy planes downed.

There are five decades of half-truths and myths surrounding this unusual personality. Many discredited Richthofen the man as well as Richthofen the soldier. A common slur against his "cowardly fighting tactics" claimed he flew above his squadron to pick off the cripples striking for home. A pilot who would paint his machine a conspicuous glaring red to invite attackers could not build such an unparalleled string of victories by fighting only damaged machines and novice pilots. His record against experienced airmen and top-notch enemy flying equipment speaks for itself. Of his 80 victories, 42 were single-seater fighters with forward-firing machine guns; Sopwith Camels, S.E.5s and Nieuports, all matched to the Albatros Scout and Fokker Dr. I. He scored eight times against the formidable two-place "fighter types," the Sopwith one-and-a-half Strutter and the deadly Bristol Fighter. Ironically, the two times Richthofen was shot down in air combat were while attacking the older, obsolete planes.

Years after the war, the rumor that the ace used his rank and position to increase his bag of victories circulated throughout England and America. Doctor Max Osborn, the German war correspondent, wrote three days after Richthofen's death: "... *they (his men) said that whenever Richthofen and another pilot fired on the same plane that crashed, Richthofen stepped back in favor of the other claimant, a habit they praised as a handsome expression of his high-minded comradeship.*"

Late in the evening of April 29, 1917, within an hour of gaining his 52nd victory, von Richthofen was interrupted at dinner by a telephone message from High command.

I have just received the message today that you have been victor in an air battle for the fiftieth time. I heartily congratulate you upon this marvelous success. The Fatherland looks with thankfulness upon its brave flier.

May God further preserve you.

—Wilhelm I. R.

April held a strange significance for Manfred von Richthofen. It was in April of 1915, before Verdun, that he decided to fight his war in the skies. In April 1916, in a clumsy two-seater, equipped with an awkward machine gun, he shot down his first enemy plane as a chaser pilot. April of 1917 was his record month for air victories.

What would April of 1918 hold?

CHAPTER FOUR

"... Shot Down to His Death"

The scattered dumplings of clouds drifted lazily under the formation of Albatros scouts as they droned in the brilliant blue at 12,000 feet. On this day, July 6, 1917, young Richthofen, accompanying the *Kette* in his all-red machine, was dealt a sudden upset in his rise to fame. Four days earlier he sent his 57th aircraft, an R.E.8 from Number 53 Squadron, R.F.C., flaming to earth with its two occupants; and now he glimpsed the kind of death he had dealt to British airmen for the past 10 months. He tumbled unchecked to within 150 feet of the pocked battlefield, his plane out of control, blood streaming down his ashen face, strength sapped, and fighting— desperately fighting away—the brink of darkness. He clutched stubbornly to every wisp of strength and through sheer force of will, held the fading light until he could reach German-held ground for a crash landing.

Coming at a time when the air-fighting staffels were being reorganized into Jagdgeschwaders, or groups, Richthofen's stumble was a serious blow. As Geschwader Kommandeur he had headed J.G.I's four Jastas (squadrons) only two weeks before this day. The group was centered around Courtrai in occupied Belgium with Jasta 4 at Cuene under von Doering, Jasta 6 at Bissegham under von Dostler, and Jasta 10 at Heuie under von Althaus. Jasta 11 was at Marcke, Richthofen's headquarters. This had been his squadron, but after his promotion to Rittmeister, he passed this command to the highly capable Kurt Wolff.

Wolff had already flown in the early morning patrol of the 6th, and was writing his 32nd victory claim when the field telephone rang to warn of enemy air activity in Jasta 11's sector. The highly efficient *Flugmeldedienst,* or Flight Reporting Service, was a network of aircraft-spotting stations that observed the number and direction of enemy planes crossing the front. The reports were channeled to a control center by telephone and the Jasta nearest the approaching flight was notified of their altitude, strength and probable point of interception. Since Jasta 11 was still on alert, Wolff snatched up his helmet and goggles and sprinted for his waiting Albatros as six others followed. On the spur of the moment, Richthofen decided to accompany the slender Staffelführer and they headed for the lines, eight strong, Wolff leading.

The weather was excellent as they climbed to patrol altitude between Ypres and Armentières without sighting the enemy formation. They patrolled the intercept area for 20 minutes before they finally saw six F.E.2s, still on the British side. They were from Number 20 Squadron at Marie-Chapelle and were out for the express purpose of seeking out and destroying any German aircraft they could draw into a scrap. They were a plucky crew, for none knew better than they that their slow, underarmed F.E.s were no match for the speedy Albatros. Thus the hunters became the hunted as Richthofen eyed the formation carefully and kept his distance. Richthofen suspected that the Britishers wanted to cross the lines but dared not risk encountering his squadron. All eyes in the flight were now watching the F.E.s closely, glancing now and then to the Rittmeister in anticipation of his signal to attack. The F.E.s retreated, but when they slipped over the lines a few miles away, Richthofen was prepared for the move. He knew the east wind that day favored the British squadron, which could use it to drift back to safety. He thought the British saw his staffel waiting for them. They had not; they were merely heading for their assigned patrol area. When he knew the enemy squadron was far enough behind the German lines to be caught, Richthofen sprung his trap. He wheeled the entire formation in one grand curve and cut off their escape.

In the tight formation, Wolff was a few yards ahead and below the Rittmeister as Richthofen singled out the leader and plunged down. The F.E. pusher biplane carried the observer-gunner in front and the pilot in the rear cockpit. Except for the engine it had no rear protection. Captain D.C. Cunnell was piloting the command plane and up front at the swivel-mounted Lewis gun was Second Lieutenant A.E. Woodbridge. Before the first shots were exchanged it became clear that a major engagement was rapidly developing. Four Sopwith triplanes of Number 10 Naval Squadron sped to the F.E.'s rescue as another German squadron edged toward the converging flights.

As the distance narrowed, Richthofen was vaguely aware of Wolff's opening burst on the lead plane and of Woodbridge's quick return fire. He calculated precisely how he would make his initial attack. If the head-on pass were unsuccessful, he would turn back and make a second pass at the enemy's blind spot under the cumbersome F.E.'s tail.

Cunnel accepted combat immediately, and as Wolff flashed past the outmoded two-seater, the Captain turned to meet the red Albatros, giving Woodbridge a clear target.

Woodbridge was surprised and excited by the sudden onslaught of the German swarm, but he singled out the attacker behind Wolff and tensed for the head-on attack. He swung his gun, aligned the sights on the looming biplane and began firing in steady bursts . . .

"Thank God my Lewis didn't jam. I kept a steady stream of lead pouring into the nose of that machine . . . I could see my tracers splashing along the barrels of his Spandaus and I knew the pilot was sitting right behind them . . ."

As yet, Richthofen had not released the safety catches

on his machine-gun triggers. He reported his dash toward the F.E. this way:

> I let him shoot, for at a distance of 300 yards and more the best marksman is helpless. One does not hit his target at such a distance.
> Now he flies toward me, and I hope that I will succeed in getting behind him and opening fire.
> Suddenly, something strikes me in the head. For a moment my whole body is paralyzed. My arm hangs down limply beside me; my legs flop loosely beyond my control. The worst was that a nerve leading to my eyes had been paralyzed and I was completely blind.

Woodbridge sensed that something had gone wrong with the enemy machine, and later he said:

> Then something happened. We could hardly have been 20 yards apart when the Albatros pointed her nose down suddenly. Zip, and she passed under us. Cunnel banked and turned. We saw the all-red plane slip into a spin. It turned over and over and round and round. It was no maneuver. He was completely out of control. His motor was going full on, so I figured I had at least wounded him. As his head was the only part of him that was not protected from my fire by his motor, I figured that's where he was hit.

Once again Richthofen's contempt for long-range fire had lured him into serious trouble. His head was the only part of his body not shielded by the engine and on the left side of his skull one of Woodbridge's bullets found its mark. The lead missile struck a glancing blow and furrowed alongside the bone. Although it did not touch his brain, it splintered the bone—and one of the splinters pressed a vital nerve. Two miles over the lines his D.V fighter went into a steep dive with power on—completely out of control. Within seconds it began to spiral viciously and later Richthofen admitted the force was so great it could have torn the wings off.

The ace acted instinctively—much as he had during his earlier emergency. In a moment he recovered the use of his arms and legs, but not his sight. He fumbled blindly for the ignition switch, found it and killed the runaway engine. He twisted his head to find the sun, but could not. Everywhere it was black. He tore off his goggles. Still there was no light. He was completely blind. Recalling that horrifying experience he later said: "At that moment the idea struck me: *This is how it feels when one is shot down to his death!*"

With power off, the Albatros slackened, then wallowed drunkenly about the sky, alternately catching itself and falling into another sickening plunge. During one gyration it stalled completely and began a loose spin. Richthofen felt the plane's movements and estimated he had dropped between four to six thousand feet.

> I concentrated all my energy and said to myself, 'I must see—I must—I must see!' Whether my energy helped me in this case I do not know. At any rate, suddenly I could discern black and white spots and more and more I regained my eyesight.

Richthofen peered dazedly through half-closed eyelids at the badly blurred altimeter. It read 2,400 feet when he carefully pulled the Albatros from its spin and listlessly he permitted the machine to glide ahead until he leveled off, shakily, at 150 feet. Below him stretched the churned battlefield and barbed wire entanglements. No landing here, and so he switched the still-windmilling Mercedes back to life and flew eastward. But his strength began to wane and his eyesight began to fail again. He knew if he blacked out again, at that low altitude, it would be the end. Fortunately there was a small patch of relatively unplowed ground directly ahead with a road nearby. Fighting to hold his sight, he glided awkwardly into the ground and took with him a string of posts and telephone wires. The battle-scarred plane settled to a stop. Weakly, Richthofen tried to crawl from the cockpit. He was halfway out before his strength left him and he fell to the ground and lay still.

While two of the Baron's pilots circled overhead, Leutnant Schroeder of the *Flugmeldedienst*, with a corporal, were the first to reach the crippled plane. They found the pilot lying on a bed of thorns, too weak to move. Blood filled his helmet and streamed over his head to the ground. Under the smeared and coagulated blood his face was a pasty white and his eyes were closed. His breathing was so shallow that both men were certain he was dead. They loosened his collar, gingerly removed the bloody helmet, and applied a field dressing. When the airman stirred, Leutnant Schroeder ordered his corporal to hurry to the nearest field telephone and summon an ambulance. Troops passed by and one soldier paused to offer the Rittmeister a drink of cognac, but Richthofen wisely waved it away in favor of water, knowing that a stimulant would not be good for the profuse bleeding. He asked to be taken immediately to Courtrai, and as soon as the ambulance drove up he was placed inside, now having lapsed into delirium and deep shock.

At Menin, the ambulance turned into an aid post, but Richthofen refused to be removed. He told the doctor he wanted to go directly to Courtrai. The doctor reflected only a moment before he nodded to the driver. The wagon bounced on.

In Courtrai the ambulance sped to St. Nicolas Hospital where alerted surgeons were already scrubbed and awaiting the famous ace. As soon as the patient was on the operating table an anesthetic was administered and his head was shaved.

The wound was four inches long. At one place the bare white skull lay exposed over an area the size of a half dollar. Hair never grew there again. Had the bullet traveled a fraction of an inch farther to the left it would have been the end. The surgeons sutured the wound and ordered complete rest and quiet. Richthofen's nurse, Katie Otersdorf, as efficient as she was attractive, hovered quietly near the Fatherland's great eagle. But despite her gentle nursing care, neither she, the physicians, nor the drugs could relieve the excruciating headache the patient suffered for the next two days. Within the week Richthofen sat up in bed to read letters and telegrams of sympathy from his friends and comrades. He even joked about his thick Richthofen skull having proved itself bulletproof. News of his fall had not as yet been released to the German people, and it was several weeks before the British learned what had happened. Certainly Jagdgeschwader I fought with no less vigor, for now they flew with vengeance. On the afternoon of July 11th, the Rittmeister stirred from his rest to see Staffelführer Wolff placed on the bed beside his. Grinning sheepishly, Wolff raised his bandaged left hand in greeting. It had been shot through in the morning's air fighting.

Nineteen days after his near scrape with death, Richthofen was back at Marcke, anxious to resume command of J.G.I. His doctors advised against a too-early return to duties, and his superiors forbade him to fly. He was thinner, quieter. The bullet that nearly killed him had robbed him of a portion of the vitality and vigor that made him what he was. Clearly the wounding and the unnerving fall had sapped his spirit, and after a few days back in the field he realized how weak he really was. His strength did not return quickly nor did his wound heal well. For months afterward he complained of severe head pains, dizziness and buzzing in his ears. He retired frequently to the solitude of his quarters to nurse his throbbing head, and twice he returned to St. Nicolas Hospital to have bone splinters pulled from the wound. If his men had cause to idolize him before, they had even greater reason now. When the pilots congratulater him on having made a safe landing under such heavy adversities, he replied matter-of-factly, "It was quite the natural thing to do under the circumstances. Any one of you would have done the same. A true chaser pilot never takes his hand from the controls until he drops dead!"

On the morning of August 16th, after five weeks out of the cockpit, Richthofen defied orders. After Jasta 11 was airborne he called for his machine to be readied and took off alone for the lines. In the air, he struggled to fight off a creeping nausea. As he broke out of cloud cover over the Houthulst Forest he sighted a lone Nieuport scout. Cautiously he maneuvered to a favorable position above and behind the unsuspecting enemy pilot, and in a single, swift pass, he shot the machine to earth. He watched over the cockpit rim as the tumbling plane fell end over end and slowly broke apart—and his sickness suddenly became acute. He turned directly for home, and once arrived, made a shaky landing. Bathed in sweat, in a state of complete exhaustion, he was helped from his plane by his mechanics and put to bed by his batman. When he finally arose some hours later, he avoided the medics, knowing they would try to send him on leave.

For the first time in his life, Manfred von Richthofen was fighting an enemy he could not see; the ghost of a shaken confidence—and it was making itself known. He finally conquered the specter, though the long struggle left mental wounds that never completely healed.

Ten days later he flew again to gain his 59th victory, a Spad. Again he had a bout with airsickness and dizziness. Again he retired to his quarters for rest.

After his 60th victory on September 2nd, the Rittmeister took leave for his beloved Schweidnitz. The Baroness Kunigunde von Richthofen noticed a great change in her son when she saw him. She confided: "When I saw him afterward, the wound on his head was still open. I think it was only natural that he longed for this rest in his old home. But he could not find it there; there was too much excitement around him."

The warrior was tired. During the few moments he found alone he pondered much over Germany's fate. He was no longer confident of victory and he expressed—for the first time—a fear for Lothar's safety. Manfred's assurance faded and he became less formal, almost relaxed, with his subordinates. When he returned to the front on October 23rd, he missed many of the smiling faces that had bade him farewell six weeks earlier. In his absence the war had not been kind to J.G.I, for among the

missing were two of his ablest fighters—both Staffelführers. Werner Voss, the latest leader of Jasta 10, and
Kurt Wolff were dead.

mysterious whirlpool, a tortured, torn expanse of muddy soil pitted with shell craters. Then a light breeze stirred from the east-northeast. The sun showed promise of rising clear overhead to burn off the ground mist. By 6:30 the surface temperature was in the mid-forties and observers looked for improved visibility.

The troops were glad for a dry day. Their dew-covered helmets gleamed softly in the early light that gave a new color to the khaki dress of the Australians and the field gray of the Germans; a color made by the sun that tried to break through the veil of overcast.

Rifle barrels were wet. The Germans rubbed the moisture from their 98 Mausers with their fingers, and the Aussies did the same to their Lee-Enfields. And all waited.

The sky was usually hung with observation balloons at this hour, but the artillery targets were still shrouded in haze, and the balloons bobbed at their winches like bloated pigs. Later they would float aloft.

It was Sunday, April 21st. Atop the ridge others were rising. At the command posts of the 11th and 14th Australian Brigades, artillerymen were stirring. There was a smell of fresh wet earth and the almost eerie trill of a morning lark. From here the Australian gunners surveyed the cauldron of battle, the meandering trenches below; from here they appraised the havoc of every shell they arced into the enemy positions. On these heights a determined array of field pieces and howitzers pointed their barrels eastward. Nearby, diggers huddled low over sheltered fires made from splintered ammunition boxes. A quiet morning meant bacon for breakfast and possibly stew at midday. But however appetizing was the aroma of frying bacon, for some the delightful scent was a sinister reminder of another lingering smell. They could recall that it was three years earlier, almost to the day, that Fritz launched the war's first gas attack.

One of the forward batteries was equipped with six 18-pounder field pieces in pits and two post-mounted Lewis guns (for anti-aircraft protection). The emplacements were perched on the bald crest a hundred feet above the now-turgid Somme where the stream curves sharply southward and flows on to Corbie. The 53rd Battery of the 14th Australian Field Artillery Brigade—part of the Fifth Division—were robust men from Queensland and New South Wales. A hundred yards to their right was a sister battery, the 55th. The 51st Battalion was centered north of Corbie, and the 52nd Battalion was dug in at Vaux-sur-Somme on the river's north shore. Eight hundred yards southeast of the 53rd Battery, on lower ground, was the 11th Australian Infantry Brigade. A thousand yards due east of its guns was a shell-shattered brick kiln whose tall, perforated chimney was a prominent landmark. Imaginative Aussies called the crest thereabout "Whistler Ridge" owing to the shell holes through the brick stack, that likened it to a fife.

The Fifth Division was formed in Egypt from artillery and infantry troops trained in the vicinity of their homeland's state capitals.

Commanding the 53rd Battery was Leslie Ellis Beavis, a Duntroon graduate from New South Wales. An erect, fair-haired and well-proportioned officer, Beavis stood just under six feet. Little that happened in his bailiwick—or in the German positions two miles distant—escaped his alert blue eyes. He was a better than average officer, and his skill in commanding a forward artillery unit was held in high regard by his superiors. He was a mere youth of 23 and he was a major. Although younger than many of his battery regulars, he met little resentment on this account and was well liked by officers and men alike. In the heaviest bombardments of Broodseinde and Passchendaele, when Australian artillery suffered the heaviest casualties of that time, Beavis directed artillery operations through deafening days and flash-filled nights of thundering, rolling H.E. and shrapnel. For weeks he had lived in a gas atmosphere. By day the Germans lobbed phosgene shells, and at night mustard shells fell into their positions. The sun, struggling through the misty air, evaporated the pools of choking, burning yellow death; officers and men removed their masks only to eat. Beavis was not as yet physically ill, but like many casualties, he had lost his voice.

Then, in the early morning hours of November 2nd, near Hannebeek Wood, a mustard shell dropped onto his headquarters dugout and settled him. With his eyes bandaged and his throat enflamed, he was taken to Wandsworth Hospital in London to recuperate. By January he was back in Flanders with the 53rd and in early April arrived on the Somme. The young tactician emplaced his guns on the high ground, slightly on the northern side of the Somme-Ancre peninsula.

The guns were light, horse-drawn English artillery pieces that fired a 3.3-inch explosive shell of 18 pounds. In battle the weapons proved flexible and effective, and although their range was understood to be four miles, they could strike an additional mile by lowering their spade and laying the elevation angle. The gun line, all 75 yards of it, faced southeast, toward Hamel.

"Normally all six guns were operative," Beavis recalls today, "but on this morning one was out of action owing to a faulty breech mechanism. Although Ordnance workshops insisted it was safe, I refused to fire it until it was replaced."

Like most forward field batteries on exposed ground, the 53rd had two light machine guns mounted head-high on wooden posts for protection against strafing by German airplanes. Gaudy, black-crossed machines would make sudden low-level darts along and behind the Allied trenches to strafe exposed troops unawares.

Behind the field pieces, 23-year-old Bombardier J. S. Seccull emerged from his dugout in the embankment. A former carpenter of Preston, Victoria, Seccull was the NCO in charge of the Lewis mounts. When the battery arrived on the Somme he had placed his two guns on the left half of the line according to Major Beavis's orders. As events would later show, this was sound tactics.

Seccull's dugout mate was Gunner Robert Buie, who had been awake for three hours and was standing near his gun. Spare drums of ammunition were at his feet.

Buie, 25, was fair, short and tubby, a quiet, shy young man from the Australian bush. His Scotch progenitors came to Australia in the 1800s to work in oyster culture and to fish the beautiful coastal waters. Before Buie volunteered he was one of an extraordinary group of professional fishermen whose families had fished the mouth of the Hawkesbury for generations. He thrived in the rough, and from his boyhood days of hunting in the wilds, this youth with the keen blue eyes had been a crack shot with a rifle. Early in training his accuracy was noted and he was trained as a machine gunner. He did his work well and had little to say.

Gunner William John Evans was on duty at the other Lewis post. Nicknamed "Snowy" because of his fair—almost white—head of hair, the former Queensland shearer was, at 27, a roustabout on the rough-and-ready side. He was light complexioned with a large straight nose, large of frame, muscular and a talker. A 53rd artilleryman described him as "a demon with the drink but a man who could truly soldier." To minimize the effects of his drinking and isolate him from the regular gun crews, he was assigned to the remaining Lewis mount. Major Beavis considered Evans a "good chap" and acknowledged that he was more of an extrovert than his fellow gunner, Buie.

"Their weapons were, in reality, not 'machine guns,'" Beavis explains, "but light automatics which, in contrast to the heavier Vickers machine gun, could be easily traversed or elevated to follow a target. Each gun had elliptical AA sights, two ellipses—for fast and slow speeds of the angular movement of the target. The manufactured sights had not yet been issued, so I arranged for Fitter Bartlett to go to the Ordnance workshops and make two sets.

"Evans was about ten yards to the left of the number six gun and Buie's gun was only some five or ten yards in the rear of the line, about the center or slightly left of center."

"We were on the reverse slope of the ridge, with good drainage. When there was traffic the soil was gray-black, but the shell craters and excavations showed the characteristic white limestone or chalk content. A narrow muddy trail ran along the back of the ridge with a bank on the side of the guns. The dugouts were in this bank, only a few yards behind. My dugout headquarters was connected to the 14th Brigade Headquarters by a field telephone. Our S.O.S.[1] lines were in front of Hamel and our O.P. [observation post] on the high spur north of the Somme completely overlooked the river and the area around."

Beavis had been keeping sharp watch on a work party of enemy soldiers across the lines. His observers followed their activities closely, and on the preceding afternoon he registered the guns on target. Toward evening the Major ordered his gunners to open fire on the activity. That evening, in the yellow-orange glow of his lamp he wrote in his diary:

> Attack suspected tomorrow morning so put down counterpreparation. Nine periods, each of two minute bursts at three rounds per gun per minute.

At night most of the cavelike dugouts were lighted with the feeble glow of issue candles. Deep resonant voices, musical in tone, came from the shadowy openings, and the scent of pipe tobacco made the men think of warm stoves and cosy rooms at home. The gun teams occupied the dugouts with the Sergeant gun layer in charge. In a pinch eight men could crowd into one. The remainder of the battery was at the wagon line in Bonnay with the field kitchens and horses. Major Beavis's dugout, centered behind the line, was also the battery headquarters. It had a pressure lamp, a box table and a sleeping bag.

There was no morning shoot but 27-year-old gun layer Sergeant H. E. Hart, with his customary alertness, was already astir. Hart was a paragon of military efficiency, a

---

[1] Closest point that guns are laid to engage the enemy, usually 100 yards in front of the friendly lines.

man who could handle men and pursue his business methodically. Earlier Major Beavis had appointed him battery clerk. Hart wrote his reports with a fine, deliberate hand and seldom forgot a name or face. Of his commander, Hart recalls, "I was his personal clerk for eight months and I felt that he had a warm regard for me. I prepared all his military correspondence and Intelligence and I feel that he relied upon me more than his own officers. The Major was a clever and brilliant artilleryman and his knowledge of the scientific side of gunnery was excellent." On this morning, after checking on his gun and crew, and with little to do except await orders, Hart relaxed in his dugout with a magazine. It contained an illustrated article on the famous German ace, Richthofen, and Hart studied the photograph and reflected on the youth's striking features.

In action the battery's three section officers took turns at the forward posts, acting as forward observation officers. This morning Lieutenant J. J. R. Punch was inside the stone windmill 2,200 yards southeast. With him was Gunner Fred Rhodes.

Lieutenant Doyle was short and robust. His face was fair, round and carried a friendly smile. Although markedly casual in his military dress and bearing, the one-time schoolteacher was considered by Beavis to be a conscientious artillery officer.

Lieutenant A. B. Ellis was the opposite of Doyle. Tall, thin and dark with a stern face, in matters of battery business he was a disciplinarian, having learned soldiering in the enlisted ranks as an ex-regular gunner. Mental and physical strain claimed Ellis, one member of the battery recalls. On August 8th, the day of the great Allied counteroffensive, the officer suffered a complete collapse and was taken from the line.

"In action," Beavis tells, "the officers wore the same jackets as gunners; breeches, leggings or puttees (worn upside down), issue boots or boots that came up to the knee (strapped at top or laced); the jackets were Australian pattern, wool and coloured grayish-khaki."

Artillerymen accepted their daily labors amid the

noisy guns. Concussion was to be avoided, and there was always a deal of pulling and shifting guns and toting shells about. The 53rd's position was fairly exposed and subsequently grew hot when the fire from Boche batteries became more than desultory and the whine of shells crossing the Somme increased in tempo. "Berthas," an uncommonly ugly breed of nine-inch shell loaded with H.E. sailed over with a querulous "squeeeee" and exploded with ear-splitting crashes and bursts of murky dull-red flame. Then the Aussie cannon came alive, the batteries atop the ridge crashed with tumult as the Anzacs answered, and both sides fell to quarelling pell-mell, snarling at one another and going one for one. Huge chunks of clay and stone flew in all directions. The air became acrid with the smoke of guns and the powder fumes were bitter on the tongue. The roar of the belching cannon made dry dirt fall from the dugout shorings. Everything quaked. In a rage, the reverberations rolled away to the rear.

At times an enemy barrage preceded an infantry attack. Small-caliber bullets made a slow whine over toward Vaux Wood, and occasionally there was the slow *wok*, *wok*, *wok*, *wok* of a Lewis gun. A good Lewis gunner could play a tune with his weapon, and it was sometimes used for signals along the line. They thumped out "All policemen have big feet" *rat-a-tat-tat—tat, tat*. The faster chatter of the Vickers guns always seemed to echo along the valley walls.

One German position before Hamel had a good view of the Somme. It was Number 1 Battery of the 16th Field Artillery Regiment. Its sudden bursts of shell fire made life hectic for the Aussie diggers who tried to requisition ownerless chickens in Sailly-le-Sec, or brew tea in the ruins of Hamelet. German snipers kept the Anzacs pinned. When light gunfire erupted across the fields there was an occasional *bingl-ockety-pockety-rockety* when a bullet struck the barbed wire and went spinning end over end. In this exposed atmosphere the best a soldier could hope to salvage from a close shell burst was a "cushy" wound that meant a trip to Blighty (England) for convalescence.

Gunner R. L. Clifford Hunt was a gun layer for one of the 53rd's guns. He recalls:

> "Each 18-pounder was manned by five or six men. Number 1 was the sergeant-in-charge, Number 2 was responsible for range, Number 3 the gun layer, Number 4, loader, and Numbers 5 and 6 looked after the ammunition and set the fuses—for shrapnel. My job as gun layer was to "lay" the gun on the correct line of fire, laterally, through a dial sight and manipulate a level to adjust the difference above or below the horizontal plane. This is rather technical, but very necessary in undulating country. We could fire from 15 to 20 rounds per minute."

The Anzacs were toughened fighters, wiry, and easily acclimated to unsheltered warfare. They fought hard, took what came, and complained as vociferously as any soldier of any army. An American officer said of them:

> "Australians were very brave men. There was an excellent spirit of comradeship between the officers and men. Adventurous, high-spirited and gay. They suffered large losses in proportion to their numbers. Death always being so near, they tried to make the most of life."

Typically, the digger insisted on credit for his achievements, and had a reputation of being fair in his judgments. While he could appreciate the fine labors of his companions, he was critically outspoken of those who fell short of their goal. Theirs was a great brotherhood, where life thrived even in the pool of danger, in the dreariness of death, and in their mutual loyalties. When they raised their voices in "Waltzing Matilda" it was for more than fellowship. It was for solidarity.

As for rations, he fared better than his enemy. In quiet moments the field kitchens brought the food forward. Gunners of the 53rd ate three meals a day, and there were a few among them who had not fared this well before the war. Bread (about four men to a loaf each day), apple jam and tea for breakfast; sometimes bacon. For lunch fresh stew meat (sometimes horse meat), cold corned beef, or if under shelling, cold or warmed tinned "Macanochie" (mixed meat and vegetables), or tinned pork and beans and hot tea. Generally the evening mess was bread with strong butter, plum jam (or cheese) and hot tea with condensed milk. The food was cooked in two-gallon round dixies and more often than not was still warm when ladled out. In winter the containers were so cold they could not be carried with bare hands. The men sat on boxes or outside their dugouts to eat, and scanned the skies for diversion. When German scouts appeared overhead, or a high-flying observation plane dared venture across the line on a recon task, white shrapnel burst high in the air, soft, like puffs of cotton batting. The diggers made bets on whether the Hun would escape. But on this Sunday morning air activity was light owing to uncommon sky conditions. The weather was strangely different. According to Major Beavis:

> "I have very distinct recollections of the weather conditions. It would be described as a hazy sky—with no direct sunlight—with a slight silvery mist round the horizon, plenty of dispersed light but little or no shadows. Probably at several thousand feet the visibility would have been poor with conditions resembling a thin fog."

Almost a thousand yards southeast of the 53rd Battery was a machine gun emplacement of the 24th Machine Gun Company (7th Infantry Brigade) commanded by Captain F. Watts. One of Watts's most capable noncoms was 27-year-old Sergeant Cedric Bassett Popkin. He was in charge of the emplacement's four belt-fed Vickers guns, of which one was postmounted for anti-aircraft defense.

Popkin's baptism of fire came on the Passchendaele front in September of 1917, where the gas attacks were among the heaviest. Popkin's assistant on the gun was Private R.F. Weston, also 27. Weston was a handsome soldier, alert and highly observant. Like many of his cobbers, he faithfully recorded his more vivid impressions in a diary. As a qualified first-class gunner, he was serving as Number 1 at the mount.

It was mid-morning when 29-year-old Private G. Sowerbutts of the 44th Battalion moved into the wood on the crest of the ridge to observe the General J. H. Cannan's 11th Brigade. He swept his glasses along the valley floor, where a few misty whirlpools still lingered in the low places.

In one of these depressions huddled first Lieutenant Fabian of the 16th Field Artillery Regiment. His shallow damp hole was the artillery observation post and, like Sowerbutts, he too, was scanning for enemy activity—in the opposite direction. The morning was strangely still.

Number 3 Squadron of the Australian Flying Corps was near Poulainville, very nearly across the road from 209 Squadron and close by the railroad stop at Bertangles. Although a part of the Commonwealth, the Australian air service was autonomous.

Major David V. J. Blake commanded the outfit, in the main a collection of patched, war-weary R.E.8s bordering on obsolescence, all flown by young Aussies who carried on daily recon, spotting and photo-mapping missions in the face of stiffening Boche air resistance. The lumbering biplanes were sitting ducks over the lines, the object of enemy anti-aircraft gunners and a favorite target of speedy Albatros fighters and Fokker Dr.Is.

The airmen of a two-plane mission being readied in the predawn had no reason to believe that this day would be different. For the past week they had been alerted to expect increased opposition. The finest German air squadrons were massed opposite Amiens to drive the British patrols from the skies. The two pilots and two observers had arisen early in anticipation of an early flight, but at daybreak, with their field huts little more than foggy outlines and the end of the field lost in mist, they were forced to wait.

The poor visibility and obscured sky prevailed until

mid-morning when, shortly before 10 o'clock, Lieutenants S. G. Garrett and A. V. Barrow of one R.E.8, with Lieutenants T. L. Simpson and E. C. Banks of a second recon plane, received word that conditions were clearing over the front. In minutes the RAF (Royal Aircraft Factory) engines were warming smoothly, and on signal the flickering propellers dissolved into walnut swirls as the two ungainly machines bounced into the air. Within minutes the steady hum of the engines disappeared in the southeast and the Corps front was about to be photographed again.

Twenty miles east, von Richthofen rose shortly after sunrise to view a sky veiled in thick haze. Low wisps of ragged stratus slipped across the aerodrome, and through the small window he saw several pilots waiting for the skies to clear. He pulled his coveralls over his gray silk monogrammed pajamas, glanced up at his square features in the small mirror on the wall and then splashed water on his face. Its bracing coldness was as spring water, and it brought to mind again the pleasant anticipation of his coming holiday in the Black Forest. The trip was the last thing he and Bodenschatz had discussed before retiring.

Although fastidious about his appearance, Richthofen declined his customary shave. There would be time after the early patrol—if indeed a patrol could be flown at all. This morning there would be time for breakfast; usually there was not. In the early light the men did not have time for food, and when they returned they were ravenously hungry. The Rittmeister admired men who could fight and die on empty stomachs.

Outside, Richthofen joined his fellow officers. The sea of ooze was less distressing, but the wet wind across the flying field was almost sticky. On the north side the road was beginning to dry, and the commander saw the thinning ground mists rise from the low-lying Somme. It swept more briskly now across the grass, wraithlike. And easterly.

Spirits were more ebullient than usual. Manfred became aware of the gaiety and joined in the conversation over a table of hot tea, milk and eggs, bread and butter with marmalade. Wolfram von Richthofen sat quietly, experiencing mingled emotions of anxiety and awe. His famous cousin had given his approval at last; if the Jastas flew this morning he would accompany them.

With the uncertain halt of the German advance, the RAF had turned from bombing, strafing and reconnaissance to checking the German fighter formations that now swept with renewed strength and deadly regularity all along the front.

Bertangles Aerodrome near Allonville in the Horseshoe Wood was on the Amiens-Albert road. Fourteen miles behind the front, it had cinder ramps and fair facilities. A large grass field that was once farmed, the aerodrome was 400 yards across and set amid level, open countryside. The road alongside was ancient and rough. But except for St. Omer, Bertangles was better known to the RAF than any other aerodrome on the Western front. Major Lanoe Hawker had flown from it the day he was killed by Richthofen. Billy Barker had also used it, and now it accommodated three flying squadrons.

Number 48 Squadron flew Bristol Fighters and housed their machines in the few wooden hangars on the field. This outfit was commanded by tall, slender Major Keith Park, a New Zealander who would gain 20 victories before the Armistice. A firm individualist, Park later commanded the Eleventh Group during the Battle of Britain and rose to air chief marshal. His pilots had good reason to remember Richthofen. On their first offensive patrol in April of 1917, only two machines of a six-plane flight returned; four fell to five Albatros D.IIIs led by the all-red machine.

A nearby cluster of tent hangars and gray huts marked Number 84 Squadron commanded by Major W. Sholto-Douglas, later Lord Douglas and Marshal of the Royal Air Force. His squadron headquarters was a small farmhouse at the edge of the field with one room assigned to each of the three flights. Here the men lunched and awaited orders to fly, but at night they supped and were billeted in the village. Pilots of 84 flew S.E.5s, and one of them, little, high-strung, swarthy Captain Beauchamp-Proctor from Capetown would see the end of the war with 54 German machines to his credit. Both squadrons were based at Flez when the German push began, and narrowly escaped being overrun by the gray wave.

Across the aerodrome were the tent hangars of 209 Camel Squadron, each tent large enough to hold a machine. The tents stood in a row before the wooden huts, and in the trees of the woods that bordered two sides of the field were smaller tents that housed 209s pilots. Sometimes the hangar tents were blown over in a high wind.

A month earlier 209 Squadron flew to England en masse to exchange their Clerget-powered Camels for the superior Bentley-powered ones. They returned to their base, then at Bray-Dunes, on the eve of the German offensive; the following day they were shelled heavily. The squadron moved hurriedly to Teteghem, outside Dunkirk, and finally reached Bertangles on April 7th. Their return to France was as naval aviators of Number 9 Squadron, but on April 1st, when the Royal Naval Air Service and the Royal Flying Corps merged to become the Royal Air Force, squadron pilots grudgingly donned their new uniforms of light blue and reluctantly accepted their new squadron designation—209. The British fighting squadron remained basically administrative; its tactical components were the five-plane flight, of which there were three flights to a squadron. The German equivalent was the *Jagdstaffel*, usually two flights of six machines each.

When night met day over Bertangles on April 21st, the pilots who were scheduled for the dawn patrol slept through call time. The unsettled sky precluded a patrol before late morning. The central weather bureaus in Paris and London reported for this morning:

> . . . the sky is overcast in the . . . northeast
> of France, rain is falling in the north of Hol-
> land at Lyons . . .

Until mid-morning this weather would ground German and Allied airplanes, then the rising sun and in-
creasing wind would thin the fog and break the overcast. There would be better visibility on the ground, but
the haze would persist.

Near the tents, shrouded in the foggy dawn, was a
gray-white hut with a tarpaper roof, spectral in its peel-
ing paint and wetness. Inside, several men were stirring,
among them Major C.H. Butler, who commanded 209
Camel.

In a nearby cone of canvas a young Englishman who
had just turned 19 slowly donned his uniform and boots.
He was trained at Chingford, commissioned in the Royal
Naval Air Service in 1916, assigned to the squadron in
June of 1917 and considered one of the more experienced pilots. He was Lieutenant Francis J.W. Mellersh,
destined to become an air vice marshal.

Other tents were coming to life. Lieutenant W. J.
Mackenzie of Ontario rolled to a sitting position on his
cot and shook his head. Then he smoothed his thick hair
with his hand. Lieutenants M. S. Taylor and C. G. Brock
of Toronto were reaching for their tunics. Lieutenant A.
W. Aird, of Victoria, was already dressed.

Lieutenant O. W. Redgate, a thin English-born pilot
with a small, drawn face, pulled on his boots and
yawned. He was temporarily in command of Captain
Stearne T. Edwards' flight—until Edwards returned
from his leave in May.

Several of the officers already had their early cup of
steaming tea and were huddled together near the flight
line, waiting for the weather to improve. An overhead
glow through the mist gave their wrinkled uniforms an
almost luminous quality. A flock of birds swept by, their
chirping deadened in the vapor. Bertangles was noted
for its abundance of birds, especially nightingales. They
swarmed to nest in the nearby wood and at night their

song kept the replacement pilots awake until they learned not to hear them.

Lieutenant Robert M. Foster, a R.F.C. pilot who had completed a full tour of operational flying on Sopwith Pups in 1917 and who had been posted to 209 Squadron in March 1918, stood with others as mechanics checked the stub-nosed Camels. Only yesterday this man who would one day be an air chief marshal of the RAF had scribbled in his log:

> Scrap with seven triplanes over Dompière. Guns frozen. Attacked four two-seaters, more gun trouble. Attacked one two-seater with one gun—250 rounds close range and did in observer with Boots and Taylor.

A second entry:

> twenty minutes target practice—guns O.K.

"The general atmosphere at the time was pretty tense," Foster reflects today. "Only by the narrowest of margins had the massive German offensive, staged in the last ten days of March, been held; the British Army had had very heavy losses and the troops holding the line in front of the key town of Amiens were exhausted."

One of the pilots was impatient for the day to begin. He was 22-year-old Wilfred R. May, the squadron's newest replacement. The tall, slender, blond-headed young man answered to "Wop," a nickname acquired years earlier. As restless as a cat, he was friendly but undemonstrative. From Carberry, Manitoba, the former motor demonstrator had joined the Sportsman's Battalion in 1916 as a way of finding a place in the R.F.C. It was a year and a half later in France that Sergeant May of the 202nd's machine-gun section finally received his orders to sail for England and flight training.

Because pilots were desperately needed to replace those lost in the recent Somme offensive, May's advanced training was abruptly shortened. "I was completing my training," May told his fellow pilots shortly after his arrival, "when I received orders to go to Scotland for a gunnery course. I arrived there one night and the following afternoon I was suddenly hustled back to London. My gunnery training was over!" He shipped to France and to the pilots' pool at St. Omer, located just west of the Belgian border. From there it was a short ride to Bertangles.

When May was a student at Alberta College South he met Arthur Roy Brown, a young man with an enthusiastic bent for "aeroplanes." May had no inkling he would meet his former schoolmate in this drab setting, or that he would soon become the catalyst in the most controversial action ever to split the ranks of the Empire's armies. He was overjoyed to see Brown on his arrival and especially pleased that this morning his old friend would lead him over the lines on his first high-offensive patrol.

But Wilfred May found Brown very unlike the square-jawed and dark-haired chap he knew at Edmonton. This was not the man who had once expressed such friendliness and warmth, who had an exuberant love of sports, sailing and track. This man was lean and haggard, his face lined with fatigue.

Roy Brown could no longer spark enthusiasm for each new day. As the gray morning lightened he slumped wearily on the edge of his cot and tried once again to shake the spectres from his tired mind. He had slept less than five hours—five fitful hours—and awakened with the same submerged tension that had become his constant companion. His stomach burned; his eyes smarted. He moved heavily from his cot and splashed cold water on his tired features. He walked like a man who was carrying the war on his shoulders, an old, young man with 14 months of the strain and uncertainty of aerial combat etched on his gaunt countenance. The pressure showed itself in shattered nerves, a refractory stomach, and a painful inflamed colon. Battle fatigue and critical gastritis.

In the past week he had lost weight—and he was already 25 pounds underweight. The glint in his once-shrewd gray eyes was no more. Now bloodshot, they moved restlessly in their darkened sockets. Raymond Collishaw, a friend who was to be victor in 60 air combats and rise to the rank of air vice marshal in World War II, had flown into Bertangles a day or so earlier for a brief visit. He later said he found his former navy comrade in a bad way, physically and mentally. For Brown, the elation of flying he once felt so strongly had at last slipped from him. There was a day when flying was everything for the adventurous young Canadian; with Stearne Edwards he had learned to fly at his own expense in Dayton at the Wright Flying School. He was commissioned a flight sub-lieutenant in September of 1915 and three months later sailed for England. While taking advanced training at Chingford he crashed and fractured a spinal vertabrae. The accident confined him to the hospital until 1917.

The airplane had been transformed into a hideous weapon of death, and Brown's love for the freedom of a clean sky and a bracing slipstream had been transformed into a nightmare of one flaming, plummeting death after another. He had once loved to fly; but fly and kill? No.

These seven Canadians, two of them flight leaders, composed almost half of 209 Squadron. In the shadow of the hangar tents, behind the line of 15 dew-streaked Camels, a slender boyish captain waited with other officers for the weather to clear. Oliver Colin LeBoutillier, "Boots" to his squadron mates, was an American volunteer from East Orange, New Jersey. As the commander of a five-plane flight, his Camel was marked with four white stripes on the side of the fuselage, two of which crossed the turtleback. Outside the cockpit, under the rear center-section strut, was a small plaque lettered "Jean"—the name of a girl he dated in London.

LeBoutillier had learned to fly at his own expense in 1915, like Brown. He soloed a vintage Wright B at Mineola, Long Island. In Canada he enlisted in the Royal Naval Air Service and after six weeks of rigorous schooling under toughened, old-line naval officers at

Crystal Palace outside London, Boots went on to Redcar
Aerodrome in the north for more flight training. At
Dover and Cranwell there were flight checkouts in combat types. He reflected, standing in the foggy damp of
the hangar opening, that one year ago his training C.O.
had written in his log book: "Ready for combat service,
and on that date Sub-Lieutenant LeBoutillier had 29
solo hours.

Tall, dashing, and with a head of curly dark hair,
LeBoutillier's ready grin and casual attitude did not go
unnoticed by his staid British superiors. But the Yank's
devil-may-care skill with the feisty Camel, coupled with
his ability to lead in combat and inspire confidence
among his subordinates, had also been noted, and pro-
motions came without delay.

Reaching back 49 years into his memory, LeBoutillier
told of that wet, foggy morning at Bertangles:

> We lived in tents, hung our laundry on a line and on
> weekends caught a lorry to Amiens for a bath. We lived
> like most fighter squadrons whose mission was to invade
> German airspace and keep the Boche planes away from
> our recon machines and bombers.
>
> There were many foggy mornings at Bertangles like the
> one of April 21st. Each pilot drew the dawn patrol two or
> three times each week. Before daybreak—about 30 minutes
> before takeoff time—the operations officer came into our
> tent and shook us. He put a bottle of Scotch on the table
> and we each had a drink. The Air Ministry would have
> raised hell if they knew about this, but it got us started.
>
> Usually the pilots of one flight slept in the same tent. By
> dawn the fire in the field stove had burned out and
> everything was wet and damp. For light we used a
> kerosene lantern or candles. The planes were already lined
> up in the darkness outside, each tended by a corporal-
> mechanic with a sergeant responsible for the five-plane
> unit. Our Camels were supposed to have red cowlings, but
> the pressure of the desperate Allied holding action had
> put our already overworked mechanics farther behind.
> Replacement machines were going into action with the
> factory brown or olive-drab noses.
>
> The armament officer checked our guns the night be-

fore. Briefing for the dawn patrol was held in our tent by the operations officer, then we got in our planes and took off to try to intercept the German bombers, cripples and recon planes returning from early predawn raids. They were easy to see silhouetted against the daybreak, and were good targets. We usually flew two patrols a day—about five hours in all.

For this morning, we were scheduled for an early high-offensive patrol. All three flights were readied, but the weather was practically on the ground, visibility was nil, and we had to wait for the fog to thin out enough for us to take off. We thought that once we were in the air we could get above the stuff and continue our patrol in the clear. Our orders were to patrol our sector, which extended south to the beginning of the French lines, then north to Albert, which would put us 15 miles behind the German front at our deepest point.

CHAPTER SIX

A Final Rendezvous

Not long before the great March offensive a German journalist visited J.G.I, and noted the strong contrast between the trenches and the flying field. The men he found at Richthofen's Geschwader were different.

> No weary legs hamper him; he does not have to crawl over the dead or stand up to his knees in the mire. He is the pampered aristocrat of the war, the golden youth of adventure.
> He leaves a comfortable bed, with bath, a good breakfast, the comradeship of a pleasant mess, the care of servants, to mount his steed. When he returns, he has only to slip out of his seat . . .

Yes, they returned—if they survived enemy bullets, anti-aircraft shrapnel, engine stoppage and structural failure—to comfortable lodgings at aerodromes in the countryside. Airmen were rarely begrudged these privileges; it was from the aviation branches that death took the largest proportionate number. Whether a fighter pilot or an observer, his chances of surviving the war were slender. And because his life was likely to be a short one, he took a special license in its rare gaiety. And this morning, because he was looking forward to leaving the war for a holiday, Manfred von Richthofen was unusually gay.

When the Rittmeister appeared on the field, a regimental band sent by a nearby division commander blared forth in recognition of his 80th victory. The ace nodded his acknowledgment stiffly and walked with Joachim Wolff to the hangars. Never a music lover, he remarked to his companion that the music was loud. The display made him uncomfortable.

He saw that the weather was still unfavorable, though the thinning sky cover indicated a change for the better. Visibility was poor, but the combination of a light wind and a rising sun was expected to burn off the mists within half an hour.

Retired General der Flieger Karl Bodenschatz lives today in Erlangen, West Germany. More than anyone in the German military forces, his was the closest official association with the Kaiser's illustrious man of the hour. Thinking back to that morning, the former adjutant remembers:

"Richthofen was always ready to fly, just as on this day of April 21st. Early in the morning there were enemy fliers reported, so he had to get ready for the frontline patrol. The fighter pilots who were on the alert were standing by, ready to board their planes, and other airmen were waiting for their flight instructions.

"Richthofen stood among them in his regular flying suit. All were in excellent spirits and the light mood that prevailed earlier swept again through the air. The Rittmeister, in the spirit of the occasion, playfully tipped over a stretcher on which Leutnant Richard Wenzl had stretched out. When the laughter subsided, Wenzl again lay down on the same stretcher and again Richthofen tipped it over. His laughter echoed across the field. Seldom had his men seen him in such good humor. They knew he was pleased with yesterday's 80th victory, though he said little about it. And they knew he was already relaxing in anticipation of his holiday in the Black Forest.

In light-hearted revenge, several pilots slipped behind a hangar and tied a heavy wooden wheel chock to the tail of Moritz, Richthofen's beloved Danish hound. Then they told the faithful animal to go to his master. Richthofen smiled when he saw the dog struggling toward him, untied the chock from his friendly mascot and stroked him—for the last time. A photographer recorded the scene and snapped another picture of the group as they waited near the field telephone. Again the commander appraised the weather. Adjutant Bodenschatz later wrote:

> The men at Supreme Headquarters were agreeable to a leave for the commander, for they were anxious that this man should not follow Boelcke and Immelmann in death. Because Richthofen was now the greatest fighter ace, they believed that in his continued exposure to danger his great service to the Fatherland would likewise be lost.
>
> Headquarters instructed me to suggest to Richthofen that he accept a safer position (such as inspector) in order to share his great experiences with others. He laughed when I brought up the subject. "Inspector? No. I will stay at the front!"

The matter was closed.

Bodenschatz approached the men to announce that the weather conditions would shortly permit flying, then left for the forward observation post. At approximately 10:30 (9:30 Allied time) the east wind cleared most of the clouds. Richthofen held a brief conference with his pilots. The telephone operator ran from the communications shack. "There are several English planes at the front." The officers hurried to their planes.

At 9:40 Richthofen, leading Jasta 11 in 425/17, took off with five machines, including one piloted by his cousin Wolfram. He had ordered Wolfram to observe the air tactics and remain clear of any engagements. Vizefeldwebel Scholz was in this first *Kette* of three planes to take to the air; behind them in a second group were Wenzl, Weiss and Karjus. The latter had lost a hand while serving as an observer earlier in the war. He wore a specially designed steel claw with which he could operate the Dr.I's controls.

The German Army was making preparations for yet another attempt to breach the Aussie defenses at Villiers-Brettoneaux. In planning his patrols to parallel the line of Marieux-Puchvilliers, Richthofen intended to protect his own reconnaissance machines as well as prevent

British observers from discovering the German troops massing behind the front. Richthofen led his flights due west, toward the battleground between Hamel and Villiers-Brettoneaux.

Conspicuous by his absence was Leutnant Ernst Udet, a pilot who had been handpicked by the Rittmeister less than a month earlier. He was on medical leave. On April 6th, the pain from his worsening ear infection was so severe that he could barely move. Udet said afterward:

> "The Rittmeister slapped my shoulder. 'You're for leave, Udet,' he announced.
>
> I protested. 'It'll probably pass off.' But Richthofen immediately cut me short. 'You'll travel tomorrow; you're no use to us until you're fit again.'
>
> It was a hard blow having to leave my flight at that moment, just when things were going so successfully, but it was obvious that I could be of little use in my present state.
>
> On the following morning I left the aerodrome, and Richthofen himself came to escort me to the old two-seater which was to carry me back to the base. As we took off he remained standing on the aerodrome, waving to me with his cap. His fair hair shone in the sun.

J.G.I had been augmented by the temporary addition of Jasta 5 and Jasta 46—which were not a part of Richthofen's Jagdgeschwader. Jasta 5 was in the air and in clear sight north of Jasta 11. Leutnant Wolff, having made a late start, soon joined Jasta 11 to make the Baron's group seven strong.

Wenzl and Weiss broke formation and curved away to join Jasta 5, leaving Richthofen, Wolfram, Scholz, Karjus and Wolff to continue the patrol. Jasta 5 was at full strength that morning and, including Jasta 11, there were approximately 25 fighter planes—a formidable force. Proceeding along the Somme River, they had reached 10,000 feet before they approached the lines.

Minutes before Richthofen's departure from Cappy, the three flights of Camels were winging their way southeastward into German airspace. LeBoutillier, the American, gives a prologue of the patrol:

As we waited in small clusters near the planes and in our tents the wind began to pick up a little and several of us noticed it was out of the east. Bad for the Germans. There was a slight chill to the air, but for the most part we weren't dressed for cold-weather flying.

Roy Brown, 'A' Flight leader, was in overall tactical command of the 15 planes. I remember him well. He was quiet and reserved but well liked by his men. Like the rest of us he was resigned to his duty, sticking it out come what may.

Brown had been flying combat patrols steadily—except for a recent rest rotation—since late 1916. With 12 victories and the Distinguished Service Cross his intended 13th victory proved to be an unlucky number. Brownie's nerves were worn thin by the kind of tension only fighter pilots can know. The strain of waiting for the next patrol could be as nerve-wracking as combat itself, and now his reserve had been drained. He had a nervous stomach that was fast developing a full-blown ulcer. But he never complained; he simply 'carried on' and kept his troubles much to himself.

'Wop' May was the freshest member of our squadron—and the least experienced. He was assigned to Brown's flight and was scheduled for his first offensive patrol that morning. He was excited of course; nothing fazed him, then or later, that I can recall. He was the type 'anything goes', so there was quite a study in contrast between May and Brown. They had been friends in Canada, and after the Armistice some fanciful stories were told how Brown took May under his wing and made several practice flights with him before this day. Another claimed that May reported late to 209 after a two-day party and that Roy went to bat for him when the C.O. ordered May's return to the pilots' pool. I'm not aware that either of these things happened, and the fact is simply this; Roy Brown had been driving himself and was far too exhausted to take on any but his regular duties. I suspect an early injury in a training crash was troubling him as well. When the German push began Brown was given additional duties as the senior flight leader. The strain was showing.

It's impossible to describe the mingled emotions and utter confusion we all experienced in a single day of air fighting. These were trying days, with the situation at the front still touch and go. The troops were barely holding the Jerries in check, and all of us could have done with a rest. The things I saw and felt have often caused me to ponder the limits of human endurance. The constant pressures of flying and fighting have drastic effects. Pressures work strangely on men. I've watched pilots change their temperament completely in a day, especially if they've been jolted suddenly, lost a close friend or had one narrow escape too many. They simply go to pieces. Fine fellows would suddenly collapse and cry like babies; with others it was a gradual thing. And strangely, a few didn't appear to be affected—at least outwardly—so it was difficult to tell how they were holding up. What eats at one may not bother another; what makes one wake up in a sweat-soaked cot would make another fellow yawn. I'm certain of this though; to a man they were all fine young officers. Outstanding? Yes, they were *all* outstanding.

Wilfred May stood beside Roy Brown as the sunlight made a feeble attempt to break through the haze. They were caught in the clamor of men and growling machines, and it was as May had imagined it would be. In the knowledge that he was about to become a part of the great adventure, his excitement mounted.

"This is it," May remarked to the haggard man at his side. He tried to restrain the eagerness in his voice and his face was flushed. Brown nodded wearily, one hand on the cockpit rim of his Camel. "Remember Wop, if we meet EAs and they decide to fight, stay clear of the general scrap. If we dive on them stay on the outside—or overhead—and watch. You can learn a lot."

May nodded. "I will, Roy."

"And above all, keep your head moving. If you're attacked, fire if you can, then dive for home. Now go ahead; it's time."

May turned and took long strides to his Camel, buckling the chin strap to his helmet as he walked.

The 15 machines stood ready in their drab colors and three-ring target insignia; engines whirled and popped, mechanics strained at the wingtips. Helmeted heads bobbed in the cockpits and Brown made a hand signal. The two aircraftsmen holding back the lower wings of his machine sprang aside and his Camel darted forward, its rudder fanning briskly. It bumped a little and headed for the elms at the end of the field. On it came and lifted lightly into the heavy, wet air. The next Camel followed, then the next, their vibrant roars blending.

Now the first flight was airborne, making off in formation over the trees and green plain, and the others hastened to follow. May was kept busy holding his place in formation; he did not want to be caught lagging when they crossed the lines.

"We were finally able to start on the patrol about 9:20," says LeBoutillier. "Brown, leading his flight, took off with Lieutenants Mackenzie, Lomas, May and Mellersh.[1] About five minutes later "C" Flight, led by Redgate, followed with Lieutenants Edward, Siddal, Aird and Drake. It was a few minutes later that I got into the air with my flight, "B," and trailing behind me in a V were Lieutenants Brock, Harker, Foster and Taylor. I remember Taylor quite well; he and I were good friends and this day in particular he was in the thick of it—got himself an Albatros.

"We climbed steadily east and south toward our lines, our three flights separated somewhat by the differences in our take-off times. The weather didn't improve as we'd hoped it would. It was very bad, with heavy fog and clouds.

"Brown's and Redgate's flights reached the extreme end of our patrol sector first and turned north. I continued to lead my flight south and about 10:20 over Le Quesnel, six and a half miles inside the German lines, we sighted a pair of Albatros two-seaters heading for our side, obviously on a photographic mission across the

---

[1] Mellersh, after a false start, returned to base (probably with engine trouble), took off in another Camel at 10:05 and rejoined his flight.

Ancre. We were at our assigned altitude of 12,000 feet, and inasmuch as the Germans were below us, I gave the signal for the attack and we dived on them. Taylor immediately got one into trouble and it went down. I went after the other one, which took cover quickly in the clouds. We milled around, nosing in and out of the clouds at 9,000 feet, trying to find it but finally satisfied that we'd lost him, I signaled to reform and we continued our flight northward. During this skirmish we'd become well separated from the other two flights; they were nowhere to be seen. We headed almost due north, climbing slowly to regain our altitude, and kept our eyes sharp for "A" and "C" Flights."

The R.E.8s from Number 3 Squadron arrived in position 7,000 feet over Hamel at approximately 10:35 and immediately began to photograph the Corps front. Garrett and Barrow flew north on the Australian side while Simpson and Banks maneuvered toward the German trenches.

Each observer had exposed less than half a dozen plates when a flight of red-nosed triplanes—part of an unidentified Jasta not belonging to Richthofen's J.G.I—appeared overhead nearest Simpson and Banks. Because of the poor visibility both airmen were late in seeing them come into view, peel off, and dive to the attack just east of Hamel.

Taken unawares, Banks dropped his camera plates and sprang to his gun. The recon planes converged for protection from the attacking Boche, and each time a triplane maneuvered on the tail of an R.E.8, the pilots banked their machines around to give their gunners clear targets. Their range was so close that German and Australian could see one another clearly. After Banks had fired 200 rounds at short range, Simpson flew into a cloud bank, and the triplanes turned their attention to Garrett and Barrow. As one triplane bobbed on the tail of the R.E.8, Barrow sent a prolonged burst into it and was overjoyed to see it turn over and fall away rapidly.

The other machine swooped in and Barrow sent splinters flying from its wings. It pulled out of the fight and dived for base; Banks followed Simpson into the cloud cover. They emerged in the clear a short time later and seeing the sky clear for the moment, resumed their photographic mission.

Five minutes later, at 10:40, von Richthofen, in company with more than 20 machines of Jasta 11 and 5, was just west of Cerisy and 4,000 yards upstream from where the German front lines crossed the Somme. Each formation of five and six planes included Albatros Scouts and Fokker triplanes flying in several V formations.

A short distance to the south, slightly higher and flying on a near-collision course with the German force, Roy Brown was leading eight of 209's Camels. Mechanical troubles had forced Edwards and Lomas to fall back and turn to the safety of their lines. West of Cerisy, a hamlet on the left bank of the Somme, a British anti-aircraft battery opened up on the circus machines. Brown sighted the white puffs and headed toward them to investigate. He saw the large German formation ahead and a few thousand feet below. They were heading directly toward the lines.

Brown paused only long enough to signal "Wop" May—flying the outside left position, to separate from the flight and climb. As May veered up and away, Brown gave the "talley-ho"—attack.

The Camel's initial attack fell on Jasta 11's flight of triplanes led by Leutnant Hans Weiss. The eight machines pounced pell-mell, head-on, into the Dr.I's and immediately attracted the attention of the other German flights.

Richthofen sighted the encounter near Hamel. Because of the poor visibility, his visual contact occurred somewhat later than usual and allowed less time for maneuvering. He wheeled his formation in a wide left turn, climbing, and prepared to single out a Camel on the edge of the melee.

LeBoutillier's flight was somewhere south, still out of sight. He records: "For about four or five minutes after we encountered the two-seaters we continued through that murky stuff without sighting anything. I recall we hadn't quite regained 12,000 feet when all hell broke loose! From above and all around us there came a swirling rush of brightly painted Fokker triplanes. I guessed from their markings that this was part of Richthofen's Circus. Brown's and Redgate's aeroplanes were already in the thick of it and my flight scattered and started after the enemy aircraft."

CHAPTER SEVEN

Encounter

The faint haze along the horizon held ground visibility to approximately three miles, but movements in the air were clearly seen by the fighting men for miles along the front.

For Robert Foster, in LeBoutillier's trailing "B" Flight, action came early. He was in the area of Warfusee-Abancourt when the enemy showed himself.

". . . the first incident was when we spotted a reconnaissance two-seater making off east as fast as he could go; but we were able to cut him off and a combined attack . . . sent the German down in flames. In those days there were very few pilots, either Allied or German, who were anything but supremely unhappy to see an aircraft catch fire in a fight—no parachutes, no means of escape from the fire: one could only hope that the crew had been killed before the fire took hold.

"We had lost some height in this action and took immediate steps to recover it, since we knew what to expect. An aircraft in flames gives away a position conspiciously; the anti-aircraft defenses opened up with vigor, and we knew that if enemy fighters were in the area and above us, we would be at a disadvantage. Shortly afterwards we saw a large formation coming for us . . ."

Private R. J. Falconer of the 26th Battalion, temporarily attached to the 7th Brigade Observers Section was, at that moment, sitting on the rising ground midway between the two villages of Buire and Rebemont, and several hundred yards north of the road that connected them.

"My attention was drawn to the scene of the air battle by the sound of heavy aerial machine-gun fire to the south," Falconer said. "Visibility being good, I was able, with glasses, to pick up clearly a big flight of planes to identify the nationalities, they were quite distinct as slightly east of the wood located on the rising ground south of the Ancre. Whilst the planes were too far away they weaved and twisted in one big 'mix-up.' "

The big "mix-up" began with the head-on clash of Brown's Camels and the gaily decorated machines of Richthofen's Geschwader. A blattering roar of engines punctuated by a sharp exhange of gunfire erupted directly over the weary heads of German infantrymen resting in the ruins of Cerisy. Many were dozing in a cluster 4,000 yards upstream from where their front line crossed the overflowing Somme. At the sound of air fighting a few stirred and looked upward.

The Camels closed with the second *kette* of Jasta 11 when it wheeled in a tight formation turn. Leutnant Hans Weiss in his all-white triplane led the pack, which was not at that moment a part of the Rittmeister's group. Behind him, separated by less than 20 seconds, the other formations of Albatros D.5s and Fokker Dr.Is rushed into the forming merry-go-round. Wolfram separated from Richthofen's *Kette* and climbed away.

Before this clash began, Brock and Aird's Camels developed serious engine trouble and they were forced to break formation and limp home. Redgate and Drake, their ammunition exhausted, were also forced to withdraw. May separated quickly up and away from the on-rushing machines. The seven remaining Camels, heavily outnumbered, careened into the German onslaught and the formations merged in the headlong rush. Wings swerved drunkenly up and down, right and left. The more rash and defiant warbirds plunged pell-mell through the opposing formation, and each spun around to single out an adversary. They whipped and whirled, engines racketing full out. Tracer smoke curled in a crazy network as machine guns crackled and their barrels jerked on the mountings.

On the ground the machine-gun fire sounded like chestnuts roasting in a fire. With others of the 53rd Battery, Major Beavis's attention was drawn to the angry drone of the many engines.

> I recollect clearly the aircraft twisting and turning in what . . . appeared to be a fairly tight group of planes over the Sailly Laurette area . . .
>
> There was a hazy sky, with no direct sunlight, and with a silvery mist round the horizon. Plenty of dispersed light with little or no shadows. We had no difficulty seeing the movements of the aircraft in the dogfight some five or six thousand yards to the east-southeast."

The hard-pressed 209 pilots maneuvered in the kaleidoscopic blur of German plumage, and after several deafening minutes neither side had yet drawn smoke or blood. Almost imperceptibly the east wind floated the slowly settling melee over no man's land. Then LeBoutillier's B Flight droned out of the mists at full tilt. They flew suddenly—and with surprisingly little choice in the matter—into the air battle. The large black crosses on the wings of the enemy machines were startling in their clarity and B Flight had no time to jockey.

The arrival of the Camels did little to improve the odds. Planes of Jasta 5 were on top of them in an instant and Leutnant Richard Wenzl of Jasta 11 spoke later of these new "Lords" that suddenly joined the battle.

Captain LeBoutillier, caught in the midst of the raucous swirl, found himself in a sky very much crowded with striped, spotted, and multicolored triplanes. It was every man for himself and a machine-gun bullet for the slow-witted.

> "I guessed from the enemy's markings that it was Richthofen's Circus. Brown's and Redgate's flights were already in the thick of it and my flight scattered and started after the enemy aircraft. We were outnumbered more than

two to one. I estimated there were about 27 German planes in the scrap and as two of Redgate's pilots had dropped out before the engagement—and right off two more Camels were forced out—we were 11 strong against more than twice that number of Fokkers. I judged that at least six of the triplanes were predominently red. I did not see the Albatros scouts over Sailly-le-Sec; some of our pilots, in rehashing the whole scrap that evening, mentioned sighting a few, but they were at a different level.

"I can assure you the details of that dogfight are vivid in my mind to this day. It was short but fast. Every third bullet fired from our Vickers was a tracer. The Germans used them, too, though I'm not sure of their spacing. In those few vicious moments the sky was literally filled with tracers; thin, white threads crisscrossing in every direction. Aeroplanes were everywhere. They flashed in and out of the clouds, above, below, and in front of me. First a Camel would flash past, then one or two Fokkers. I had my hands full trying to get onto an enemy's tail, avoid a collision, and get a burst off. In a fight like that you work down all the time to keep flying speed. It was like trying to catch lightning in a bottle!

"To add to the chaos, my left Vickers had been jamming for the past few days and I was trying to get it to work. The aluminum clips connecting the bullets were causing a crossfeed. I finally got it working spasmodically and got off a few fair bursts at an all-red triplane that I chased into a cloud. Then, at about 5,000 feet, another triplane got on my tail and managed to put a few healthy bursts into my Camel. I dived into some cloud cover to shake him off. I kept right on going because the fight was beginning to break up and thin out. Actual fighting time was almost always short; it wasn't something we dragged out to the bitter end. We engaged, got in a few bursts if we could, and then got out. I don't mind telling you that in this particular fight we were all glad to see it break up early, as hot as it was and as outnumbered as we were.

The visibility was still rotten at my level, though we could see straight down and up fairly well. I continued to let down in a northerly direction because I wanted to check my controls to see if I could still fly. Earlier in the war I had my aileron and elevator controls shot up while flying a Sopwith Pup and crashed just short of the French lines. Naturally, I was afraid the same thing might happen again."

Brown fell briefly on two triplanes at the fringe of the fight north of Sailly-le-Sec. In half a minute the tables were turned and he found them perched behind him; their combined fire uncomfortably accurate. The Captain nosed his Camel toward the trenches and when the struts and interplane wires reached a high pitch, he fingered the spring-loaded ignition button on the control stick and the whirling rotary muffled and slowed. The Dr.Is followed for a short distance, then broke away. Brown brought the windmilling rotary popping to life, recovered and turned back toward the fight.

Wolff, darting about in the swarm, kept one eye on his leader. At this stage of the fight he noted: ". . . . I saw the Rittmeister several times not far off, but as yet I had not seen him bring down a plane."

Had Richthofen been able to select a target from among 209's Camels, the ending of the battle would have been different. But he had obviously not selected a target, for it was the lead party of Jasta 11 that made first contact. Scholz became involved in the fighting over Sailly-le-Sec before Richthofen's group met Brown's Camels. Then Jasta 5 joined the fray. With two German machines for each Allied plane, Richthofen was obliged to mill around in the role of circus master and hope for a battle partner or a lone enemy on the outskirts of the fight. If he saw May overhead, he considered him out of reach at the moment.

Lieutenant Mellersh had followed closely behind Brown, singled out the nearest triplane, a Jasta 5 machine with a distinctive blue tail. He chased it westward, deeper into enemy territory. When he closed the gap he let his Aldis sight drift across the decorated fuselage. He tripped the twin Vickers in a deflection burst—the way a trap shooter leads a clay pigeon. Half a hundred rounds rattled from his guns. The track of the tracers told him that his aim was true; the triplane rolled drunkenly, nosed over and fell toward the ground without smoking. Then it leveled unsteadily and turned toward Cerisy. Mellersh went after it to insure the victory, but as he closed in for a second time two Fokkers fastened themselves behind his Camel. Likely they were Wolff and Karjus. Before Mellersh was forced to abandon his chase, he turned his head in time to see his blue-tailed adversary crashland at a point three miles inside German-held ground. It was later considered a decisive victory.

The pilot of any rotary-powered fighter had to divide his attention constantly between firing at the enemy, avoiding becoming a target—and keeping his engine running. A hand pump had to be used at intervals to hold between two to three pounds of air pressure in the fuel tank and if, in the heat of combat he forgot this, a violent maneuver could interrupt the fuel flow and the touchy rotary would simply quit. The fuel and air levers had to be readjusted for different altitudes. An ordinary bullet through the tank would stop the feed; an incendiary could end it all. Suddenly.

Evidence that one of the triplanes following Mellersh was Hans Joachim Wolff is shown in Wolff's written report of his encounter. He said he "...took good aim and brought down a Camel." But Mellersh's rapid descent was only to shake his attacker's blistering bursts. When another Camel came to Mellersh's aid, it veered into the triplanes and sprayed them with steady gunfire. Wolff and Karjus abandoned the chase.

Mellersh recovered control and oriented himself behind the German lines. He was at near treetop level along the Somme—with a badly misfiring engine. A low-level dash for base was the only alternative. It was touch and go. Added to the suspense of the backfiring Bentley that threatened to quit cold was the steady *crack-crack* of pot shots from German Mausers.

"The dogfight had fairly well centered slightly east of Sailly-le-Sec," LeBoutillier recalls, "where the river and the front lines met. The wind had drifted the entire engagement over the British lines, so by now I was very nearly over Sailly-le-Sec and quite close to the Somme

River." Scholz, also in the vicinity of Sailly-le-Sec, fired at several jinking Camels. It was likely his gunfire that struck Lieutenant Mackenzie as the Canadian brought his guns to bear on another curving triplane. From behind, Mackenzie heard a clear and sudden fusillade of shots at his left rear. In the same instant something crackled directly behind him. The back of his wicker seat was splintered away and momentarily he felt a sharp sting in his back. A Spandau slug had nicked him and Mackenzie flicked his Camel into a steep left bank. Out of the corner of his eye Mackenzie saw the German turn right and in five seconds the Canadian was firing into the triplane. Then he remembered his wound. In 1927 Mackenzie recalled that moment.

In the excitement I didn't know I was wounded, but when I put my hand back I felt the tear in my flying suit.

I went into a spin somewhere between 3,000 and 4,000 feet, with the motor off. One of the Germans followed me to see the crash . . . I was quite low, so I headed back toward our lines, still afraid that something might happen because of my wound—maybe a faint—although I felt all right.

Despite the slowly mounting pain and loss of blood, Mackenzie was able to reach Bertangles and land safely. He was the only 209 casualty that day.

Lieutenant Foster made note of the fierce aggressiveness of the German fighters in that air battle.

On this occasion . . . there was no doubt about the determination with which Richthofen and his 'circus' pressed their attack. In a matter of moments there was a complete melee. At first we managed to maintain our flight formations, but as the mix-up intensified, it became a matter of individual action in violent maneuvers and in short bursts at very fleeting targets. For myself, I recorded at the time one or two passing and ineffective shots at Richthofen's red triplane and a substantial encounter with another German aircraft, tastefully and impressively painted in a combination of light blue and sea green.

At 12,000 feet, Wilfred May circled and watched the whirlwind of action over his cockpit rim. The fight slowly settled under him and drifted with the wind. Except for the deafening roar of his engine the youngster could hear nothing—not even the popping machine guns below. From practice firing he remembered how his own guns sounded, and he knew from pilot talk that a machine gun crackling sharp behind him meant he was the target.

As fate would have it, the two greenest fighter pilots in that sector of the Western front—each under similar instructions—met as they circled over the dogfight. May was pleasantly surprised to find himself advantageously over a triplane gaily decorated with purple wings and a silver fuselage. A sitting duck.

Wolfram von Richthofen, hypnotized by the swirling aerial spectacle forgot that he, too, was fair game. May, slightly higher, found the aimless circling of the unsuspecting pilot too tempting to resist. He pushed his fighter down, pell-mell, opened fire—and missed. The surprised Wolfram, jolted from his role of observer by the "chukking" guns behind him, dived impulsively—directly into the center of the fray with May after him, still trying to bring his guns to bear. Wolfram leveled off and retreated toward Cappy, leaving his pursuer trapped in the middle of the battle. May had blundered —and into the next chaotic five minutes he crammed the most chilling and unforgettable adventure of his lifetime.

It seemed to May that the gaudy Fokkers converged on him from every direction on collision and near-collision courses. They missed him by inches as he dodged them instinctively. He could not remember what to do or what to think or of any plan to follow. He simply reacted. One Fokker shot from a cluster and came directly for him, head-on, machine guns winking orange-red flashes. May saw the tracers streak past his upper planes, then he pressed his gun trips and held them down as they converged. At the last second each swerved. May glanced back. The German appeared to be descending out of control, but there was no time to follow him down.

Then May recalled Brown's instructions to avoid all contact, and he tried to extricate himself from the melee. Frantically he rolled his Camel into a tight vertical spiral and held both guns open, spraying bullets at every triplane that crossed his sight. The dodging and shooting and twisting seemed to take hours. Planes flashed past so close that he could see the pilots' grimaces behind their helmets and goggles. It was all a dizzying mass of winged hatred and growling defiance.

May forgot that machine guns would not operate continuously; first one jammed, then the other. He tried to clear them but could not. Now defenseless in the center of the swarm, in desperation he spun out of the battle and dropped clear. In his words: "I kept dodging and spinning down until I ran out of sky and had to hedge-hop along the ground. After I leveled out I looked around but nobody was following. I checked the sun's position and headed west for home. I started up the Somme Valley at a very low altitude, feeling pretty good at having extricated myself . . ."

May tried again to clear his guns, but they would not release. It was no matter now for the die was cast. East of Sailly-le-Sec at 6,000 feet, Manfred von Richthofen's calculating eye caught sight of the fleeing Camel. He rolled his machine into a diving turn. Young Lieutenant May would have no further need of his guns that day.

Overhead, Wolff and Karjus were pairing off with another set of Camels as Richthofen's red triplane flashed past them in a steep dive, Wolff said later ". . . I suddenly saw the Rittmeister's red machine close to me engaging a Camel which, apparently hit, dropped down and then retreated to the west . . ."

At that precise moment, Roy Brown was free and heading west. He scanned the sky. May was not overhead. Then, low and to his left, he saw an awkwardly maneuvering Camel drop from the fight east of Sailly-le-Sec and head along the valley floor toward the Australian lines. At first Brown thought it was out of danger and beyond the notice of the German fighters. But then he noticed an all-red triplane dart from the battle and dash after it. It closed the gap rapidly.

Wilfred May heard machine-gun fire behind him. Tracers arced between his wings. He snapped bolt upright in his seat, fighting a rush of panic. He remembered it this way:

> For about two miles all went well. Suddenly the whiz of bullets began again. From the direction they came I knew I was being fired on from above and behind. The bullets with their line of blue-black smoke streaked the air beside and ahead of me, passing altogether too close to be comfortable. I wheeled to get out of their way, and twisting my head I saw a red triplane in close pursuit!

CHAPTER EIGHT

The Chase

"A telephone message came from the battery observation post," Major Beavis reported, "situated near the stone windmill on the north side of the Somme, about midway between the battery and the air fight, that a British aeroplane and a red aeroplane which was pursuing it were flying in the general direction of the battery. In a very short time the aeroplanes appeared in view flying low along the west-east valley of the Somme."

Private Falconer, still observing near Buire, could not take his glasses from the dogfight. The noisy melee fascinated him; then some motion below the fight caught his eye.

> After a few minutes had elapsed, during which time no casualties were observed, a plane was seen to break off action and head back to our rear area, in the general direction of . . . Corbie. This plane was immediately followed by a second plane . . . I naturally thought they were two of our planes which were out of ammunition or otherwise in trouble.
>
> The leading plane lost altitude rapidly, the following plane conforming with this manoeuvre.

Overhead, Lieutenant Foster sensed the fight would soon draw to a close.

> I could claim no positive success; and, as so often happened, the sky, which at one time had seemed overfull of milling aeroplanes, suddenly became empty. The en-

gagement had started at 12,000 feet and we finished up
right down to the ground. In those days it was a sound
maxim that when one found oneself all alone down on the
other side of the lines, with a lot of unfriendly Germans
letting off their guns at one, the wise thing to do was to
retire westwards with all despatch literally at ground level
and with maximum manoeuvre. This I did.

Captain LeBoutillier, east and north of Sailly-le-Sec,
continued his let-down over the front and turned toward
the Australian lines. "When I reached 2,000 feet I started slowly to come out of my dive and turned westward
toward home, hoping to sight a Fokker and make one
more pass. To the right and below me I saw two Camels
heading in my direction. Off to my left, two or three
triplanes whizzed past in the opposite direction. Apparently everyone had had enough for that morning."

Near the "Brickfields" on the Bray-Corbie Road, Gunner George Ridgway of the 29th Battery had a clear
view eastward down the valley. Something distracted
him as he repaired a telephone line. ". . .I heard machine-
gun bullets fall around and saw that three aeroplanes
had broken away from the crowd of machines that were
fighting several thousand feet up. When the three were
several hundred feet from the ground, I saw that the
first one was British, the second German, the third British."

Wilfred May, bathed in a cold sweat, turned his head
to see the ugly nose of the all-red Dr.I. Its machine guns
were winking tiny flickers of pale yellow. Death was
stalking him. He remembered that dreadful moment this
way:

Richthofen thought I would be an easy mark. I was
crippled because both my guns were jammed. Richthofen
dived and went for me.
I could not go any faster—my only hope of safety was in
changing course so often that he could not train his guns
on me. But—twists take time—and the red plane gained on
me.

They swept along the right bank of the muddy Somme south of Sally Laurette, and Wilfred May heard the harsh clatter of the Baron's guns close behind. To May and the observers along the canal it was clear that Richthofen was trying frantically to get a bead on the wildly weaving plane ahead—but the Camel appeared to be just out of his reach. His Spandaus pounded as May's shoulders and helmeted head crossed and recrossed his sight. Both ammunition tracks trembled as the cartridges raced to the breeches in a dull metallic blur. But his bullets would not go where he wanted them.

Or—*were* they going precisely where he wanted them to go?

Was Richthofen's intention at this stage of the chase to kill May or, as in his similar pursuit of Lanoe Hawker earlier, merely to drive May lower and lower to force him to land and be captured alive?

There were marked similarities in this chase and the one that claimed Hawker. Each of the British pilots were based at Bertangles. An east wind was blowing. Each chase started in German-held ground and progressed toward the Allied lines. Both Hawker and May made a dash for the safety of their lines and maneuvered vigorously to avoid the bullets of their pursuer. Richthofen had steadily forced each pilot lower and lower. Did the ace recognize the parallels—and did he intend to follow a like plan with his enemy machine?

With Hawker, Richthofen had found the chase quite simple:

> He had to decide whether he would land on German ground or whether he would fly back to the English lines. Of course he tried the latter, having endeavored in vain to escape me. . .
>
> While he came down he tried to escape by flying in a zigzag course during which, as is well known, it is difficult for one to shoot into an enemy machine. That was my most favorable moment. I followed him to an altitude of 150 feet, firing all the time.
>
> He could not help falling.

Sailly Laurette moved backward past their right wings but May did not notice. He was vaguely aware of a blur of trees just below—of a flash of muddy water here and there.

I kept coming lower and lower, edging west at every opportunity. It could not have been long—although it seemed so to me—before we crossed the German lines.

The sinuous trench system lay like a broad and ugly stream that meandered from horizon to horizon. It flashed below their wheels, broken posts jutting up to entangle a bramble bush of barbed wire. A shell-pocked crossroads off the right wing tip, a cluster of roofless farm buildings, now a row of hemlocks directly ahead... German infantrymen looked up as the buff-colored underside of the British machine passed—then they saw the darker reddish belly of the triplane close behind. In a few seconds Aussies and New Zealanders saw the same scene. Mausers and Lee-Enfields cracked out. From somewhere on the brown, torn, blasted battlefield with its flat greasy shine in the diffused light, came the *wok-wok-wok* slow fire of an automatic weapon.

Any escape at tree-top level across no man's land held hazards in addition to the chase plane's blistering fire. Ironically, Allied pilots sometimes suffered from friendly—as well as enemy—groundfire. The feeling ran strongly among British airmen that the Anzacs in particular were inclined to spray the skies at the sight of any low-flying machine, whether it carried the Cross or Cockade. Numerous English and Canadian fighter pilots claimed that the Anzac's reputation for this was notorious. Thus, a low-level dash across the Aussie lines was not without its qualmish moments for the British flying officer who, with a little imagination, could see himself zeroed in by a hardened, brawny, rough-and-ready Anzac gunner with a limited knowledge of the different insignias.

"I knew it by the roar of the guns below, (May recalled) for the machine guns and infantry opened up on us and the Baron's guns never seemed to cease for a moment. Our own guns peppered us too. While they were directing their fire at my pursuer they were just as likely to hit me—we were so close. I was still losing height in turnings and twistings; I could see the ground distinctly and the men who looked up at us. Still the red plane came on—he was determined to get me."

Obviously Richthofen was not aware that he had crossed the lines, so intense was his concentration on the plane ahead. In firing without interruption he had made a serious mistake; he had not divided his attention. He was about to make another mistake; pressing a low-level pursuit behind the enemy's lines.

Now Sailly-le-Sec flashed backward on their right. Ahead was another bombed-out village on the north shore. Lieutenant J. J. R. Punch of the 53rd Battery was at an observation post near the stone windmill 750 yards east of Vaux-sur-Somme and the same distance north of the Somme Canal. With Gunner Fred Rhodes he watched the triplane follow hotly after the Camel, keeping up a spirited firing. Punch later exclaimed: "The red plane was right alongside our position on the cliff... 80 feet above the Somme and within pistol shot!" At this point a fleeting Camel made a sudden and unexpected appearance from the northeast—just as the two machines left the vicinity of Sailly-le-Sec and headed westward along the Somme. Roy Brown nosed his Camel into a dive and gathered momentum. The distance to the twisting planes diminished quickly. At his high rate of speed the right rear of the red Dr.I loomed up rapidly. Brown pressed the triggers on his spade-shaped control stick. His Vickers guns came to life and sent a ripple through the cockpit. The sting of powder flew into his nostrils, and ahead of him the deceptive tracers made slow, arcing streaks.

It was this action between Richthofen and Brown 3,000 yards east of the 53rd Battery that captured the attention of Lieutenant J. M. Prentice of the 39th Battalion; action that was, paradoxically, largely ignored by many other ground observers.

"I recognized the well-known Richthofen plane," Prentice said in 1962," which was flying very low and chased by an RAF plane which I subsequently learnt was piloted by the Canadian, Captain Brown.

"After directing a heavy burst of fire at Richthofen, the RAF plane zoomed away and disappeared in a northerly direction. Apparently the pilot had abandoned the fight."

Gunner Ridgway also saw it. By now he had forgotten all about the telephone line he was ordered to splice, so intently was he absorbed with the oncoming air chase. "The first plane was dodging to escape the second. The third plane was following above the second, at a slightly greater interval. The third then passed out of the picture but the other two went on."

R. A. Wood, an officer of the 51st Battalion in Vaux, heard the shouts of cooks and mess orderlies from his nearby field kitchen. A large cooking vessel had been struck by a machine-gun bullet. He then saw the three low-flying machines roar overhead in time to notice the trailing plane—a Camel—fire his burst at the red triplane. At lunch that day, judging from the bitter remarks of his men, Wood was convinced the only target the Camel pilot hit in his dive was their cooker, which resulted in a substantial loss of their rations.

From a point near the Mericourt-Corbie Road south of Heilly, and close to the 53rd Battery, Lieutenant Wiltshire saw: "...three airplanes dive out of the fight...one British plane dived out toward the Somme. The other, with the German on his tail, continued toward the ground, out of my sight."

To more than one witness, it appeared as though Brown had apparently "abandoned" the fight.

Would a flight leader of proven courage and 12 victories set out with such determination to rescue his former schoolmate only to abandon him to the fate of two machine guns less than 30 yards from the victim's back? Why did Brown pull away? Did his gunfire strike its target? Did it affect Richthofen's ability to press the pursuit?

Major Blair Wark, V. C., D. S. O. of the 32nd Battalion, did not think so. Brown had now passed out of the picture and Wark, after telling of seeing only May and Richthofen at that moment, added: "...the red triplane which was following it was firing keenly, and there could be no possibility of the pilot already having received a wound such as the one which killed him."

May was not aware of Brown's high-speed pass on his pursuer east of Vaux. He was too busy trying to spoil Richthofen's aim. He drove his Camel below the level of the hills and treetops, and although he zigzagged wildly over the marshy meander of the Somme, the red triplane hung on grimly. At the beginning of the chase, Richthofen confirmed his suspicion that May was green to the game when he deliberately fired on the Camel early to test the enemy pilot's reaction. The old tactic worked again, for May revealed himself as a novice by beginning to twist and turn. He lost speed rapidly.

Now the gap narrowed steadily.

As the planes roared in low over Vaux-sur-Somme, the chase became markedly more desperate. And so determined was Richthofen to force down the plane ahead of him, that his own position did not enter his mind. This must be so, for not once did he pause in his maneuvering and firing. Lieutenant-Colonel J. L. Whitham, commanding the 52nd Battalion in Vaux-sur-Somme, noted, "They 'flattened out' as they passed over Vaux-sur-Somme, less than a hundred feet from the valley level."

Captain R. L. Forsyth, a regimental medical officer, stood at the back door of his billet in the western end of Vaux-sur-Somme. He marveled at the skillful maneuvering of the red triplane and the remarkable ability of the Camel pilot to avoid his gunfire. Later that day he wrote this account in his diary.

"The red triplane ... was evidently better managed, as our boy got lower and lower and finally came skimming along a few hundred feet above the earth with the big 'plane on his tail. I ran through the house to the front door just in time to see him almost tip the tiles of our gate, and after him, lower than I have ever seen a 'plane, came the big triplane. Julin with me gave a yell and grabbed for his revolver . . . Over the village they went and skimmed up the hill behind it, the triplane stuttering its guns off in short gasps at what looked like a 30-foot range."

Corporal J. E. MacLean, also of the 52nd, said afterward: "My companions and I were startled to hear a plane flying so low that it seemed almost on the roof. We rushed out in the road in time to see a plane flying very low and skim over the houses, followed by a red three-decker German plane. The German fired short bursts while overhead, apparently without effect."

Wolff, southeast of Vaire, made a quick look-around for his red leader. "We had a fairly strong east wind and most probably the Rittmeister had forgotten this fact . . . (a short time later) I looked for the Rittmeister and saw him at a very low height somewhere over the Somme and not far from Corbie. He was still pursuing the Camel. I shook my head and wondered why the Rittmeister was following a machine so far behind the enemy's lines."

Wolff became distracted when he turned his attention back to the Camel he had fired upon. As he watched it descend to what he thought would be a sure crash, another 209 pilot surprised him from behind and, with a long burst of fire, put 20 holes through his Dr.I.

For G. E. Golding, late of the 15th Machine Gun Company, the appearance of the two hedgehopping machines was equally sudden. "We had what you might call a grandstand view of the whole affair," he said. "We, my three mates and I, were sitting down along the wall of the last house in a village named Vaux-sur-Somme, about 10 A.M. All of a sudden two planes swept over our heads flying just above the trees, the Allied plane going for dear life for the back of our lines with this red triplane on his tail and firing bursts at him.

There was no other plane in the vicinity when we saw them."

As they contour-chased madly along the river, May struggled desperately to fight away a growing sense of panic. "Still I kept my machine twisting and dodging. When the bullets were at my left I turned to the right; when they were just above me I dropped a little. But I had not much more distance below me and I could not get above him."

Richthofen was mildly surprised that the chase was taking so long. He did not know precisely where he was although he suspected he would not long remain safe from attack.

He would have to decide soon whether he could deliver a quick *coup de grace* or abandon the chase.

Corporal Norman H. Ramsden, a linesman attached to the 8th Field Artillery Brigade, followed the hare and hound chase intently. He had the impression the pilot in the red machine was so intent on getting the Camel pilot that he was unaware he was rapidly becoming a perfect target for the dozens of post-mounted Lewis guns in the vicinity. He thought the Britisher gave the best exhibition of "aerial acrobats" he had ever seen. "He did everything to avoid being in a straight line for more than a second; he flung his machine about in all manner of crazy turns, and all the time kept losing height!"

Richthofen was not accustomed to a long chase without result, especially when his hedgehopping target was mere yards ahead of him and contrasted so well against the ridge. Already the chase had covered almost two miles and the enemy had shown no sign of surrender. Richthofen reassessed his chances of forcing the plane to earth and decided it was necessary to finish the Camel pilot off, and soon. His aim became more calculating, but the more anxiously Richthofen expected the bobbing Camel to fall, the more tenaciously it resisted the fatal strike. Now that he was firing in deadly earnest Richthofen was disturbed when the pilot's weaving back kept eluding his aim. Again and again he tried to zero in. But the Britisher was proving to be all the more difficult a target to score.

As frustration mounted in the Fokker's cockpit, caution faded. The east wind was likely forgotten now; the business at hand crowded out all else. As yet there had been no concentrated ground fire to distract the Baron; many Aussies were so fearful of striking the lead plane they withheld their fire.

May zigzagged frantically as they passed close to the brow of the peninsula west of Vaux where Lieutenant Jenkins, of the 212th Seige Battery Royal Garrison Artillery, got a close—very nearly level—view of the hot pursuit. Half a minute before the climax of the chase, he saw: ". . . the German ace . . . sitting alone in his red triplane some 200 feet above the Somme and at only 120 yards distance from me. Lieutenant May was zigzagging and Richthofen was keenly following him less than 50 yards behind the tail of May's machine. Suddenly Lieutenant May turned left across the copse . . . and I thought they would both crash in the treetops."

Another officer saw something else. Lieutenant Quinlan of the 55th Battery observing on the southern bank of the Somme said: "Richthofen was very close to the hunted plane when I first noticed him, and his machine gun was in action . . . a third plane was certainly there, but not close enough to engage with Richthofen."

Sergeant Popkin saw them coming. He reasoned if they continued on their present path along the canal, they would pass close to his gun. "They were flying very low," he said, "just above the treetops." He assumed the stance of Number 1 at the Vickers and waited. Weston stepped aside to act as Number 2 man to steady the belt feed.

Popkin squinted along the dark cylinder and estimated the Britisher's height at 60 feet. He knew both machines were below the ridge and the copse of wood on the brow of the hill toward which they were heading.

May was desperate. The chase that began southeast of Sailly Laurette had become a scudding, frenzied treetop level dash of more than three miles. The dry bursts of the red plane's guns were louder. The tracers whizzed past his cabane struts. Ahead, a 30-caliber Spandau slug struck the water of the Somme and spouted a muddy fountain.

"Close to Corbie, I started around a curve in the river, but Richthofen beat me to it by cutting over a hill and at that point I was a sitting duck. I was down too low between the river banks to turn away. He had me cold. I was in such mental turmoil that I had to restrain myself from pushing the control stick forward and disappearing into the Somme. I knew this was the end. . ."

But it was not the end, for from Vaux, Lieutenant-Colonel Witham saw the Sopwith Camel break away from the valley floor and make a sudden dash toward the side of the hundred-foot slope. "It seemed certain," Witham said, "that both would crash into the spur immediately west of the sharp bend of the Somme where it turns southward toward Corbie, but we saw the leading plane rise at the spur, closely followed by the triplane. The triplane seemed to be definitely under control of its pilot as it passed over Vaux . . ."

Rupert Weston recorded the moment in his diary. He wrote:

> ". . . Our plane was at the mercy of the pursuing plane; both planes came directly towards our gun position, the pilot of the all-red Fokker was continually firing bursts at the pursued plane to within 100 to 150 yards of our position. It was at this point that we opened fire."

The planes approached almost in line, and Popkin later said: "On came the planes, the Britisher in front and about 60 feet in the air. They were so close together that I had to wait for the Britisher to pass. Then I opened up on the German machine . . . I fired about 80[1] rounds and he immediately turned at right angles to my position and banked to clear the top of the ridge . . ."

As the vibrating Vickers tracked with the trailing

---

[1] Approximately six to seven seconds—a "long burst" by any standard.

plane, Weston thought the red plane became somewhat unsteady, but it lifted itself over the copse of wood and banked left to clear the ridge. A deliberate, guiding hand was still in control. The Fokker flew on.

Private Sowerbutts watched the planes skim nearer along the valley floor; the roar of their oncoming engines mounted. Less than 400 yards away he saw Popkin angle his Vickers gun, with Weston at his side looking upward. He heard the crackling bursts rattle from the gun as the metal cartridges sped into the breech. The plane came on and Sowerbutts, in a crouch, raised his Lee-Enfield and took quick aim on the triplane's whirling rotary engine. He had time to squeeze off one round as the Dr.I flashed overhead at less than 40 feet. "I thought the gunner got him," Sowerbutts said, "as the plane gave a swerve to the right, but he straightened out again and went after the English plane. I saw him cross the Bray-Corbie road and heard the Lewis guns from the [53rd] battery firing . . ."

Action became brisk now, for the machines were flying into an area of concentrated Australian firepower. Perched high above the valley, almost on the crest of the ridge northwest of Vaux, 8th Brigade gunner Ray McDiarmid and his mate, Joe Hill, watched as the red plane came across their Lewis gun at an inviting angle. It had not yet reached the crest of the Morlancourt ridge. Writing in 1959, McDiarmid recalled:

I still have a vivid recollection of what took place. There was a good dogfight on somewhere in front of Corbie, and one of the Pom[2] planes dropped out and Richthofen got on his tail. I had a crack at him as he passed but did no good. Our position was fairly high above the valley and I think Richthofen's altitude would be about 300 feet above the valley when I fired. Unfortunately I didn't lead enough and as both planes were

---

[2] Short for "Pommy" an early Australian term for Englishman. It originated in the early convict days when English prisoners served their terms in Australia as "Prisoners of Mother England" (P.O.M.E). Hence the Australianese Pom.

coming into the line of sight I only fired 20 rounds at about 150 yards. I recall that the English plane just cleared Vaire wood.

An intelligence officer and interpreter for the 11th Infantry Brigade was in the wood on the hilltop. Lieutenant Donald Fraser later reported "a strong burst of M.G. fire coming from the direction of southeast corner of the wood."

Gunner R. L. Clifford Hunt was at work on the left end 18-pounder of the 53rd Battery. He related, "we had had an all night 'shoot' and had been 'stood down.' One of my duties was to clean the gun, and when this was completed I was lowering the camouflage net over it when I heard the roar of planes coming toward me. A big red plane was driving one of our scouts down. The red plane was firing at the scout but the leading plane at this point was not maneuvering at all. He seemed to be trying to get as close to the ground as possible for his safety." To Jack Hocking at the 108th Howitzers, there came the distinct impression at this point of the chase that the triplane was flying almost horizontally with its engine throttled back, as though to check itself from overrunning the Camel.

May half cringed and half braced for the slug he felt sure would enter his back—or his head. He remembered, "at the end I was flying right down above the ground and couldn't go any lower!"

At the 53rd Battery, bombardier Seccull watched the oncoming pair, heard the sporadic popping and cracking of scattered rifle firing and the short rattling bursts from machine guns. The red plane, he knew, was a common target for every digger with a weapon at hand.

Less than two minutes earlier, Lieutenant Wiltshire, just behind the 53rd Battery, had lost sight of the Camel and the triplane because he was almost 40 feet below the level of the ridge. Now, suddenly, they appeared again—and he never forgot the dramatic entrance they made into his field of vision.

Within minutes, from the east, they appeared over the rise and, flying about 40 feet from the ground, passed almost overhead. The British plane was flying up and down, the German trying to imitate and giving quick bursts with his gun. The German seemed to crouch forward as he gave each burst. The British plane steeplechased a group of trees and swooped down over the Ancre . . .

Richthofen was trying to end it—and anger was clouding his judgment.

CHAPTER NINE

The Kill

"I was lying on the ground," said Lieutenant G. M. Travers, "about 50 yards from 11th Brigade Headquarters, setting my map and having a general look round with my glasses. My runner, Private Webber, was with me and I had the two planes in view, coming straight toward us ... Both planes were flying so low that they almost crashed into the trees at the top of the hill."

As the oncoming fighters swept toward the 53rd Battery, more riflemen, elated with the prospect of a rare, low-flying target, took hasty aim. Major Beavis recalls: "I was standing near Evans, slightly in the rear toward Number 6 gun. Richthofen was a perfect target for our two guns. The plane approached generally east-west, that is, in line with the Lewis guns. We faced more southeast than east and Richthofen seemed to fly straight at us." For the *Official History*, Beavis said:

> Keeping on this general course ... brought them ... close to the crest of the transverse spur on which we were stationed. At the time I estimated their height as 150 feet. The British Sopwith Camel was deviating to right and left for protection, and the red 'plane was trying to keep dead on his tail. The Lewis gunners were standing to their two guns ...

Standing a few feet behind Buie was Tom G. Lovell, a Sapper in the 11th Field Company Engineers. Later he said:

As they came over us it looked as if Richthofen was actually trying to ram our plane . . . we could see both pilots quite well. Richthofen was alive at that moment because we could see him looking around.

The enemy plane came into range but neither gunner could shoot because the Camel was in the line of fire. Bullets and tracers continued to spit from the Spandaus, zip past the Canadian and smack into the earth on the Battery side. An artillery officer later marveled: ". . . no one knows why we were not hit by the bullets which flew all around us."

Then Evans began firing. Lieutenant Doyle, standing beside Evans, reported:

Owing to our plane being in the line of fire, fire was not opened on the enemy plane until it was less than 100 yards off. The enemy plane was then firing at the British machine. After several bursts of fire (from Evan's gun) the Hun plane turned N.E. and wobbled as if out of control.

"As he came over us," Tom Lovell said, "Bob [Buie] lined him up in his sights and fired." Lieutenant Ellis referred to Buie when he observed that:

The gunner was able to fire direct on the body of the enemy pilot. As soon as fire was opened the plane turned north.

Although Ray McDiarmid was unable to see the Lewis gunners, he could still see the plane clearly. He remembers:

About ten seconds after I fired, I heard a gun on our left open up. I saw the plane stagger and get out of control. Something was thrown from the plane, which proved to be Richthofen's goggles, but I can't remember the bloke who picked them up, though I knew him—a 30th Battalion man.[8] The only thing I'm crooked about is that I missed him . . .

---

[8] E. E. Hardaker, with the 11th Brigade.

According to R. L. C. Hunt, the moment of truth came to Germany's famous son simply and quickly—though violently.

I claim that, apart from Gunner Evans, I was the nearest to the ill-fated airman.

Gunner Evans was 20 to 30 yards from my end gun and on slightly higher ground. I could see Evans clearly although my attention was directed mainly at the German airman. I saw Richthofen as clearly as I would see any man at 30 to 40 feet and at that moment the camouflage net flapped violently. He banked sharply over the battery and I looked directly into the cockpit. I don't think the flapping net attracted his attention—it would have been too late then. He realized his danger when on top of the enemy post, banked, and completely exposed himself. It was then that Evans fired his fatal burst—at point-blank range.

I did not notice Richthofen's actions when struck. His plane immediately regained an even keel and went into a shallow dive—until it crashed.

In the midst of a small grove on the slope, an Australian named Inch watched Richthofen fire his guns. As the red plane came nearer the ground, still chasing the Camel, Inch saw the gunfire stop abruptly.

Seccull, between the guns, judged the effectiveness of his gunner's fire. He adamantly declared: "Richthofen might have been fired at before we got him, but he had not been hit."

Richthofen had clearly been struck mortally. Several men saw fragments flying. Someone yelled as the red machine lurched drunkenly.

Beavis observed, "Immediately the red triplane turned sharply to the north, became somewhat unsteady in its flight. . .

"Richthofen was following the maneuverings of the Camel right up until he turned away to the north and northeast. My recollection is that the triplane did not proceed behind our line of guns as I am certain I did not have to turn about to watch Richthofen's course. In my opinion there would be little to choose between their chances of hitting Richthofen. There was no third plane within a radius of at least 2,000 yards."

Lieutenant Travers noted:

> Almost directly over the spot where I was lying the enemy plane swerved to the right so suddenly that it seemed almost to turn over. Our plane went straight on from that moment.

And a few yards downhill from Travers, Lieutenant Fraser observed:

> I lost sight of the British machine as my attention was concentrated on the enemy plane which was flying as if not under complete control, being wobbly and irregular in flight, it swerved north, then eastwards, rocking a great deal and suddenly dived out of my sight . . .

The sharp bank and brief climb also permitted F. L. Carter of the 42nd Battalion to see directly into the plane's cockpit. Jack Hocking said it seemed to gain more power momentarily—as though the pilot had "lurched over the engine throttle," for the engine burst into a brief full-throttle roar.

Sitting on the ground at one side of the Mericourt-Corbie road 500 yards north of the 53rd Battery was a stretcher bearer of the 3rd Pioneer Battalion. Private James Work was resting to nurse a painful molar. As he watched the ending of the great air battle he recognized at once the gaily painted red machine as the one that had previously dived on the trenches to spray his companions with machine-gun bullets. "He was very game and had no fear" was Work's recollection. As he watched he saw the red plane drive one of the Allied planes toward the ground, "up near the Seven Oaks. Our machine gunners opened fire on him when he was. . .still firing on our plane. I could see the pilot in the cockpit, and there were other British planes in the air, but they were quite a distance away. One of our planes turned and circled once . . . and then flew off."

At the Vickers post, Weston assessed the accuracy of Popkin's first burst at the German. "This, in my opinion, did some damage and made the pilot aware of his danger...but the pilot was still in charge, for instead of continuing the chase he doubled on his tracks and returned to attack us ... It was only a matter of who fired first."

The triplane's turn caused considerable—though unnecessary—anxiety between Weston and Popkin. Neither man realized the turn was the result of fire from the 53rd Battery, but Captain Forsyth recorded in his diary:

> At the brow of the hill . . . the triplane ran into a direct stream of bullets from a machine gun in amongst a battery. He . . . turned sharply as if going to attack the gun . . .

At that time, Lieutenant Prentice saw: "a burst of fire from the Australian battery, which apparently scored a direct hit."

From his nearer position at the brick stack, George Ridgway could also see the German aviator quite distinctly. He passed to the gunner's right, very low, and the soldier saw the pilot's head fall over to the left. Immediately the plane curved right. Ridgway marveled that of the hail of bullets fired at the German, it was incredible the only one to hit him was at that late moment.

Unaware that the Fokker had run squarely into a withering crossfire a thousand yards beyond their gun, Popkin braced himself and pressed the trip again as the plane sloughed around in a drunken glide. The weapon vibrated out another 80 rounds at a range of more than 600 yards. He reported:

> As it came toward me, I opened fire a second time and observed at once that my fire took effect.

The second burst ended in a jam caused by the prolonged firing. Weston worked frantically over the hot, crackling weapon to clear the breech.

"He's coming on!" Popkin cried, trying to help Weston, who cast a quick glance over his shoulder. The triplane completed its semicircle and nosed down as though to head directly toward them for a strafing run. Popkin and Weston were prepared to take cover, but a few seconds later when the breech was clear, the Dr.1 was swerving shakily in the opposite direction. To the gunners, it was obvious their last burst had done its work.

Lieutenant Quinlan saw the ending of the fight this way:

> Richthofen appeared to be intent upon finishing the hunted 'plane. His machine gun was in action until just prior, say 200 to 300 yards before his crash. The third plane (Brown) was at that time practically over Corbie Church . . . from 800 to 1,200 yards distant and . . . hundreds of feet higher.

A hundred yards from the 53rd Battery, near the crest of the Morlancourt Ridge, Sergeant E. C. Tibbets was walking along the Mericourt-Corbie Road with his cobber, when they saw the red Fokker close behind the weaving Sopwith Scout. "When our plane was over the gunners," Tibbets recalled, "he seemed to 'bank' and Richthofen did the same, and it was then that the machine-gun burst ended the battle!"

Still holding a sideslipping curve toward the northeast, the unstable machine wallowed drunkenly in what appeared to be a loosely controlled glide. The engine slowed quickly, and its sound dropped to a rushing whine. The propeller had flickered almost to a standstill when the undercarriage thumped down and sheared into the churned earth. There was splintering and a muffled rumble as it settled on its belly in a slithering skid. For a split second it appeared as though it would stop so abruptly it would flip over, but it checked itself and stopped nose first in a low earthcovered heap of rubble and mangel-wurzel roots on the south side of the Bray-Corbie Road. Two hundred yards away were the remains of the partially demolished brick kiln, recently used as a temporary prisoner of war compound. The tail of the machine was in the air; the front of the fuselage had buckled in absorbing the brunt of the impact. Beneath the fuselage the undercarriage lay crushed and broken. Both wheels had separated. The fuel and oil tanks had burst. They dripped their contents on the hot rotary and spilled to the ground in warm little pools—a mixture of pungent petrol and sickening-sweet castor oil. A propeller blade was splintered, and one of the lower wing panels was greatly crumpled. Its nose was pointed almost toward Bonnay. A hundred yards away, where the 8th Brigade Field Artillery was hidden in a little copse of woods, Corporal Ramsden had stood spellbound for the last 15 seconds of the Fokker's flight and crash. "I'll never forget that air fight and finale!" he said. "It was a beauty!"

The Dr.I came down in front of the 53rd Battery. Major Beavis estimated that it "hit the ground 400 yards north-northeast of where the Lewis guns were," and that "the point of impact was just out of sight over the brow of the rise in front of the guns."

To Falconer, still observing through his glasses in the distance, the machine appeared to plummet to earth with the left wing and tail making contact first. He claimed that a "shower of debris flying into the air" could be clearly seen. Simultaneously he heard the slow rate Lewis gun burst and remarked to his mate: "That's a feather in *his* cap."

Richthofen's brilliantly colored machine had long announced his presence in the air to the Allied soldiers along the Western front. Now it suddenly became even more conspicuous; the broken red wreckage was in plain view of German positions for miles.

And what of Wilfred May who had been plucked from the very pit of death? He did not comprehend—at that moment or perhaps ever—what had actually happened. He knew only what he saw—and from this vivid and shocking experience he drew his own conclusion.

"If I had been experienced, Richthofen would have got me," May reflected, "because he would have known what I was going to do next. As it was, I didn't know myself, and my erratic maneuvers baffled him.

"I was beginning to despair—then something happened. Watching over my shoulder I saw something so wonderful I could not believe it—the red plane—rolled drunkenly . . . and fell to the ground with a great crash and cloud of dust . . . There came up beside me my Flight Commander, Captain Roy Brown. I guess I was pretty nearly all in. I didn't know anything. I had no idea where I was, but he led the way to the aerodrome."

It was what Wilfred May saw, and what Roy Brown didn't see, that accidently combined to create the "almost-logical" conclusion that Richthofen met death in the air by an enemy pilot.

But, at the moment Brown and May were winging home, Sgt. E. C. Tibbets mused: *"Richthofen's plane came down a few hundred yards away. Under the circumstances it made a remarkable landing and the way it came down with the pilot dead, my cobber and I just wondered if he lived sufficiently to bring his machine down."*

CHAPTER TEN

The Diggers

All eyes—friend and foe—became fixed on the triplane that rested, awry, beside the dirt road. In muddy depressions on the valley floor across the barbed wire, men of the 238th German Field Artillery and the 10th Foot Artillery Regiments stared at the broken red airplane on the slope of the brown hillside. Rangefinders went into action.

Captain A. Koster, a German infantry officer stationed in the line, remarked, "We could not accept, because of his glide, that he was dead, although we had to take into consideration that because of a defect he had to make an emergency landing and could not return to our lines."

From the bald expanse of the ridge, New Zealanders and dark-complexioned Aussies, with their square chins and withered eyelids, watched for movement in the cockpit; but the pilot made no attempt to exit.

Eight hundred yards due north of the crash, Aussies of the 108th Howitzer Battery exchanged shouts and, although all troopers were under general orders not to expose themselves on the heights, a few men moved out at a brisk pace. Artillerymen of the 53rd Battery, 400 yards due west, were jubilant. "Lieutenant Ellis rushed past me on his way to the crash," L. E. Beavis remembers. Clifford Hunt forgot all about the camouflage net and sprinted toward the wreckage, followed closely by Tom Lovell. Major Beavis called to the NCO in charge of the guns: "Get the identification, Secculll" and the bombardier trotted off on the double.

Now a scattering of men came from all sides to converge on the stilled machine. Norman Ramsden was already running from the copse of wood that hid his 8th Brigade Headquarters. While McDiarmid looked to his still-smoking Lewis gun and changed to a full pannier, Joe Hill, his mate, started out for the downed triplane.

A dozen men claim to have been the first to reach the plane, but the honor belongs to an unnamed digger who left his post near the ruined brick compound. The man approached cautiously, and saw the plane's stilled occupant slumped over the controls, his blond head leaning against one side of the cockpit rim. It was obvious at once that when the machine skidded to its abrupt stop, the pilot was thrown against the gun butts—with violence. Blood flowed from his mouth and nostrils and spattered on the knees of his dark brown coveralls. He was dead.

Digger Inch was not far behind. He noticed a bullet wound on the right side of the man's back, down low. The Aussie lifted the German's arm and found no resistance, no movement. Years later he could remember that scene, how the dead airman's eyes were wide open— and very blue—and that his blond hair was closely-cropped.

Tibbets and his cobber did not have far to go. He later remembered:

> We were among the first to arrive at the plane and saw the pilot slumped forward with his head over the side. His fur cap had fallen off on the ground and was picked up. There was more or less silence amongst those present; that feeling of gladness and sorrow—you will readily understand what I mean. We did not examine him for wounds— we just knew he was dead and nothing could be done.

Corporal J. Homewood of B Company, 44th Battalion, sprinted to the fallen machine. In his billet on the sharp slope of the ridge a hundred yards distant, his card game was interrupted by the approaching planes skimming up the slope. He heard a Lewis gun chatter and rushed outside in time to see the triplane crash land beside the road.

The highest ranking officer to witness the plane's fall was [then] Brigadier General James H. Cannan who commanded the 11th Brigade. He was standing at the door of his Infantry Brigade Headquarters when the plane came to earth several hundred yards away. "Donald Fraser was my Intelligence Officer," Cannan recalled, "and he proceeded to the site immediately."

Private Webber ran ahead and reached the scene before Lieutenant Travers and Captain Cruikshank of the 11th Brigade. The first officer was already on the scene. It was Lieutenant Fraser, who had joined less than a dozen men now at the wreckage. Fraser immediately pulled the airman's shoulders back and braced himself against the body. He reached down to release the clasp on the safety harness. He worked quickly in hopes of saving the airman should some signs of life be present.

"Give a hand, you men!" he called, and Ramsden, Homewood and another digger helped him tug on the limp and unwieldy form until it was lifted clear of the cockpit. Together they lowered the body gently to the earth. One glance told Fraser the man was beyond help. ". . . he was quite dead," Fraser reported, "and was considerably cut about the face and was apparently shot through the chest and body."

"He's a goner, sir," one digger said in a tone edged with awe. He had not seen a German airman before, and like most ground soldiers he greatly respected the men who flew and fought high above the battlefield.

Fraser knelt beside the still form. From behind him came the sound of ripping fabric. Fraser did not look up; the "souvenir kings" were already at work.

Hunt strode up, looked briefly at the dead airman and like a few others, mistook the fresh facial injuries for bullet wounds. Years later he remembered seeing the pilot's chin "marked as by a bullet." Then Hunt turned his attention to the wrecked Fokker to collect a few mementos.

Lovell thought the plane was relatively intact compared with other machines he had seen smashed and burned. He saw the dead airman and noted what to him were clearly trunk and abdomen wounds.

"We rushed up to the plane in less than five minutes. When we got there we could see that Bob's bullets had got him," Tom Lovell remarked. "He had not suffered very bad head injuries—it was the bullet wounds that killed him, the one in the chest and the one in the abdomen. I did not notice others.

"There were quite a lot of other troops round gathering souvenirs...There was a photo of a very charming fraulein taken out of his wallet. I heard it was supposed to be the girl he was to marry."

At the height of the gunnery action, Private James V. Rake, a 3rd Division Headquarters Signaler attached to the 11th Brigade, was inside his usual signal post—a small covered trench—a short distance from the 53rd Battery. The muffled shouts, drone of the engines and the softened clatter of the automatic weapons aroused his curiosity. He crawled from the trench and looked northeast toward the old brick kiln where, on its near side and scarcely 100 yards away, a German plane had come down. He reached the wreckage soon after Fraser, Ramsden and another digger had removed the airman and laid him beside the plane. Rake saw a reddish mass staining the clothing over the left breast of the corpse. "The airman was wearing a black leather jacket and boots," Rake recalled in 1962 shortly before his own death. "His face was fair and his hair was sufficiently fair to be quite noticeable. One of our chaps—A.I.F.—a stranger to me who'd come up, said, 'He flew that low over us, we couldn't miss him' [Bombardier Seccull]. The plane was sufficiently smashed to prove positively that it hit the ground nose first—or nose and one wing together—and not on its wheels alone."

As Falconer watched the rush to the wreckage from a distance, the impression of the crash was burned in his mind when, almost simultaneously, an anti-aircraft shell burst overhead at 500 feet. But the Private had good cause to remember the event for another reason. Immediately after the crash, in following standing orders, he telephoned Brigade Headquarters to report the action. "In doing so, I gave the wrong map reference and was duly hauled over the coals for my carelessness."

By now there were scores of diggers present. Clifford Hunt reported, in the language of the times, that the remains were "ratted" of anything in the way of souvenirs—personal or otherwise. . .

Private Edward Burrow of the 52nd Battalion who arrived soon after the crash, observed: "There was such a scramble for souvenirs that, although only minutes had elapsed from the time he struck the ground till I got there, someone had relieved him of his boots." As he looked at the dead airman, Burrow had the impression that a bullet had entered the airman's face near the lower jaw on the left side and had come out behind his right eye.

It was Corporal Ramsden who, with others, pulled the pilot's fur-lined boots from his feet. Soon afterward the padre, "Red" Perry from Norwood, South Australia, took them away. "So we stripped the plane of its Spandau guns and propeller," Ramsden said. This was no sooner done than an officer of "Tivey's crowd"—8th Australian Infantry—arrived on the scene and chased them away. "We later cut the prop into bits and made paperweights with small shields cut from the cowling to put on them . . ."

George Ridgway, who was a little more than a hundred yards from the site where the Fokker crashed, took a piece of wood from the structure. L. H. Wincey of the 108th Howitzer Battery, saw a small brass clock that had just been removed from the instrument panel already in the hands of a British soldier of the Royal Engineers. He bought the timepiece for a few francs.

How the fur-lined boots—as well as the machine guns— were later recovered by Number 3 Squadron's salvage crew officer is not clear, but it was Lieutenant Warneford who later donated one boot to the Australian War Memorial. And McDiarmid volunteered: "My Battalion had Richthofen's guns in their possession for a short time. . .but they were handed over to the R.A.F."

The guns were temporarily stacked—or hidden—in the 7th Platoon gun pit where Corporal Homewood pilfered one of the gunsights, much to the later consternation of the A.F.C. crew who discovered the loss.

Joe Hill "got a chunk" of the petrol tank. He gave Ray McDiarmid a piece and the Lewis gunner cut it into the shape of Australia to fashion a "dead meat"[1] ticket from it.

Practically every digger who visited the scene came away with a scrap of the deep red fabric. Others, likewise hopeful of getting their hands on some fragment of the famed airman's red plane as a keepsake of his downfall, set to work more earnestly. Adjustable wrenches and screwdrivers appeared as if by magic; hammering, pounding and tearing sounds prevailed as the crowd grew. Instruments disappeared.

Lieutenant Fraser noted the growing number of infantrymen and requested Captain Adams of the 44th Battalion to place a guard over the plane to prevent looting and to disperse the crowd.

Laurie Stamp of the First Australian Bicycle Battalion arrived soon after the body had been removed from the machine. He picked up a small book from the ground. It measured about one and a half by one inches and lay as though it could have fallen from one of the airman's pockets. On its black cover was a gilt German cross and inside was German printing and a few handwritten notes. Most of the tiny pages were blank. Stamp took it back to Australia as a souvenir.

One set of prized souvenirs—the Baron's gloves—changed hands three times within five minutes. A signaler of the 108th Howitzers removed Richthofen's gauntlets and stuffed them, none too carefully, into the

---

[1] Identification tag worn around the neck.

front of his tunic. In a few minutes Lieutenant R. B. O'Carrol of B Company, 44th Battalion, arrived under orders of Colonel Clark to post a guard and check the looting. O'Carrol promptly ordered all gunners to return to their stations and the signaler, miffed at having his souveniring interrupted, shot back: "Yes, while *you* rat him!" to which O'Carrol replied cooly "Yes. . .and I'll begin with those gloves. Give them to me, please." The signaler did so and stalked off. A few moments later the Lieutenant saw a sergeant [Popkin?] souveniring and called him down. "Sergeant, you should be helping me, not showing a bad example to the men." The sergeant replied matter-of-factly: "Sir, I shot the bastard down . . . I ought to have *something*." O'Carrol looked at the man and reflected. He handed him the gloves. "Take these, Sergeant. That was mighty fine shooting!" What ultimately became of them is unknown. The machine-gun belts were cut up and distributed to Aussies throughout Corbie Hill. Richthofen's ring, watch and identification disc were never seen again.

Infantry officers who tried to check the swarm of light-fingered spectators found their efforts in vain. The Divisional report mentions this guard was "soon afterward dispersed by shellfire." Warrant Officer H. J. Tesch of the 41st Battalion picked up the plane's cardan-mounted *Kompass* 100 yards from where the machine rested. Mounted on a slender post in the right side of the plane's cockpit, it had snapped off on first impact and was hurled through the fuselage fabric. Except for the cracked glass, it was intact. James Work said he salvaged "some metal from the cockpit, fashioned a set of knives from it and sent them home to his brother in Melbourne." Lieutenant Travers souvenired one of the black insignia crosses that measured about four feet square. It too, eventually went to the War Memorial. Hunt lost his mementos when he was wounded later, except for two bits of plywood, one of which was presented to the War Memorial. On a piece of the machine's plywood, one aircraftsman made a sketch, with a dark-red fabric insert, and sent it to his brother as a memento.

Gunnery officers, who had watched Richthofen pursue his prey almost 3,000 yards behind the front lines before he had the misfortune to run head-on against the Lewis gunners, were already commenting on the fact that had he passed a hundred yards to either flank the Lewis guns would have been almost useless. "There was a great relief amongst the troops at the escape of the leading aeroplane," one digger at the site remarked.

Down the slope, Sergeant Popkin quickly turned his gun over to Weston when the plane crash landed.

> I immediately rushed up the hill and on arrival a couple of minutes after the crash found the wrecked plane surrounded by infantry officers, who would not allow anybody to touch it. However, I stepped in and wrenched a piece off one of the wings for a souvenir.

When Popkin saw the aviator's body he noted first that the airman had bled freely from multiple wounds. Popkin later mentioned in his official report there were "at least three machine-gun bullets through his body." Seccull, on the scene, also had the distinct impression the airman's chest was "riddled," and R. G. McLeod, late of the 14th Brigade, saw the dead airman "with quite a number of bullet holes in his legs and chest." When Weston saw the body, he took especial notice of a bullet wound that passed through the trunk from right to left and came out a little higher in the front of the chest, " ... this wound I saw personally ... there was also another bullet embedded half-way in what I took to be a Bible, taken from one of the pockets in Richthofen's jacket; if my memory serves me right, it was on the left side."

The fact that the pilot was thrown so violently against the gun butts suggests that at some time during the pursuit he may have loosened his shoulder harness to lean forward over his sight, the better to concentrate on hitting his prey. This tends to support Wiltshire's observation that the German "seemed to crouch forward as he gave each burst."

The prevention of souveniring was not the only reason officers attempted to disperse the crowd, for, as a signaler reported, "German artillery quickly laid a barrage on the plane and made it dangerous to approach." Sergeant Hart reported that following the crash the German artillery ringed the plane with fire and Buie's impression clarifies this with: "the Germans refrained from shelling the downed plane itself, as they wanted to allow time for our Diggers to remove the body. As darkness fell however, they opened fire with a barrage intended to destroy the plane and the troops moving it."

Several diggers—especially those near the 108th Howitzers—were struck by shrapnel shards, and at least two men who were under the chase path were wounded by gunfire from the triplane or Camel.

Oddly, many at the wreck made no mention of shellfire. This has never been clearly explained. Was it an indifference to shellfire? James Rake did not think so.

I do not think that anyone is "indifferent" to shellfire, although some experienced hands may seem almost casual. I believe, deep down in themselves, the majority of infantrymen expected to be hit before the war was over and they hoped it would be only a wound. Strangely enough, I had a "premonition" that I'd be wounded, and the day before the Hamel stunt of July 4th I said to a cobber of mine, "We'll get to Blighty (England) out of this." That's what happened to me. We went "over the top" with the Infantry at 3 A.M. that morning to set up the signal post in the area to be captured. I returned to Australia aboard the hospital ship *Morvada* and was discharged in 1919.

Shelling or not, the busy depredation was to continue for the greater part of the afternoon.

CHAPTER ELEVEN

"This Is Richthofen . . . !"

For James Rake, the drama of the German airman's identification remained ever vivid. "Lieutenant Fraser, the Brigade Intelligence Officer, was kneeling on the ground beside the pilot. He opened the dead airman's jacket and removed his papers and wallet. Then he cut the name of the man from his shirt front as a souvenir[1] and remarked to us, 'Do you know who this is'?

"Someone said, 'a Fritz.'

"Fraser replied calmly, 'This is Richthofen—Germany's crack airman'!"

There was, immediately around the body, a momentary awed hush. In respectful silence the Anzacs gazed on the face of a handsome, clean-shaven young man with light hair and a well-shaped head—the famed terror of the air.

Fraser searched the corpse thoroughly and collected whatever papers and personal effects he could find. These consisted of a silver watch and a gold chain with a medallion attached. These he passed to Captain Hilliary of the 11th Brigade Staff who referred them to the interpreter, Corporal Peters, and he confirmed that this was in fact, Richthofen. Fraser at once reported this to General Cannan and to the Third Australian Division. Cannan directed the tall Intelligence Officer to take

---

[1] The scrap Fraser cut from Richthofen's clothing were the monogrammed initials *MvR* from the dead airman's silk pajama shirt.

149

statements from the machine gunners who brought the plane down. The General knew of the firing by the gunners at the 14th Field Artillery Brigade, but Fraser misunderstood Cannan's inference. It was a logical error in judgment, for the roaring engines of the low-flying planes deadened Fraser's hearing of the gunfire from the 53rd.

No one at the scene seemed to notice the absence of the pilot's flying goggles, the item Ray McDiarmid saw "thrown" from the low-flying triplane as it came on to the 53rd Battery. Twice before, Richthofen had lost his goggles overboard—and in each instance he had been in serious difficulty. When he fell under Lieutenant Wood-bridge's gun: " . . . One cannot fly without sight. I forced my eyes open—tore off my goggles . . ." In his early foolhardy flight through the center of a thunderstorm: "When I took off, the rain began falling and I had to throw away my goggles, otherwise I would not have seen anything." And now, suddenly struck with bullets low frontally, followed quickly with another slug across his chest, the goggles flew away from the plane again. Did Richthofen claw them loose and throw them clear in a final desperate attempt to prolong his failing sight after the bullets struck him? Or did a convulsive whip of his head and shoulders snap the goggles from his helmet and catapult them overboard? How quickly death came to Richthofen became a speculative topic for days afterward. Unfortunately, none of the early arrivals at the site noticed whether the throttle had been closed—or the ignition switched off. There was some reason for the Dr.I's steady reduction of power in the shaky gliding turn. A unique grouping of trips, levers and a button on the versatile Dr.I's control stick enabled the pilot to fire the synchronized guns separately or simultaneously, cut the engine ignition momentarily with the spring-loaded coupe button, or adjust a small auxiliary throttle lever, while controlling the airplane's flight—all with one hand. It is entirely reasonable to assume that either rationally—or as the result of his death spasms—Richthofen's last act was to move the auxiliary throttle toward the "closed" position. This would account for the marked decrease in r.p.m. after the Fokker crossed the battery. The engine was still under reduced power when the triplane's forward section made contact with the ground; had groundfire interrupted the fuel flow the rotary engine would have stopped during the glide.[2] When the swarm of souvenir collectors finished their work, they had disturbed all clues that could tell what engine controls the pilot might have moved before he took his final breath. Those who knew the spirit of Richthofen, his aggressive determination, have pondered this in the light of his dictum: "A true chaser pilot never takes his hand from the controls until he drops dead!"

The German observers who watched from afar were hopeful the pilot was injured, for they emphasized in their immediate reports how well the red machine landed. Leutnant Fabian, an artillery observer, reported a good landing on Hill 102. The report attributed to him said: *Red triplane landed on hill near Corbie. Landed all right. Passenger has not left plane.* But another officer, Leutnant Schoenemann who was observing for Number 1 Battery, 16 Feld Artillerie Regiment before Hamel, felt a strange and overwhelming sense of dread. It was his impression that the machine struck the ground violently and that its gleaming all-red color meant only one thing: Richthofen! "I rang up the battery at once, but my superior refused to believe the news; he allayed my anxiety by telling me that all machines of Richthofen's squadron were painted red."

Like a shock wave, news of the airman's identity spread among the troops, and there was a great surge from all sides in a scramble for mementos. It was this rush—reported to have been seen by an observer riding in the basket of a swaying German kite balloon two miles away—that led to the mistaken impression that

---

[2] There appears to be no evidence from the diggers or from Number 3 Squadron personnel to indicate the fuel or oil tank was struck by gunfire.

Richthofen was murdered after landing. The belief became so widespread it was included in the History of the 238th Field-Artillery Regiment.

The souveniring attracted a much respected individual to the site—a chaplain of the 8th Brigade Field Battery. An imposing figure even without clerical garb, padre "Red" Perry passed among the diggers, bantering here, joshing there, and in short, delivered capsule admonishments to those who would "tea-leaf"[3] a dead man's personal property. Most of the men relinquished their spoils sheepishly—however reluctantly—and in a quarter of an hour, the strapping ex-footballer for the South Australia State team had retrieved—for the moment—the Baron's fur-lined boots and several of his personal items.

Richthofen was wearing a Heinecke parachute and harness. Although crude affairs, they were in use before 1918 by balloon observers. A number of German flyers were saved by them—Ernst Udet, Germany's second ranking ace, among them. In one of the last pictures taken of Richthofen he stood with Karjus and Scholz in front of their machines, wearing a harness. The baglike pack itself was fastened to the harness by clips, once the pilot was seated in the cockpit. There was no manual ripcord; upon abandoning the machine the pilot's falling body pulled the canopy from its pack. This allowed little opportunity for free fall before the shroud lines and canopy streamed. Safe parachute escapes occurred as often as not, for many times the canopy and lines fouled in the falling aircraft and carried the pilot to his death. There is no recorded evidence that Number 3 Squadron salvage detail recovered this item; but one member at the Squadron confirmed that night: "He was wearing a parachute harness ... removed before I saw him, with the pack on the fuselage or seat of the triplane." The souveniring diggers apparently scored again by recovering the silk canopy early in their looting.

---

[3] Argot of 18th Century England used by Australians, meaning thievery.

Major Beavis recalls the excitement and activity that shortly followed the crash.

I was told the Germans shelled the area of the wreck 15 to 30 minutes after the crash but it did not prevent visitors from coming to the machine.

About 30 to 60 minutes after the crash I sent my hospital folding stretcher (issued to the battery as an Army Medical Corps stretcher) to the aircraft, and my boys put Richthofen on it and carried him back to just outside the front entrance of my dugout in the side of the sunken road. This was in broad daylight, in the middle of the day. Any other accounts are imaginary. I reported the crash to my 14th Brigade Headquarters and that I had Richthofen's body at my dugout.

I opened Richthofen's flying jackets and saw a jagged wound one and a half to two inches in diameter in his left breast, which I first took to be the point of entry of [several] bullets, but apparently he was hit under the front of the right armpit and the bullets were deflected by his spine. The bullet passed out the front of the chest to the left of the center line. I was upset to see Richthofen's body and did not examine any further. When it was realized that life was gone, the corpse was wrapped in a blanket.

Major Beavis's original report said the wounds were "mainly in the chest and stomach" because he thought more than one bullet had entered the chest in the vicinity of the heart. ("I naturally had no desire to do any more examination and made a wrong assumption, based on the bursts of fire at the 'plane—at almost point-blank range.")

"Apparently the first bursts of fire were effective," Beavis said. "Both guns inflicted wounds on the pilot in my opinion."

Meanwhile, Lt. Quinlan was preparing to take bearings with his prismatic compass by which he would prove to his satisfaction that the ace had been shot down—not by Popkin and Weston—but shot down by the 53rd Battery gunner. Lieutenant Travers prepared to undertake the task of organizing his report—a fairly simple one, to his mind. When it was completed, he handed it to his 52nd Battalion C.O., Colonel Whitham.

But Private Weston felt confident they would ultimately receive the recognition due them, owing to the favorable nature of Fraser's and Travers' reports. Weston remarked: "Many of the 5th Division who witnessed the incident, also gave us the credit; during the day many congratulations were offered by different officers, including Lieutenant-Colonel J. Murray and Major Hinton.

That the RAF was obviously striving for sole recognition could not be discounted. Lieutenant P. Hutton of the Royal Field Artillery recalled in a letter to the Sydney *Daily Mail* some time later: "Later in the day the Air Force came to me for confirmation of their claim, which was then the rule, but I could not substantiate it."

It proved to be a surprisingly short time—a matter of a day or two—before German Intelligence had an unusually accurate confirmation as to how their famous son had died. It did not come from an analysis of observers' reports; it came from cloak-and-dagger activity behind the Aussie line. A former German spy who visited Australia some years after the war told, in a letter to the *Newcastle Sun* (New South Wales), how he came to report Richthofen's death to the German High Command.

At the time of the occurrence, I was attached to the Army Corps which was defending our front against the Australians, and as I was a good deal behind the enemy lines you do not need much imagination to know what I was. I was seeking information about the Australian artillery that day, when I spotted a plane flying very low, closely followed by another; there was a third plane, but it was too far away to be in the fight and Baron Richthofen was too good an air fighter to be caught like that with another on his tail. Another thing that bears out my point is that when he was examined, the bullet that killed him penetrated his chest. As far as I can remember it was the 55th Battery.[4] I was the one who reported his death

---

[4] A reasonable error. The 55th Battery was located to the immediate right of the 53rd Battery.

to the High Commander and in my report I stated that the Baron had met his death from bullet wounds inflicted by an Australian machine gunner. (The report). . .was written on Y.M.C.A. paper in Aubigny, signed "106." For obvious reasons I am not disclosing my identity, hoping that your readers do not bear any animosity to me. I do not, for I used to take off my hat to the Aussies—one always had to be so particular when you were about their lines; they used to ask too many questions.

In the years to follow, many would claim the honor of having put the famous flier out of action. Foremost to challenge the 53rd Battery gunners was ex-Sergeant-Major Alfred G. Franklyn of the 110th Section of F Anti-Aircraft Battery, Royal Garrison Artillery, temporarily attached to the Australian Field Batteries. He lives today in Leigh-on-Sea in Essex, England. Franklyn first made his claim in 1929, after reading an account that said Richthofen was brought down by a Canadian pilot. He restated the claim in 1961 and again in 1963. The former gunner told of his action while in charge of two anti-aircraft guns mounted on lorries in a sunken road 800 yards east of Bonnay. He said he observed Richthofen's circus patrolling the lines at 10,000 to 15,-000 feet, and his battery engaged them first with their two 13/18 pound AA guns.

Franklyn related how Richthofen suddenly left his circus and dived toward them as he chased two Sopwith Camels that were returning to their side of the lines. He said his A.A. guns could not fire on Richthofen owing to his stunting and low altitude, so he rushed to the battery's tripod-mounted Lewis gun, fired 30 rounds at very close range and saw the plane crash.

A statement by Corporal R.H. Barron, late of the same battery, tends to support Franklyn's claim in part. Barron said: "Just before mid-day, our attention was attracted by the rattle of machine guns, and there suddenly appeared two Sopwith Camels flying in from the German lines at full speed, and so low that they only just cleared the top of the ridge.

"Immediately behind them, and sitting on their tails, was the red plane which events subsequently proved was flown by Baron von Richthofen. He was putting bursts of machine gun fire into both the Camels without, however, doing any apparent damage." The Barron report contradicts Franklyn's statement by saying: "We promptly came into the action, and with the object of saving the British planes, put up a barrage of shrapnel between them and the Fokker . . ." Then Barron went on to tell how Sergeant Franklyn manned the Lewis gun, fired at the triplane and how it "went down at a steep angle over the ridge."

While the sincerity of these men cannot be disputed, their accuracy can.

Franklyn pinpointed his gun position at 800 yards east of Bonnay and said the plane crashed 200 yards beyond this. The scaled map distance from Franklyn's position to the recorded crash site, however, is slightly over 1,000 yards. Thus, if a Fokker fell 200 yards from Franklyn's gun, logically it could not have been Richthofen's. Were there two separate air-ground actions in that vicinity that morning?

Frank R. McGuire, a long-time researcher in the matter of Richthofen's death, has advanced a theory. Aside from the distance factor, McGuire establishes a second factor: *time*. Writing in the Summer 1963 issue of *Cross and Cockade*, the Canadian historian says:

Franklyn gives the time of the incident as 11:03 A.M.— but what date? It was on April 23, two days after Richthofen's death, that he read about the German ace's having been shot down "yesterday." That the report itself was dated the 22nd evidently did not register at the time. When he eventually noticed the actual date of that account, "Yesterday" naturally became, to him April 21. According to the war diary of the Fourth Army A.A. Defences, however, it was on the 22nd . . . not the 21st . . . that someone in F Battery, R.G.A. (no doubt Sergeant Franklyn) brought down an enemy plane.

Of course it was Sergeant Franklyn's job to discourage, and if possible, destroy enemy aeroplanes ... and he did it well! That a particular target was not, and could not have been the Baron's machine is hardly to his discredit; neither can he be blamed for supposing, in retrospect, that his victim was Richthofen. In any number of eyewitness accounts—British, Australian, German—we encounter the same tendency.[5]

Sooner or later, any German plane that fell anywhere near the junction of the Somme and the Ancre on or about April 21, 1918, was apt to become von Richthofen's!

In support of McGuire's contention is an earlier comment by a British Squadron Commander. "Every new lad in my squadron thought he was fighting Richthofen."

Still, if Franklyn downed a plane on the 22nd, it must have been a quiet "shoot," for no surviving member of the 53rd Battery who was queried about it can recall another Dr.I—or another enemy machine of any type—being shot down by ground fire in that immediate area for at least a week after Richthofen's death. And today Franklyn clearly recalls these significant details about the afternoon of April 21: "About an hour afterwards a large motor car came to our position from the aerodrome with a high official of the R.A.F. with the pilot of one of the two Camels which were being chased by Richthofen." He also recalls the R.A.F. tender that came up and took Richthofen's body away.

Regardless of the confusion in dates as recorded in the war diary of the Fourth Army A.A. Defences, Franklyn *did* fire on Richthofen's plane on April 21st in its curving descent—after it had passed over the 53rd Battery and at a time coinciding with Sergeant Popkin's fire from the slope of the ridge.

At the 53rd Battery dugout, officers and men from nearby units, curious as to the appearance of the most lionized fighter pilot of all time, came to pause over the body and pay their last respects. There was no rejoicing

---

[5] One such account, for instance, depicts a pursuit down the Ancre, another up the Somme, and so on. F. R. M.

among the men, although they would neither hide nor minimize the significance of their accomplishment. McDiarmid summed the feeling of the time when he said: "It was later that we were told that the plane belonged to the famous 'Red Knight.' It came out in Routine Orders ... Strangely enough, the news caused a mild sort of regret amongst us, for we knew of Richthofen's exploits and he commanded our respect and admiration—enemy or not—just as Rommel did in the last war."

Von Richthofen in the cockpit of an Albatros Scout,
early in 1917.

The Richthofen family at Schweidnitz. Left to right: Manfred, the
Baroness Kunigunde, Lothar, Major Albrecht von Richthofen (seated), Karlo Bolko, Ilse. *Courtesy Verlag Ullstein*

Baron Manfred von Richthofen; shy, handsome, "Red Dragon" of the Air, downed eighty enemy planes in individual air-to-air combat over the Western front. While pursuing his intended eighty-first victim, Lieutenant W. R. May of 209 Squadron, he was plucked from the sky as he flew at tree-top level over the 53rd Battery of the Australian Field Artillery.

Die Jagdstaffel des Freiherrn von Richthofen, im Apparat sitzend Rittmeister Freiherr von Richthofen.

Richthofen, in the cockpit of his Albatros fighter, and his Staffel—1917. *Australian War Memorial Photo*

Von Richthofen's Albatros D5, where he landed it in a field near Wervicq after being wounded and temporarily blinded by a bullet from Lt. Woodbridge's gun on July 6, 1917.

The F.E. 2. It was from this antiquated type that Lt. A. E. Woodbridge, with Captain D. C. Cunnell as pilot, shot down the famous German ace on July 6, 1917. This machine had various armament installations, including an arrangement whereby the observer could shoot backward over the top wing with his Lewis gun. Equipped with 120 or 160 horsepower engines, Richthofen shot down fifteen F.E. 2's. *Photo courtesy the Imperial War Museum*

Manfred von Richthofen several days after he was shot down by Lt. A. E. Woodbridge on July 6, 1917. The wounding changed his life in many ways and altered his thoughts about the war and ultimate German victory. *Courtesy Verlag Ullstein*

Lieutenant Lothar von Richthofen is assisted from his Albatros fighter by his batman. The brother of the remarkable ace, he downed forty Allied planes in seventy-seven days at the front. *Imperial War Museum Photograph*

Lothar von Richthofen crashed on March 13, 1918 and was hospitalized because of injuries. It was while in hospital that he learned of his brother's death. *Courtesy Verlag Ullstein*

Rittmeister von Richthofen and his fellow pilots chat with a captured English pilot of the Royal Flying Corps, who appears none too concerned about his fate as a prisoner of war. *Courtesy Knorr and Hirth Verlag*

A snapshot of Lieutenant D. G. Lewis and his Camel *Rhodesia*, taken shortly before he fell, burning, as von Richthofen's final victim. *Courtesy D. G. Lewis*

Richthofen's "Red Devil" Dr.1 425/17 as it appeared on the day he was shot down. The aircraft was dark red overall, including the cowling and wheel covers. The rudder was white. Only a few days before his death, the old style cross insignia was removed from the plane and replaced with the straight type that continued throughout the war. These crosses were edged with a thin white border. Many triplanes in J.G. 1 were predominantly red, but only the Rittmeister retained the all red coloration.

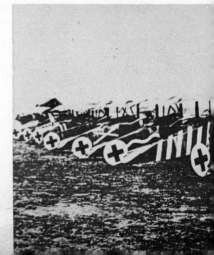

From the appearance of this part of Richthofen's "Circus," there is small wonder that the gaily decorated and brilliantly colored planes were named after their counterpart, the traveling circus. *Imperial War Museum photo*

Von Richthofen and pilots. He wears the silk scarf taken from his body by Brigade Intelligence Officer, Lieutenant Donald L. Fraser.

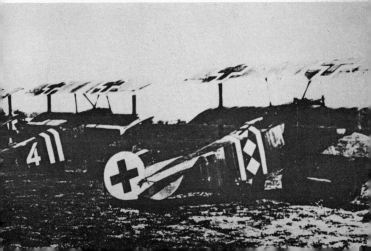

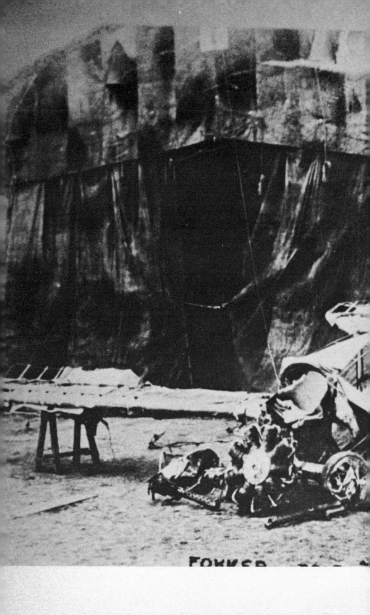
FOKKER

Richthofen's dismantled machine after the souvenir kings picked it over. The picture is somewhat misleading, for the only damage sustained was the crumpling of one lower wing, the undercarriage and the engine mounting section. A typical tent hangar is in the background. *Imperial War Museum photo*

Number 3 Squadron officers and men inspect the dismantled wreckage of von Richthofen's Fokker DR-1 at Poulainville the day after the crash. Left to Right: Captain E. J. Jones, Corporal E. P. L. deBomford (hand on tail section), 1st/Sgt. A. M. Sidey, Captain R. D. G. Francis (with pipe, facing camera), Lt. N. Mulroney (lifting wing), 2nd A/M G. A. Read (next to guns), and Sgt. V. Smith, extreme right.

Number 3 Squadron officers Left to Right: Lt. N. Mulroney; Pilot, Lt. O. G. Witcomb and Lt. F. J. Mart; Observers, examine Richthofen's twin death-dealers at Poulainville. *Australian War Memorial photo*

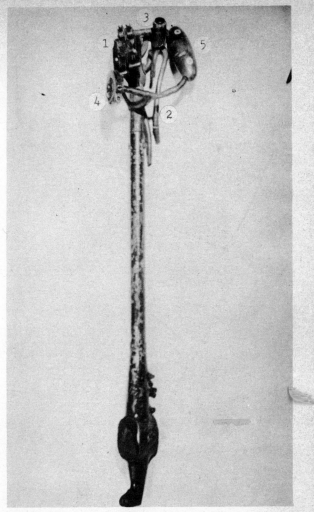

The control stick of von Richthofen's triplane. With the thumb and fingers of the right hand, a Fokker DR-1 pilot could fire the right or left machine gun independently (1) fire both guns simultaneously (2) interrupt the engine ignition system by pressing the *coupe* button (3) adjust engine power with the auxiliary throttle (the small knob is missing from the pivot) (4) and, control the flight of the airplane with his hand on the control stick grip (5). *Courtesy Australian War Memorial*

The right fur boot worn by von Richthofen on his last patrol. It bears evidence of the conflict in the form of a bullet hole near the top and thus verifies the statements of several diggers that the ace was struck by more than one bullet. *Australian War Memorial photo.*

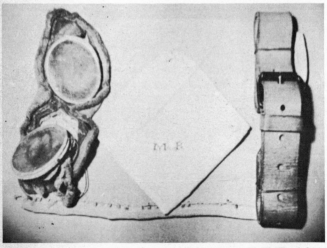

Von Richthofen's flying goggles were picked up by E. E. Hardaker of the 11th Brigade. The Baron's scarf and monogrammed handkerchief were recovered by Lt. Donald Fraser and the airman's leather belt was souvenired by J. B. Cunningham. These items are in the Carisella Collection of Richthofania. *Courtesy Daedalus Publishers*

The engine from Richthofen's triplane is displayed in the Imperial War Museum, Lambeth Road, London. The card bears the inscription: "Shot down by Captain Roy Brown, 209 Squadron." The practically undamaged condition verifies that Richthofen crashed with light to moderate impact. The engine has often been described as French due to the LeRhone nomenclature. It is actually of French LeRhone design and patent, although manufactured by German Oberursal. *Imperial War Museum photo*

"LE RHONE ENGINE"
Horse Power 110 Makers Nº 2478.
Ex Capt Von Richthofen's Machine
Fokker Triplane."
Shot down by Capt. Brown. 209. Squad.

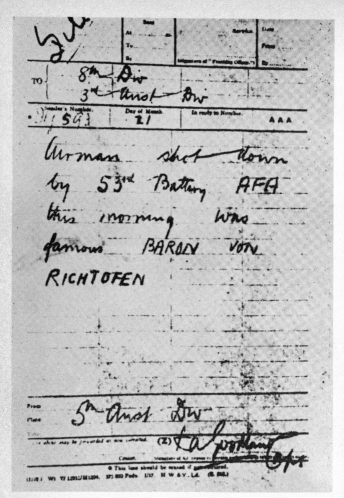

TO:
8ᵗʰ Div
3ʳᵈ Aust Div

Sender's Number: 593 Day of Month: 21 In reply to Number: AAA

Airman shot down
by 53ʳᵈ Battery AFA
this morning was
famous BARON VON
RICHTOFEN

From
Place 5ᵗʰ Aust Div

General T. J. Hobb's communication implies that there was no question as to the 53rd Battery's responsibility for Richthofen's death. *British Crown copyright*

The best-known photograph of Baron Manfred von Richthofen, the Kaiser's deadliest ace and Germany's man of the hour. About to add his eighty-first victory to this long string of kills, he was plucked from the air by gunners of the 53rd Battery, Australian Field Artillery, who fired at point-blank range as the red triplane roared overhead at an altitude of less than fifty feet.

The funeral procession of Rittmeister Baron Manfred von Richthofen at Bertangles, April 22, 1918. The cortege of Number 3 Squadron, Australian Flying Corps personnel. *Imperial War Museum photograph*

Firing party leading, the tender moves slowly through open ranks of Australian soldiers as the pall bearers follow on the last mile. *Courtesy Imperial War Museum*

At the gates of Bertangles Cemetery, the Chaplain met the procession, then preceded the flower-covered coffin through the gate, between the ranks of the Australian firing party. *Courtesy Imperial War Museum*

Baron von Richthofen's wartime resting place; his first grave at Bertangles, France, shown immediately following his burial on April 22, 1918. With other photos, this one was dropped to the German Flying Corps by British airmen the following day. *Imperial War Museum photo*

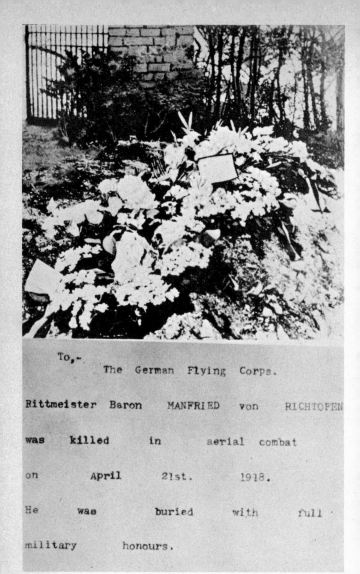

To,-

The German Flying Corps.

Rittmeister Baron MANFRIED von RICHTOFEN

was killed in aerial combat

on April 21st. 1918.

He was buried with full

military honours.

This message and photo was dropped at several locations behind the German lines following the burial of the German ace. *Imperial War Museum photo*

Enlisted personnel of Number 3 Squadron buying milk from farm girls. Taken at Flissels Aerodrome in 1918. Left to Right: E. P. L. deBomford, R. T. Ince, C. P. Holdenson, Unknown, C. E. Symons.

The R.E.8, the type of airplane with which Number 3 Squadron was largely equipped. Used for observation, artillery spotting, photo reconnaissance work, it carried one fixed Vickers machine gun on the left side of the fuselage and a ring-mounted Lewis gun for the Observer. With the 150 horsepower Royal Aircraft Factory air-cooled engine, it had a maximum speed of 102 miles per hour and a rate of climb of approximately 350 feet per minute. Von Richthofen shot down eight of this type. *Imperial War Museum photo*

A. R. Brown

The battlefield near Hamel, showing the desolation after the July 4 Allied offensive spearheaded by the Australian Corps. Richthofen's last dogfight and his tree-top chase of Lieutenant May occurred over this ground. *Photo courtesy James V. Rake*

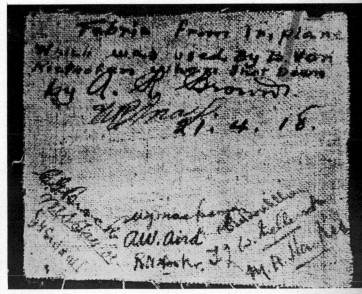

The fabric taken from von Richthofen's DR-1 triplane and signed by the eleven members of 209 Squadron who participated in the morning's action. That there was no doubt at that time as to who allegedly shot down the *Red Devil*, is shown by the words at top. *Courtesy O. C. LeBoutillier*

Lieutenant W. J. Mackenzie—"Bill" and his Camel at 209 Squadron. Born in Memphis, reared in Port Robinson, Ontario, he was—miraculously—the only Allied casualty in one of the most unforgettable air battles ever waged over the Western front. *Courtesy Mrs. George Bridge*

Sergeant-Major Alfred G. Franklyn (foreground) stands before a gun of the 110th Section of "F" Anti-aircraft Battery, Royal Garrison Artillery. The Battery is shown in action at Omiecourt, on March 24, 1918. The gun is a 13 pounder, 9 counterweight, antiaircraft type on a Mrk. IV Motor Lorry Mounting. Between the lorry and the tree a typical post mounting for the light automatic Lewis gun is seen. *Imperial War Museum photograph*

Sergeant-Major Alfred George Franklyn of the Royal Garrison Artillery, was a member of the 110th Section, F Battery, A.A., British Expeditionary Force, attached to the A.I.F. He fired on the red triplane after it passed over the 53rd Battery, during its curve. *Courtesy Alfred George Franklyn*

With men of his machine gun company, Gunner Cedric Bassett Popkin poses behind a Vickers 30 calibre machine gun of the type he fired at the red triplane.

Gunner Robert Buie, 3801, was mentioned in official dispatches as one of the two men whose Lewis gun fire fatally struck von Richthofen over the 53rd Morlancourt Ridge. *Portrait taken in 1919*

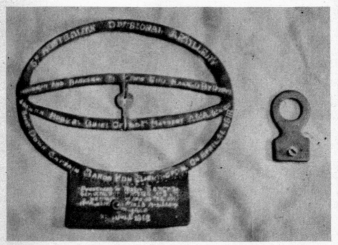

The backsight (left) and the foresight fashioned from a discarded 18-pounder shell case by Fitter Bartlett, was mounted on Gunner Buie's Lewis gun. Eventually all Lewis anti-aircraft posts were equipped with manufactured sights of this design. Presented to General Hobbs. Now on display in the Australian War Memorial. *Australian War Memorial photo*

our loving son
Oliver

Lieutenant Oliver LeBoutillier

The re-interment of von Richthofen in Berlin, November, 1925. Brought from a cemetery for the German war dead at Fricourt, the body is carried through the streets of Berlin enroute to its final resting place—Invaliden Cemetery.

President of the German Republic, former Field Marshal von Hindenburg throws the first handful of earth into the open grave at Invaliden Cemetery to conclude the reburial rites in November of 1925.

At final rest today, in Russian-held ground. Richthofen's grave at Invaliden Cemetery, East Berlin.

CHAPTER TWELVE

Afternoon

"I well remember the excitement in the squadron," said ex-Corporal E.P.L. deBomford of Number 3 Squadron, "when news came that Baron von Richthofen, leader of the well-known 'Red Circus' had been shot down in a sector not far from our aerodrome.

"A salvage detail, consisting of a party of mechanics from our squadron, in charge of Lieutenant W. J. Warneford, went out to bring in the remains of Richthofen's cracked triplane. Among the group was Corporal Bigum, Colin Collins, A. Waldron and others."

The other men were the detail sergeant, Richard Foale, Corporal J. A. Porter, J. A. Kitts, A. G. Bond and Air Mechanic 1st Class A. A. Boxall-Chapman, later of Lincoln, England, and Mick Worsley, the driver. Warneford was assistant to the squadron equipment officer, Captain Roderick Ross, who in turn was responsible for the filing of a technical report on the broken plane. Within minutes of receiving the pinpoint location of the crash site, the crew headed east along the Poulainville-Querrieu Road in a Crosley open-bed tender.

Ten miles away the 14th Australian Brigade began to host the visits of officers directed to carry out the orders of Rawlinson to look into the matter of Richthofen's death. The parade of dashing staff officers, with their red tabs, swagger sticks and superbly cut riding boots would continue for days. They were men who squinted through monocles, and with colored pins on maps calmly worked out attacks and defenses along the waterlogged

Somme. To meet the requirements of Generals Haig and Gough, many were cavalrymen. In the main they were not accustomed to the hardships of forward positions; they lived well, wined and dined one another at mess. Their polished boots echoed along the gleaming halls of chateau quarters. They found time to hunt and fish, take walks and occasionally flirt with the better-class mademoiselles. In the hours and days that followed, Major Beavis remembers he and his officers were host to several such men.

> Several airmen called in the afternoon—no recollection in my diary—one was a Major or Lieutenant-Colonel and one a pilot or flying officer or equivalent. The Senior Air Officer—probably the Wing Commander—brought a pilot along. Possibly, whilst being polite, I did not take their claims seriously, as it was so fantastic to suggest that Richthofen could have been killed from the air. To those actually on the spot all the circumstances are so definite and clear that he could only have been shot down from the ground ... the whole controversy was ridiculous since the evidence of actual eye-witnesses is so simple, direct and clear, all the other evidence is merely to try and justify an assumption. There were no conflicting Australian claims and the Germans on the hill behind Hamel who saw the pursuit and escape of the Camel, and Richthofen's descent, agreed that no third plane was firing on the triplane as it swooped along the Somme valley.

When Brown arrived at 14th Brigade Headquarters with Cairnes and another officer who was not immediately identified, they were directed to the officers of the 53rd Battery. After customary formalities, Cairnes explained that the objective of their mission was to clarify conflicting claims in regard to the shooting down of the red machine. Battery personnel registered mingled surprise and bewilderment. A few were mildly amused. But when it became clear the pilot's claim was a serious one, the Australian attitude changed and they firmly contested the air claim. Among others, Buie was called. He shook hands with Brown. Then, with Major Beavis and

Captain Ellis, he pointed out the Lewis guns, traced the triplane's flight path down the valley, described the gunnery action and located the wreckage. Brown remained politely attentive and appeared, outwardly at least, to accept the word of the artilleryman. To a man, the Aussie observers all agreed there were only two planes—Richthofen's "tripe" and May's Camel—over the battery at the critical firing. As the R.A.F. officers prepared to leave, Brown commented that he "was certain he'd brought down a red triplane," but added that possibly it was "in another sector." He did not visit the wreckage over the slope and this precluded any personal satisfaction he might have gained from examing the plane for the bullet holes he felt certain he fired into it.

But Roy Brown was in no mood to altercate the issue. Rebuffed, how could he contradict the statements of the senior officers and battery personnel? No doubt he disguised his real feelings well, for one digger commented: "He went away, apparently satisfied."

The body of the dead ace had arrived at the dugout shortly before the R.A.F. officers appeared, and there Brown saw the corpse on Major Beavis's cot. He was unprepared for this. The experience proved a considerable shock to the young and sensitive airman who, for the first time, saw his enemy counterpart—a flier cold in death. In air fighting, the brief brutality of machine-gun bullets piercing a fellow man was something fleeting—and detached. Now, on a balmy April afternoon the violence of it all came suddenly and painfully home to the young Canadian—who was all too willing to believe the much-admired German hero had died by his hand.

There was—at another time and another place—a scene much like this, when a German flyer, young Leutnant Hermann Becker, the leader of Jasta 12, with 23 victories and who, like Richthofen, wore the *Ordre pour le mérite* proudly on his breast, paused thoughtfully over a fallen Allied airman. Perhaps, like Roy Brown at that moment, Becker comprehended more deeply the brutality, the senselessness, the inhumanity of war. He left behind these words: "Despite the victory, and even if it is a hard-wrested victory, there is always that sad regret, that human sympathy for the victim, who was, after all, another pilot like oneself . . . "

Brown did not linger beside the stretcher; the strain was overwhelming his ragged nerves and knotted insides. He retreated unsteadily to the car, nauseated and weak. He leaned against the side and awaited the others—and was sick.

Sergeant Popkin remained at his post and gave much thought to the morning's happenings. He felt confident it was his second burst that was fatal to the German. But there were several factors of which Popkin was unaware.

The Vickers gunner had no way of evaluating the effectiveness of the gunfire that began as his first burst was ending. He was aware however, that the red triplane was below the ridge and copse of woods on the brow of the hill when he began firing his first burst. These shots, hastily aimed, likely struck some nonmetal parts of the machine, but certainly not the pilot. Weston and Popkin saw the Fokker fly onward under power and *lift itself* over the copse of the woods, and over the ridge.

Popkin was not alone in the belief that he was responsible. Lieutenant Fraser's first impression was that the gunner in the southwest corner of the wood had caused the fall. Fraser sought out and found the Sergeant at his weapon.

On General Cannan's direction I went out to get particulars of the machine gunners who had brought the plane down, and found Sergeant Popkin of the 24th M.G. Company at his anti-aircraft M.G. at J.25.b.3.7. (approx) (Somme valley).

At this time I was not aware that any other M.G. had been firing at this plane. I congratulated Sergeant Popkin on his successful shoot, but afterwards found out that two A.A. Lewis Guns belonging to the 53rd Battery A.F.A. had also fired at this plane when it was directly over my head, but the noise of the engine prevented my hearing the shooting.

In summing up his official findings Donald Fraser concluded:

> The 53rd Battery Lewis gunners probably assisted in sealing the fate of this airman, as he apparently flew right into their line of fire. I am strongly of the opinion that he was first hit by Sergeant Popkin's shooting, as he was unsteady from the moment of that first burst of fire.

Popkin recalled his interview with Lieutenant Fraser. "About an hour later an intelligence officer of the 11th Brigade came and took my regimental particulars and told me who I had shot down.

"About six o'clock the same evening a liaison officer of the 52nd Battalion, with his report written out, saw me and also took my regimental particulars to support my claim. The Colonel of the 52nd Battalion also supported my claim, but owing to the report from my Company going in a week after the incident I am afraid I got very little consideration."

Years later, Popkin was to receive more consideration than he realized. But the man who made a conscientious effort to pinpoint who—in fact—fired the fatal burst, C. E. W. Bean, was plagued by indecision.

Bean first recorded the honors in favor of the 53rd's Lewis gunners. Then, in 1928, he became involved in the broadening controversy and said that one bullet had entered Richthofen's jaw and passed out the left side of the face beneath his right eye. This was a gross error. Then Bean added: "I do not think the three Australian gunners [Popkin, Buie and Evans] themselves could determine with any approach to certainty, which of them fired the fatal shot." After he had consulted with other authorities and reviewed the medical records, Bean formed yet another opinion. He considered much of the supposedly "new" material that continually cropped up was actually long-neglected material. After sifting a mountain of evidence he wrote in the appendix of his fifth volume of the war history published in 1937, that neither Buie nor Evans could be credited "since it [the bullet] came almost directly from the right and from behind the aviator." Bean concluded that Popkin's second burst was fatal, but he overlooked two facts; that the range was 600 yards, and that the pilot chased May up and over the ridge *after* the first burst had ended. Granting that Richthofen's right side was exposed to Popkin at that distance, the tilt of the Fokker as it banked in its final turn would have caused a fatal bullet from Popkin's Vickers to travel *downward* through Richthofen's chest, not *upward* as it did.

Under the general routine order, all downed enemy aircraft were the property of the Air Service, and so it was that Major Beavis recorded that "a few hours after the crash a tender came from Number 3 Squadron to pick up the body and the 'plane." Lieutenant Warneford and party arrived at 2 P.M. and in his report said the plane was being shelled by German artillery. The ticking Crosley crawled cautiously along the sunken road that led past the openings of the 53rd's dugouts. Typical of rear-echelon aircraftsmen unaccustomed to exposure in forward positions, they parked the tender on the road behind the sloping protection of the knoll, and walked the short distance to the wreck which was still being briskly "souvenired." Shrapnel-shy, the aircraftsmen took their time in dismantling the tattered triplane, already greatly stripped of instruments and small gear. Much of the work was completed after nightfall. Meanwhile, Corporal Porter had located Richthofen's body on the stretcher at the 53rd. He learned that a medic had been there and declared all life extinct.

Despite the forbidden use of cameras except by official photographers, at some time during the salvage operation, Richthofen's body was photographed. Rumor had it that J. E. Wellard of the 41st Battalion made two exposures, and another member of the outfit, David Gillingham, claimed Wellard showed them to him several days afterward. "Someone ... may still have his copy of Richthofen's photo," Corporal Ramsden said later. "He was propped up in a sitting position against the wall of a shed when he was photographed."

"The officer of Number 3 Squadron, A.F.C., in charge of the salvage detail," Beavis explained, "brought the tender to my dugout and stated he had been sent to pick the body up. I do not know who gave these orders, but I handed it over and it was transferred to the vehicle. I had not realized our R.E.8s of that squadron had seriously claimed Richthofen. The officer said one of his people had shot him down. I did not treat it seriously; his claim was as sound as Brown's."

The aircraftsmen maneuvered the corpse onto the bed of the tender, being careful to brace it against the side of the bed. One mechanic pointed to the dead airman's head.

"What's that?" he asked, indicating a darkened ring around the neck of the corpse.

His companion frowned and shook his head. "Hanged if I know. Broken brace wire probably. Whipped 'round his throat when 'e smashed."

But the external brace wires on the Dr.I, those supporting the center section of the upper wing, were intact. The ring was actually a radial bruise, an injury characteristic of a crash in which the head is suddenly snapped forward—then back. The sudden whiplike motion and attendant stretching of the neck muscles had burst the small blood vessels and caused the ringlike bruise to appear.

While dismantling the triplane some hours after the crash, Boxall-Chapman took careful notice of two details. He saw a single bullet hole in the right side of the plane at the cockpit level—and he saw that the engine's magneto switch had been turned off. Did Richthofen turn it off—or had a souveniring digger?

The tender departed with Lieutenant Warneford, and Worsley driving. The corpse, bundled in the truck bed, bumped heavily along the muddy road to Poulainville. Major Beavis turned again to battery duties. He reflects:

> I did not do anything to establish our claim as I thought—wrongly—that the facts would speak for themselves.

Later that afternoon we resumed our usual activities, calibrating guns and engaging targets.

A former staff officer of the 5th Brigade, Australian Field Artillery, 2nd Division, recalls visiting the crash site a short time after Richthofen's demise:

So far as I can remember, the time of my arrival on that scene must have been in the early afternoon. .... Aircraftsmen of the R.A.F. were dismantling the red triplane when we got to the scene; I presumed for easier handling and transportation to the back area. I recall that I was somewhat amazed at the apparent condition of the aircraft. Though not in any way an expert in such matters I had, nevertheless, seen quite a few of the remains of crashed planes during my active service years. Most of those had either burned in the air, or on impact, and were little more than a smear of ashes. The remainder had been a shattered pile of struts and fabric, which little resembled any form of a plane.

I was therefore rather astounded to discover that, to my untrained eyes at least, Richthofen's aircraft was still quite recognizable as a fighting aircraft, and evidently not too badly damaged at that. The fore end of the ship was quite a bit broken up; the rest of the fuselage structure seemed not damaged at all. One wing appeared to have a crimp in it and the ship, when we saw it, appeared to be tilted drunkenly to one side, but considering that the salvage crew had apparently been working on it for some little time, it was difficult to decide what was the actual damage and what was the result of breaking down for transportation.

I do not remember seeing the prop, so cannot remark on its condition. But I heard later from the person who sold me a fragment, that at least one section of it had been shattered on impact. It was plain to see that the "souvenir kings" from the adjacent batteries, etc, had given the red tripe a good working over before the R.A.F. salvage crew had arrived.

I clearly remember that one of the A.S.C. chaps with me, somewhat doubting that the famed German ace had been brought down while in full possession of normal fighting capability, inquired, "What happened to him, did he run out of ammunition?" The R.A.F. bloke, or whatever his unit was, replied, "Damned if I know. Some thieving bastard stripped the guns off before we got here!" Until then we had not been aware that the guns were missing from their mounts and it was not until a few days later that I heard they had been recovered.

In conversation with eyewitnesses of the happenings on the scene of the crash, or in later discussions with others who had authoritative knowledge of this event, I remember hearing no evidence to corroborate the Roy Brown version of Richthofen's death. Those in a position of knowing the actual facts, so far as I am aware, appeared to be strongly in support of the ground fire—apparently of Buie—having done the trick. I can recall no one who was on the spot mentioning the fact of another plane in pursuit of Richthofen's at the time he went down. It was only later that I heard these rumors voiced by individuals who had no first-hand knowledge of the actual event. I have therefore given credence to the views of those who actually saw what transpired rather than those who only heard what happened.

From a distant ridge near Vaux, diffused in the gathering dusk, a "spook" crouched over his semaphore and blinked to another post low in the bend of the Somme. There was an answering glimmer and the beams flickered across shell holes that held ghastly secrets. White vapor crept stealthily over the edges and slipped eerily away. In the first light of tomorrow's dawn the mist would again lie in long flaxen streaks that stretched from crater to crater.

An almost spectral red glow lingered along the sky line from one end to the other. At the partly disassembled triplane, one-time seaman Colin Collins squinted his experienced eye along the horizon and opined there'd "likely be fair weather for the Baron's funeral."

VIGIL

CHAPTER THIRTEEN
J.G.1

Shortly after mid-day, the scattering of planes returned to Cappy aerodrome. One after another, they bumped down and rolled to the line. Mechanics rushed forward to grasp their wingtips, turn them around and chock the wheels. As each Dr.I trundled to a stop, there was a final burst of power with flippers full up before the pilot cut the magneto.

Holzapfel and Menzke were the first to suspect something was amiss. A familiar machine had not yet appeared among the group. Captain Reinhard was in charge of the aerodrome during Richthofen's absence. Hearing the returning fighters, he walked to the line as the last of the Fokkers dropped down and flared easily onto the grass with a muffled thump. As the planes taxied to the line, all but one were accounted for. The all-red one. The Rittmeister. At first Reinhard was not unduly alarmed. He spoke to a pilot who thought he had seen Richthofen closely pressed by several Camels.

Now Bodenschatz was aware of the Commander's absence. Karjus and Wenzl of Weiss's *Kette* were nearest to him. As they climbed from their machines, he strode toward them hurriedly, a look of concern on his fine features. In an unsteady voice he demanded: "Where is Richthofen?"

Wenzl's eyes told the Adjutant the answer would not be good. "I have ... an ominous feeling," Wenzl replied hesitantly. "We were just over the lines when we were attacked by seven Sopwiths with red noses ... We were

171

outnumbered for a time and no one could get a good shot. The Rittmeister came into the fight and then seven or eight more Lords attacked. It developed into a very large battle. We all lost altitude gradually and when we could, we broke off the engagement and returned over the lines. As I was coming back I looked down to the east and saw a small plane on the ground." He paused; a catch in his breath. "I believe it was a red one."

The men stared at one another for a heavy moment. Scholz came up hurriedly with the disturbing news that he saw Richthofen land behind the enemy lines.

"Land?" Reinhard echoed. "Behind the enemy's lines?"

Then Wolff ran to the group, much excited, and told them how he had watched the Rittmeister follow a lone Camel along the Somme. Had he seen Richthofen go down? No, Wolff replied, but the Rittmeister was well behind the British lines—and very low. No, it was not Richthofen whom a pilot had seen hotly pursued by several planes, it had been he—Wolff.

"We were all terribly shocked when Richthofen did not return from his mission," Karl Bodenschatz recalls. "A search—rescue squad was immediately sent out. All stations were alerted to be on the lookout for him."

Reinhard ordered Karjus, Wenzl and Wolfram von Richthofen back to the front to find the Commander's plane. In minutes the three were again airborne, but having agreed on no search plan beforehand, they scattered and lost one another near the lines. Meanwhile Bodenschatz and Reinhart rang up the front.

Richard Wenzl set a straight course for Corbie. As he neared the lines he descended to 600 feet the better to locate the plane he had seen earlier. He sighted the triplane on the ground; then, in the same general area he saw another machine which he did not describe. Aside from Richthofen, there were no machines missing from J.G.I. A machine of Jasta 5? No, every one of their machines had returned. Possibly it was a wrecked machine from another, earlier, air fight that could not be

safely reached for salvage. Or perhaps it was an object
that appeared as an aircraft to Wenzl.

The young officer had great difficulty in viewing the
activity around the red machine so he started a dash
across the lines for a better look. It was a game try. A
hail of small caliber fire and anti-aircraft shrapnel
greeted him. Then suddenly the firing stopped—and a
few seconds later he knew why. A British fighter fastened itself on his tail. Wenzl continued in a shallow
dive toward the red mark that stood out against the
Morlancourt ridge. Now three Sopwith Camels were on
his tail, firing. Wenzl wisely aborted his mission,
wheeled about and dived for his lines with the Camels
steadily narrowing the gap. He flew over an observation
balloon at 60 feet, dropped to within a few feet of the
ground and stayed there all the way back to base. He
landed, unable to add anything to what was already
reported. Karjus and Wolfram likewise returned empty-
handed. Every man of J.G.I stood about silent and glum.

Meanwhile Bodenschatz hounded the *Flugmeldedienst*
for more word. Anxious calls were put through to the
front. The men gathered about the telephone, hoped,
prayed, but secretly feared the worst. The *Flugmeldedienst* had word.

It was true. Richthofen was down on enemy ground.

There was a message from Leutnant Fabian of the
16 Feld Artillerie Regiment to the effect that a red
triplane had made a "good landing on a flat hill north of
Corbie." For a time the news raised the spirits of the
men but there was now the growing uncertainty as to
whether Richthofen was alive or dead.

Leutnant Fabian's report was telephoned immediately
to Second Army Headquarters, and on to Supreme Headquarters.

Oberleutnant Bodenschatz requested permission to go
to the forward artillery observation post. The trip in a
rocking motorcycle sidecar took several minutes, then a
trek through the winding trench network to the sand-
bagged outpost. Bodenschatz stared through the powerful binoculars, swept the hill foot by foot, but was un-

able to determine anything of his commander's fate. He returned to Cappy shortly after 2:00 P.M., highly dejected.

German Headquarters had announced Richthofen's 79th and 80th victories while he prepared for the morning's patrol. Soon afterward, while congratulations were being relayed to J.G.I, Headquarters was struck with the bombshell that Richthofen was missing in action. Suddenly, High Command was faced with the dilemma of how to break the news to the nation. They could not delay for long; the British would surely announce the fact of Richthofen's capture—or worse—as soon as they identified him. But of course, the Generals agreed, the next of kin must be the first to know.

Army Headquarters made an unprecedented move— the Commanding General sent a message to the enemy.

> *Rittmeister von Richthofen landed behind your lines. Request news of his condition.*

The query was not acknowledged.

As the long afternoon wore on, spirits continued to sink as the officers and men waited morosely, impatiently. The east wind strengthened and took on a noticeable chill.

Toward evening Karl Bodenshatz resigned himself to the sad task he knew must be performed—the notification of Father Richthofen who had been recalled to duty as Garrison Commandant at Kortryk.

"I was flown to Kortryk in the two-seat observation plane," Bodenshatz remembers. "When I landed I went immediately to the inn where Major Albrecht von Richthofen was quartered and requested permission to see him."

The sun struck low as the afternoon light began to fade. Bodenschatz waited for Manfred's father in a twilight-lit room. Presently he heard a step. An elderly bearded gentleman entered, erect, and walked toward Bodenschatz. He recognized the Adjutant from J.G.I and his features clouded. "I have a feeling that something has happened to Manfred," the old man said quietly. Bodenschatz looked directly into the officer's eyes. "Major, I must report that the Rittmeister has not returned from the morning patrol. As far as we can determine, he is still alive."

The senior officer's eyes searched the Adjutant's face. *Manfred is alive?* He shook his head and his eyes took on a faraway gaze. He knew this was not so, and half to Bodenschatz, half to himself, he replied slowly and softly: "Then he has fulfilled his highest duty."

"There was no outward sign of grief on the old man's face," Bodenschatz recalls. "Father Richthofen turned and walked slowly to his room in the half-light. I saw his walk as one through the deepest of darkness. I think the old soldier expected this to happen to his son. He knew his fate."

The Adjutant returned to Cappy where he prepared telegrams for Richthofen's Mother at Schweidnitz and for Lothar, convalescing in a Düsseldorf hospital. Lothar had crashed on March 13th while landing his triplane and had suffered head and facial injuries when he was thrown against the gun butts and instruments. Manfred had visited him daily in the hospital until J.G.I's constant moves limited his trips. In the absence of his brother, the assigned Staffelführer, Manfred led Jasta 11.

The telegrams read:

> Manfred has not returned from patrol, and from present reports, landed unharmed behind enemy lines.

Lothar received the news quietly, but with bitterness. A desire for revenge welled in him. "This would not have happened if I had been there," was his only comment. In combat they had afforded one another their mutual protection.

At Schweidnitz, where the meadows were softly pastel and the trunks of the white birches contrasted with the deep green firs of the rolling forests, the Baroness had stepped into her sunlit garden, kaleidoscopic with early color, to cut a bouquet of spring flowers. As she snipped at the stems she overheard some children playing nearby. One mentioned her son's name and half-listening, she heard the child say the Rittmeister had fallen. She paused, puzzled, and gathering the cluster of buds, went into the large house with an uncomfortable foreboding. Presently the message arrived from Bodenschatz. Now began the vigil. The longest and darkest vigil was suffered at Schweidnitz where Mother Richthofen waited quietly and alone for the final word she had long feared would someday come. Manfred was his mother's favorite—and his father's. Secretly and silently she had worried for his safety, but never did she reveal it outwardly. Bad news had come to the old home before: when Manfred was isolated in Russia, when he was nearly killed by Lieutenant Woodbridge. But this . . . this, she knew, would end differently.

Reinhard paced nervously in the operations building. In the mess the pilots conversed in low tones. Some still had a dazed and distracted appearance and many wondered whether the morale of the *Luftstreitkäfte* would ever again recover. Had the pilots been aware of the crushing and victorious Allied offensive to come, they would have been even more dispirited.

In the Rittmeister's quarters, Menzke tidied the Commander's desk for the third time. Outside, near a hangar tent, Holzapfel stared at the darkened sky as though half-expecting to hear the distant popping of an Oberursel and see the red triplane burst out of the darkness and swoop down. Mechanics clustered in the shadowy gloom redolent of damp wool, tobacco, lacquer and castor oil.

Was it possible that Richthofen could be dead? True, he was mortal, but it did not seem that he could come to the same fate that had befallen so many of his comrades. He was exceptional; extraordinary. He had chosen to follow a profession so dangerous, so daring, that ordinary men lacked the courage to try. Richthofen must be alive!

Bodenschatz absently watched Reinhard pace, then suddenly remembered another duty he was obliged to perform. He took a small strongbox from the safe and unlocked it. He removed a gray folder, closed with the seal of the squadron. Slowly he opened the folder. Inside was a small note in Richthofen's hand. The Adjutant studied it for a moment, then gave it to Reinhard. The Staffelführer read the order:

10-3-18

In the event that I do not return from a patrol, Oberleutnant Reinhard of Jasta 6 is to command the Geschwader.

—Freiherr von Richthofen
Rittmeister

These few words were his whole will. There was nothing of personal concern, nothing of his private life. There was no farewell to his father, his mother, his brothers or sister, no request for the resolution of his personal affairs. The message was a simple and complete soldierly act addressed only to his squadron and to his men. Without condition, his life belonged to the Fatherland. He had provided that even should death overtake him, his last act would be for the welfare of his men—that they should have the best leadership.

Early on the 22nd, German Intelligence intercepted a fragmentary British broadcast in International code:

"... *famous German pursuit pilot Richthofen was shot down over Corbie and after landing near Australian troops* ..."

The interruption of the broadcast caused greater confusion among the Germans. Was he alive or dead? Why was the enemy silent? Their victory was certainly a great one; why did they not announce it to the world? Suspicions arose that foul play was afoot in the ace's death. Bitter rumors rippled through the back areas. Had Richthofen been beaten to death by the enemy troops? High Command ordered that all Allied prisoners and captured airmen were to be thoroughly interrogated. But fresh prisoners of war knew only that Richthofen was dead—or that a "heavily wounded pilot" whose name had been closely guarded, was taken to a hospital near Amiens. Hope at J.G.I was dying.

Until it could be officially reported that Richthofen was dead, the press could make no firm statement, but one news release from a neutral source cautiously said:

> Rittmeister von Richthofen failed to
> return from a flying raid over the
> Somme, April 21st.

On the afternoon of the 22nd, in Munich, Udet was strolling with his fiancé, Lo.

> At the time, the war seemed very, very remote ... we saw a crowd of people standing in front of a notice on a wall. "Probably news of some victory at the front," I said, and walked across to see what it was all about.
>
> A hard blow was in store for me, a blow which struck right at my heart.
>
> *Rittmeister Freiherr von Richthofen is missing*, the notice said. The letters faded before my eyes. I saw nobody, and thought of nobody, but elbowed my way through the crowd until I had reached the front row. *Failed to return from a flight*, I read ... *no traces have yet been discovered*.
>
> But I knew—knew with unfailing certainty that the Rittmeister was dead.
>
> What a man he was! ... Richthofen lived always on the other side of the boundary which we crossed only in our great moments. When he fought, his private life was thrust ruthlessly behind him. Eating, drinking and sleeping were all that he granted life, and then only the minimum that was necessary to keep flesh and blood in working order. He was the simplest man I ever met. He was a Prussian through and through. A great soldier.
>
> The news of Richthofen's death affected me profoundly
> ...

At Schweidnitz, shortly after the Baroness received a telegram that said her son was believed to be alive but

in captivity, the telephone rang. The newspapers
wanted to know whether the *Baronin* "had received bad
news from the front." Conflicting reports arrived
throughout the 22nd and until the evening of the 23rd
when—finally—she received the official announcement.
Late in the evening of the preceding day a German
soldier at an advanced airfield had picked up the first of
several dispatch tubes dropped by Robert Foster and
other fighter pilots. It was a message from the Royal
Flying Corps. It crushed forever all German hopes that
Richthofen was alive. It read:

> *Rittmeister von Richthofen was fatally wounded in
> aerial combat and was buried with full military honors.*

Shortly afterward, at 9:55 P.M. a pronouncement from
the British was relayed by Reuters to neutral services
and thence to German newspapers on the 23rd.

There was no longer any question.

Reinhard's first act on learning the official word was
to telegraph a message of condolence to Manfred's father. From Kortryk the elder Richthofen wired:

*To Jagdgeschwader Nr. I. My son still lives as your
model.*

> *Father Richthofen.*

CHAPTER FOURTEEN

209 Squadron

One by one and in scattered pairs, all but two Camels of 209 straggled homeward. The low-level flight from the Somme was a short 12 miles over farmlands bisected with dirt roads and narrow streams. West by northwest on the compass. Pont-Noyelle came first, then Querrieu off the left wing, next Cardonette, Rainneville to the right, over Coisy and just ahead lay the broad field at the side of Bertangles.

The planes swung low along the outskirts of Bertangles and blipped their engines in let-down. They passed across Monash's château where it overlooked the aerodrome, dipped over the trees that bordered the field, and flared out. Brown stared unblinkingly as the earth came up, fell off below the Camel's stub nose, and began its bumping and rustling under the roll of the wheels.

All of Brown's flight returned to Bertangles about 11:05 A.M. with the exception of Lomas who landed fifteen minutes later. Drake and Redgate, forced out of the fight, had arrived a half hour before Brown and May. Aird, of Redgate's flight, had engine trouble and had landed at Camblain. He returned to base at 2:00 P.M.

LeBoutillier's flight came in and rumbled down behind Mellersh. Brock was temporarily delayed. A forced landing seven miles north at Vert Galand Farm at 11:40 delayed his return until 3:55 in the afternoon.

Mackenzie made a shaky landing and taxied to a fast

180

stop. The Corporal mechanic knew by the gray grimace on the Lieutenant's face that his pilot was wounded. Mechanics crowded around to assist the airman from the cockpit. He was driven immediately to the hospital for treatment. There medics found he had been grazed by an explosive machine-gun bullet.

Brown taxied to the line, weak. He did not leave the cockpit immediately. All through the patrol and battle he had been unusually queasy and shaky. As his engine shut down he glanced to one side to see mechanics hold back May's Camel as its rotary engine came to a standstill. Behind them on the field, two Camels had quit cold on landing and their pilots, unable to taxi, abandoned them and walked toward Operations.

"When things got sorted out after landing back," Robert Foster recalls, "it transpired that we had lost nobody, but had much damage to our aircraft. This was the only patrol for that day because there was a great deal of repair work to be done on our aircraft as a result of that encounter, and we had insufficient serviceable aircraft for afternoon operations."

And there the machines rested, trailing fabric and dripping oil, until the "grease monkeys" came to push them to the hangars. For those devoted artificers who patched the bullet holes and repaired the damage, worked longer hours than any pilot, and sweated out every patrol just as anxiously, the only reward for work well done seemed to be more work. And this day they would have much to do.

When Mackenzie's ground crew inspected his plane, they discovered that one of the mounting points of his Bentley engine had been shot cleanly through by machine-gun fire.

The pilots assembled and said little. After a patrol each man knew the state of the other man's mind, the innermost sensations of weariness mingled with tension. It was not easy to unwind from a fight of this ferocity. It would take a little more time than usual.

Except for May, whose boundless reserve of energy afforded him a quick recovery from the harrowing effects of his near-death. Greatly excited and flushed, he joined Brown. "When we landed," May said, "Brown told me he had seen the red triplane chasing me and followed." The young man's thanks poured out and Brown dazedly nodded acknowledgement.

It was R.A.F. policy for the combat details to be recorded as quickly as possible. The haggard pilots with oil smeared faces filed into Operations and made out their reports, all of which came to the attention of Lieutenant Shelly, 209's Records Officer. Under his supervision they were typed and passed on to Intelligence and higher authority. Once recorded, the combat reports were rigidly official, irreversible—and could not be altered.

Lieutenant Taylor, awarded a "decisive," prepared this narrative for file:

> Attacked a two-seater Albatross at 12,000 feet over Beaucourt and after firing 300 rounds, the E.A. [enemy aircraft] started to emit dense clouds of smoke. It put its nose down and when at about 5,000 feet went vertically down and crashed. It burst into flames just before hitting the ground. Confirmed by Captain Brown and Lieutenant Foster.

LeBoutillier, still feeling the particular viciousness of the morning's encounter, wrote a report that reflected the heavy action from start to finish.

Sopwith B.R.   April 21st 1918
B3858 B3338 B7200   10:25 A.M.
Two Vickers syn. Guns.   as stated below
                                      H.O.P.

Captain O.C. LeBoutillier, Lieuts.
    Taylor and Foster
(1) 12,000 feet. (2) 7,000 feet.
(1) I observed two Albatross two-seaters over Le Quesnel. Lieuts. Foster, Taylor and myself fired on one when he burst into flames and crashed at Beaucourt.
(2) Engaged Fokker triplane over Cerisy (about 18–20

machines) and fired about 100 rounds at a mottled colored one but did not get him. Also fired on a red triplane which was shot down by Captain Brown and crashed our side of lines.

(3) After coming out of the engagement with the Fokker triplanes, Lieuts. Taylor and Foster dived on three two-seaters close to Albert. Both got in good bursts and E.A. dived away East. Owing to the fact that five E.A. scouts appeared above and that our ammunition was all used up, we had to break off the combat without decisive results.

(sgd) O. C. LeBoutillier
Captain

C. H. Butler
Major

Mellersh, who had scored toward the end of the battle, wrote this account:

I followed Captain Brown down into a large formation of Fokker Triplanes and Albatross D 5's. A dogfight ensued and I managed to get on the tail of a triplane, with a blue tail. I fired about 50 rounds into him when he turned and I got a long burst into him when he was turned up. The triplane then dropped his nose and went down in a vertical dive. I followed, still firing, and saw the machine crash near Cerisy.

Two other triplanes then dived onto me and I was forced to spindive to the ground and return to our lines at about 50 feet. Whilst so returning a bright red triplane crashed quite close to me and in looking up I saw Captain Brown's machine.

May took pains that his first combat report contain the essentials, and little more. Seated at a small table, he prepared this report:

Sopwith B.R.   April 21, 1918

D332810:45 A.M.
62 D.Q.
H.O.P.

Two Vickers syn. guns
2/Lt. W.R. May
7000 feet
Single-seater Fokker triplane, blue camouflaged wings. Attacked large formation of about 15-20 machines. Engaged
one E.A., firing bursts head-on into his engine, he went
over and dived down. I was unable to observe the result
as a second machine attacked me from behind.

I fired at the second machine, but without result. I then
went down and was attacked by a red triplane which
chased me over the lines low to the ground. While he was
on my tail, Captain Brown attacked and shot it down. I
observed it crash to the ground.

W. R. May
2/Lieut.

C. H. Butler

Paradoxically, though May insisted then—and later—
that Brown shot the red triplane from his tail, nowhere
in his narrative does he say he saw Brown's attack. He
states only that he observed the triplane crash. *Then* he
sighted Brown's Camel. The brevity of May's report also
gives the impression that he was in the fight from the
start. It says nothing about his guns jamming or the fact
that during most of the chase he was disoriented. Nevertheless, and despite the tendency for May's later recol-
lections to be largely in conflict with his official account,
the combat report is a sincere record of May's experiences; what he did, what he saw, what he assumed
happened.

Brown, exhausted and numb, sat heavily in a chair
and made out an even more brief report with an unsteady hand—a record of events visualized under the
stress of great anxiety for May's safety.

COMBATS IN THE AIR

Squadron 209 R.A.F.   Date: April 21st, 1918
Type and No. of Aeroplane: Time: 10:45 A.M.

Sopwith BR B 7270   Locality: 62 D.Q. 2
Armament: Two Vickers Syn   Duty: H.O.P.
Guns.   Height: 5000 feet
Pilot: Captain A.R. Brown D.S.C.   (Destroyed . . . . .

Engagement with red triplane: Result: (Driven down
Time: about 11:00 A.M.   out of control
Locality: Vaux-sur-Somme   Driven down . . . .

Remarks on Hostile Aircraft—Type, Armament, Speed, etc.
Fokker triplane, pure red wings with small black crosses.

Narrative.
(1) At 10:35 A.M. I observed two Albatross burst into
flames and crash.
(2) Dived on large formation of 15-20 Albatross Scouts D
5's and Fokker triplanes, two of which got on my tail
and I came out. Went back again and dived on pure
red triplane which was firing on Lieut. May. I got a
long burst into him and he went down vertical and
was observed to crash by Lieut. Mellersh and Lieut.
May. I fired on two more, but did not get them.

A.R. BROWN
Captain

C.H. BUTLER
Major

Although Brown's combat report suggests that he did
not personally witness the actual crash of the red
triplane (". . . *he went down vertical and was observed
to crash by Lieut. Mellersh and Lieut. May*"), there can
be no doubt that he did see the impact. In a later
statement he said in effect: "*Mellersh saw it, May saw
it, and I saw it.*"

It was not until later in the afternoon that Lieutenant
Mackenzie could file his report:

One triplane came on to me from left side; firing, and
hit me in the back, the bullet just grazing me. I then did a
steep left-hand bank and he did a right-hand turn. I then

gave him a good burst from behind and at about his own level. He turned over on his back and seemed to hang there. I did not see him afterwards as I was compelled to leave owing to pain from wound.

"After we made the necessary reports, we assembled for the noon mess," LeBoutillier recalls. "Mess was a large canvas tent with a long table and chairs. Our regular noon meal was usually steak and eggs, or bully, Macanochie, coffee or tea. The tea was rank."

Even while 209's pilots were finishing their reports and preparing for mess, an upsetting situation was rapidly reaching a head in the nearby Château of Bertangles, headquarters of Lieutenant General Sir John Monash, Commander of the Australian Corps.

Lieutenant Jack Willats of the A.F.C. was officer-in-charge of the Australian Corps Signal Company with headquarters adjacent to the château. When, in the mid-morning (before Brown's return) a dispatch arrived from the 5th Division on the Doullens-Amiens line, to the effect that the leader of the "Red Circus" had been brought down, there was great excitement. Soon afterward the excitement was heightened when Brown's claim for a red triplane was received. It was evident that his report claimed the same machine, for no other German plane was downed on the Allied side—in that section—that morning.

Those final 60 seconds were destined to become the most controversial minute in the history of aerial warfare.

The confusion was further compounded when the earlier arrival—from Number 3 Squadron—of Lieutenants Barrow and Garret's claim for one of the circus planes also demanded consideration. This latter claim was easily put aside however, for it was quickly established that the two R.E.8 airmen were not in the air action from which Richthofen descended. Some indignantly expressed opinions went so far as to say that at the time of the R.E.8 triplane engagement over Hamel, Brown's flight had not yet departed Bertangles.

It was coincidental that Number 3 Squadron at

Poulainville had the nearest salvage facilities, and the orders—with the map coordinates—were promptly dispatched.

Lieutenant Willats, in the center of the confusion, remembered that "several messages passed between the Brigadier [undoubtedly Cannan] and Sir John . . ." There was ample reason for Monash to be concerned. Dick Casey (later Sir Richard Casey), a Major on his staff, saw Richthofen crash from a half mile away."

The mess tent at 209 Squadron was 75 feet from the commander's office, which also served as Communications. It was from this building that Lieutenant Simpson hurried. The pilots were dining quietly when he burst into the tent to announce excitedly that a plane downed in the morning's engagement was von Richthofen's. And he had fallen in their patrol sector. The clatter of cutlery stopped, then the chatter began with vigor. A few men thoughtfully searched their memories for a picture of their targets—a distinct recollection that perhaps they may have exchanged gunfire with the Kaiser's much-feared "Siegfried of the Air"—if indeed the fighters encountered little more than an hour and a half earlier had included his Jasta.

Brown sat thoughtfully, eating little. He reacted to the news with little more than a raised eyebrow. Then—as always—it was difficult to fathom his thoughts.

When the noon mess ended, the pilots moved off to their tents, but Brown was asked to report to the Squadron Commander's office. As he entered he saw a staff car parked outside with a waiting driver. "From the general appearance of things," LeBoutillier commented, "we sensed something was amiss—but didn't know what it was."

Brown entered the building to face his Wing Commander, Lieutenant-Colonel Cairnes, and Major Butler. On the Major's desk were Brown's and May's recent reports. Cairnes was no stranger to Brown and after the usual amenities Cairnes settled directly to business. The discussion was confidential and—gathering from the expression reported to have been on Cairnes's face—

serious. If a precise account of the meeting was recorded, it has never come to light, and Brown said little
about their conversation later.

Cairnes told Brown the dead pilot of the red plane
shot down that morning had been identified as von
Richthofen. Brown evinced interest. In essence, Cairnes
then asked Brown if he claimed to have shot down
Richthofen. Brown, surprised, replied in the negative.
He claimed only a red triplane, and added that he was
totally unaware of the pilot's identity when he fired on
it. The discussion continued in subdued tones and shortly the three officers got in the car and drove off,
southeast toward Allonville and the front. They left behind no hint of their mission and for the next two and
one-half hours, the Squadron was a beehive.

Robert Foster was a candid observer to all of this. In a
paper he later prepared on the Richthofen matter he
had this to say:

> Richthofen had crashed on our side of the lines, and we
> claimed two other aircraft destroyed as well as the origi-
> nal two-seater in flames. A complication had also promptly
> arisen. This was a claim from an Australian ground gunner
> that he had shot Richthofen down. This we naturally took
> good-heartedly, because we had operated over the Anzac
> lines very frequently. We had a great admiration for the
> Anzacs; we were always the best of friends whenever we
> met in the local taverns, and we had many friends in their
> Corps Headquarters, at the time established in the village
> of Bertangles, where we also had our airfield. But we
> knew from experience that they were a trigger-happy lot,
> who used to fire at any aircraft which came their way,
> whatever markings it had on it. In fact it was our practice
> to weave about with special energy when we had, as was
> often the case, to get back to our side of the lines at a low
> height over the Anzac positions: this gave to their ma-
> chine gunners a better chance of seeing our British roun-
> dels, and to ourselves a better chance of avoiding their
> fire. In view of the prominence of the German pilot who
> had been killed, the Australian pressed his claim with
> vigor; but the doctor's report showed that the bullet
> which killed Richthofen had come from above and behind

and so tallied with Brown's account of his attack on the red triplane. To support the Australian claim, von Richthofen's aircraft would have had to have been in an inverted position close to the ground,[1] whereas it struck the earth at quite a slight angle and was by no means smashed to pieces.

Brown returned to Bertangles sober, morose, pale. He had the stare of disillusionment. Yet there was something about the set of his chin that told others he was nevertheless convinced of his responsibility in the fall of the red Fokker. He *knew* he had fired a burst into it during his dive; he *knew* the triplane veered under his burst, and he *knew* when he next looked down, the same all-red Dr.I was about to strike the ground. He shook his head and mulled over the long conversation with Cairns and Butler on their drive back. It had been a somewhat one-sided monologue. Roy Brown's junior rank obliged him to do most of the listening.

At that moment no human intelligence could have fathomed the frustration in the Captain's mind or the bewilderment in his expression. Whether he fully comprehended what happened, whether he remembered all or only part of the fast-paced events of a few hours earlier—no one could determine. Yet one conclusion appeared to express itself in his manner; he would never become even remotely convinced of the honesty of the Australian claim.

Thus, he chose not to accept any outside explanation that would tend to alter his impressions. To Roy Brown the matter was quite simple; he had fired on a red *Dreidecker*, it lurched aside, and when he next saw it, it was crashing onto the brow of the Morlancourt ridge.

Put together, all the evidence indicates that Roy Brown was confused—and at that time no man in the RAF had more right to be.

It was soon evident to Brown's comrades that he

---

[1] Considered by Sir Robert as an accurate account of how the 209 Squadron pilots in the engagement assessed the combat results at that time.

either did not care to discuss the matter or that he had been privily cautioned to say nothing. They could not draw him out and, rather than invite friction, they dropped the matter. Not one of Brown's flying mates—those who survived the war and those who didn't—ever doubted the sincerity of the Canadian's claim.

Was there a web of interservice conflict somewhere in this undercurrent of confusion?

Five days after Richthofen's burial, a dispatch from General John Salmond at RAF Headquarters openhandedly gave credit to Brown in a communiqué. Communications between the RAF and the Australian Corps were not so lax that Salmond's Headquarters would not know of Rawlinson's detailed inquiry then going on. The ultimate finding of Rawlinson's board of inquiry was a clear counterclaim, crediting the 53rd Battery gunners.

Something proud and something defiant would not give ground. The scene of this struggle was not the battlefield, but in conference rooms and headquarters buildings—and in the upper ranks of the Commonwealth Armies.

Nevertheless, and despite the Rawlinson Report, the defiant RAF considered itself justified in claiming credit. Roy Brown was decorated for shooting down the red machine with the award of a Bar to his Distinguished Service Cross. The accompanying citation, as was customary, omitted the enemy pilot's name. It read:

For conspicious gallantry and devotion to duty. On the 21st April, 1918, while leading a patrol of six scouts he attacked a formation of twenty hostile scouts. He personally engaged two Fokker triplanes which he drove off; then, seeing that one of our machines was being attacked and apparently hand pressed, he dived on the hostile scout, firing the while. This scout, a Fokker triplane, nose dived and crashed to the ground. Since the award of the Distinguished Service Cross he has destroyed several other enemy aircraft and has shown great dash and enterprise in attacking enemy troops from low altitudes, despite heavy anti-aircraft fire.

Brown had received his D.S.C. (an award for bravery and the only purely naval decoration) while a member of the Royal Naval Air Service. The addition of a Bar signified he had earned the decoration again. Although the British have been regarded as being somewhat parsimonious with their awards, one former combat pilot avows that if the RAF was indeed certain Brown deserved the credit for Richthofen's finish, they would surely have considered him for a higher award than a Bar for his D.S.C.

Sitting in the quiet of the Sunday evening, Wilfred May was not aware that in the years to come he would be frequently quoted and misquoted, hounded to relate the details of his miraculous escape, and forced again and again to defend the man whom he regarded as his rescuer. In his personal log, May wrote: "We afterward found out that the triplane (red) was the famous German airman Baron Richthofen."

"I have little doubt that von Richthofen had the same fatalistic outlook which was held by the vast majority of fighter pilots at the time," Robert Foster says in retrospect. "It seemed inevitable that sooner or later one couldn't avoid being killed in an air fight, or by fire from the ground, through engine or structural failure, or by running into bad weather. The more experienced of course had better prospects of survival, but even against them the odds were formidable. As it turned out, in spite of this experience and skill, von Richthofen also met the fatal chance and was killed. In 1918 the war in the air was a gentleman's war, and that applied equally to the Allied and German sides. Von Richthofen was an outstanding exponent, whom we all much admired, of how to fight in the air with courage, skill, and meticulous fairness."

Robert Foster also kept a daily record. In his log he preserved the memory of this day's happenings:

21.4.18 Sop. Camel 3858. 1hr. 50 mins. 12,000 feet. Got a two-seater Albatross in flames near Villiers-Bretonneaux with Redgate and Taylor. Met circus of triplanes over Cerisy. Brown got Richthofen on this side. Two of others seen to crash.

But whatever led to the disputes that were to be revived time and again in the coming years, the immediate argument over "who did what" was relatively short lived. With preparations already mounting for the July Allied offensive, the day in—day out business of fighting the war forced the question gradually to fade. Brown, May, 209 Squadron, the 53rd Battery and the redoubtable von Richthofen dissolved into the immediate past.

"To us it was conclusive that the pilot had been killed in the air," reflects Air Chief Marshal Sir Robert M. Foster today, "and that the aircraft had carried on in a shallow dive till it hit the ground.

"At any rate Brown was definitely awarded the kill."

CHAPTER FIFTEEN
Number 3 Squadron

"Brown's Camels" at Bertangles were a familiar sight to the men of Number 3 Squadron. One Aussie pilot described their neighboring field as a place where there was "a great group of about six squadrons or more, too close together," and a member of Number 3 recalled that "the Huns bombed the tripe out of this concentration . . . they were always having a shot at it!"

The mission of Number 3 Squadron was reconnaissance, aerial photography, and artillery spotting. Their wireless-equipped R.E.8s were battered, patched and war weary. Most of the planes were manufactured early in 1917 and were equipped with 150 horsepower Royal Aircraft Factory aircooled engines that turned huge, ridiculously huge, four-bladed propellers. This machine was not popular with most artillery fliers. One pilot of the squadron summed up its objectionable characteristics with: "It was a horrible job with a weak undercarriage and a red-hot engine in front of the petrol tank, too prone to burn with a bad landing." He knew of four that went that way at Bertangles, and their vulnerability led to the nickname of "flaming coffin."

Like most aerodromes, Number 3 bordered on a road, near which was a line of circus-like tents—the ubiquitous Besneau hangars—storage lean-to's and a few wooden structures for quarters. Housed in umbrella tents, officers and enlisted men alike were veterans who could trace their war service from the early days of Palestine, Egypt and the shores of Gallipoli.

Dusk had slipped into darkness when the tender, its lights faint, drew off the roadway near the end tent hangar and stopped outside a spare marquee. Worsley stepped down from the seat and asked R. E. Douglas and A. D. Craven to have a look at what was in the back of the tender. Warneford's Flight Sergeant, Joe Knapp, came up and together they slid the body onto a piece of corrugated metal, as a stretcher, carried it into the hangar and set it on the dirt floor. Knapp was curious about the German machine and queried Warneford who replied, "They were shelling the place, but now that it's dark we're going back for it. Should be back about midnight." He asked Knapp what he wanted in the way of souvenirs. Knapp replied he wasn't interested. Warneford said he was going to get the control stick.

In charge of the aerodrome's night guard was Corporal Edwin P. L. deBomford. The vehicle was already being unloaded when he arrived. Today, retired in Melbourne, deBomford remembers:

> The dismantled Fokker arrived late in the evening by motor transport, and to our amazement the salvage party had also brought in Richthofen's body!
>
> When I first saw the body, it was lying on a sheet of galvanized, corrugated iron on the ground in one of our tent hangars, just as it had been brought in and dumped there. It was not on a raised platform of any kind nor had it been covered with a blanket. It was lying on its back in flying kit, a dirty, well-worn leather coat, small-footed black knee boots, breeches and tunic.
>
> I was in charge of the body until the burial. My impressions, I recall, were of a short, sturdy figure with close-cropped fair hair and what appeared to be a determined grin on his face, as if he were saying, 'Now I've got you!' There was no fixed light in the hangar . . .
>
> It had been rumored that he was wearing two pairs of breeches, and that in the inner pair several thousand francs had been found by one of the doctors who carried out the post mortem later. However, I went through all the pockets I could find pretty thoroughly, but had no

luck, so if the rumor was true, all I can say is that I must have been "stiff."

Our medical orderly, Corporal Ted McCarty, told us that there were three bullet holes ... the marks on his upper lip and hand could have been injuries, but the chest wound was definitely a bullet hole as there was more blood around it than around the other two.

I have a button cut from his tunic and a piece of red fabric from his plane as souvenirs.

The next morning, and until the funeral, several officers came to view the remains, and I believe some members of 209 Squadron, R.A.F. were there, but I did not know or speak with any of them.

Soon after the body arrived, Major Blake, Captain G. E. Knox (later Sir Errol Knox), the Recording Officer (Adjutant) entered the tent with Sergeant John Alexander and other noncommissioned officers. Blake studied the body thoughtfully for a few minutes, then directed Knox to have the body photographed, explaining that Headquarters wanted them to prove to the Germans that Richthofen was actually dead and not a prisoner. The job fell to Sergeant Alexander, who assembled his apparatus in the tent.

The Sergeant's impression was that the pilot had been shot through the chin, heart and legs. A fastidious craftsman, Alexander noticed the German's face was darkened and dirty as a result of the long ride from the 53rd Battery. He directed his assistants to find some white powder to lighten the features. When they returned empty-handed, Alexander obtained some baking soda and dusted it over the face to allow the film to record more detail when the flash powder was triggered in the gloomy hangar.

Alexander next instructed the guards, Corporals McLeod and Grant, to prop the galvanized sheet with the body (wrapped around with ropes for rigidity) at a 60° angle against the nearest tent pole. A moment later the official death photograph, full face and shoulders, sharp and detailed, was made.

Roderick Ross was a Captain and the Squadron's

Technical Officer at the time. Headquarters promptly channeled his report to the Air Ministry in London. Now a consulting engineer in Melbourne, he said in 1960:

> I was the officer who examined Richthofen's plane and rendered the technical report on it.
> At our squadron, we discovered that the souveniring "diggers" had "ratted" the contents of Richthofen's pockets but somehow had missed his wallet. The wallet contained several thousand marks and a wedding photograph of Baron von Richthofen and his bride taken only a few weeks previously; also several other items. The picture was a black and white photograph. Richthofen was in uniform, and the girl was in street dress wearing a large hat. We received this information and the date of the picture from a note—in German of course—that had been written on the back. Probably a couple of dozen of us saw the photo, but whatever became of it I cannot say.

Von Richthofen and his bride? The same young lady whose likeness Tom Lovell saw at the wreckage? Admittedly there was much speculation about a secret romance, and the press, in a pique of frustrated curiosity, constantly hinted—but failed to produce anything concrete—of such a relationship.

One of the most intriguing of these rumors had to do with a series of letters in a distinctive and readily recognizable hand. Allegedly, they were carefully separated from the Rittmeister's usual flood of mail and personally given to the ace by his orderly. According to the gossip of the time, they arrived almost daily and were from a young lady whom the Baron loved and intended to marry if he survived the war. But if she did indeed exist, he never mentioned her name to anyone in the Geschwader, unless it was to his brother, Lothar.

Floyd Gibbons, an early biographer, alleges that the Baroness revealed to him that Manfred loved a girl and she returned his affection. They were to marry if he survived the war. But if this tale is as reliable as his version of Richthofen's death, we may safely assume that no such woman existed, and that Manfred's mother was likely misquoted.

Karl Bodenschatz, the man who was closest to the Rittmeister in the field, and who was in a position to survey—even handle—much of the commander's incoming correspondence, said in response to a query in the mid-Fifties: "There was no such series of letters that I know of. He received much mail and possibly they were mistaken for the letters he received from his mother."

And there is the comment of Karl Bolko, Manfred's youngest brother. When questioned in the late 1950s about a possible romance he replied with an air of finality: "There were no women in Manfred's life!"

If there is any truth to a secret romance, the woman has never revealed herself, nor has the Richthofen family wavered in its proud determination to set the topic aside. In April of 1957, on the 39th anniversary of her son's death, the Baroness Kunigunde von Richthofen responded in this way to a direct question on the oft-discussed subject:

> It was not Manfred's intention to leave a mourning wife or bride behind when he died. He never spoke of his intentions after wartime. It is not my affair to break his silence now . . .

But . . . perhaps there was a young lady who was Manfred's confidant and inspiration in the dark days when, in solitude, he came to realize that Germany would not prevail. When his name was mentioned with those of Hindenburg and Ludendorff, he—in the knowledge that her thoughts were with him as he stood on the pinnacle of fame and glory—may have found the inner peace and strength to sustain himself. Perhaps, if there was such a person, she was the only one who understood the real Manfred.

Many men, aware of Richthofen's fame, came to view his body. Across a span of 40-odd years, H. D. Billings, a wireless operator mechanic and signalman in Number 3 Squadron, recalled the scene vividly:

> When I saw the body it had just been brought in and was in flying kit. The facial markings did not strike me as bullet wounds. I had seen too many smashed-up pilots that looked the same, so think they were the result of the final crash.
>
> After the body had been searched for military papers, etc., it was left with Joe Porter, who was later to prepare it for burial, and another chap. In the search, Porter's assistant found a bundle of French money in the hip pocket—several thousand francs (worth 10d each at the time) and loudly said: "Look what I've found!" (Just as an officer walked in!) Need I finish? The officer said, "I'll take that!" before Porter—who was too keen to have said anything if *he* had found it—could do anything. Porter was not pleased. The money was never seen again.
>
> Richthofen had very small feet, size five boots, and Porter took possession of them. I think he sent them home.[1]

Porter is thought to have entered the tent around 11 P.M. and with the sanction of the guards, went through the clothing for souvenirs. He found nothing until he noticed Richthofen's black leather boots. These he removed and tried on. They fit perfectly. Porter then put his own low cuts on the body and neatly tied the laces.

During the night, work in some of the hangar tents went on. Mechanics labored in the subdued orange-tinted glow of pressure lamps to put their aircraft on the line for the morning's recon missions.

In the hangar, Corporal Porter erected a makeshift dais with two wooden sawhorses and elevated the body.

Soon after the glass negatives were developed and a few prints made, the plates were deliberately smashed to prevent the men from obtaining copies and circulat-

---

[1] In May of 1934, J. A. Porter sailed from Melbourne and presented the black boots to the Baroness at the Schweidnitz Museum. She refused to accept them, unconvinced they were those of her son.

ing them. The sole purpose in photographing the remains was, according to Captain Ross, "to combat possible German propaganda. Copies, together with photographs of his flower-covered grave and an account of the
whole incident, were dropped on the German side of
the battle line."

At least one member of the squadron managed to get
one of the prized prints before the plates were destroyed. He is Robert Barker, former First Class Air
Mechanic who resides today in Victoria.

> I remember the incident very well when Richthofen was
> brought down near Sailly-le-Sec. I was not among the
> party that brought him in.
>
> Richthofen's body was in one of the hangars where it
> had been brought and placed the evening of that day. I
> did not see the wounds or anything souvenired from his
> body, though I know he had a sum of money in one of his
> pockets. I feel sure he was wearing silk pajamas under his
> flying suit.
>
> I was the one who made the cross for his grave from
> one of our R.E.8 propellers.
>
> There was a big crowd souveniring at the plane on the
> day of the funeral and afterward. I think Collins had the
> locks from Richthofen's machine guns, but they were
> stolen from him when he went to hospital.

What of the other remains—the famous blood-red
flying machine? What became of it?

No efforts were made to restore it because another
Dr.I, captured intact, was undergoing flying tests by
Royal Air Force engineers. Strangely enough, it was the
forced landing of Leutnant Stapenhorst of Richthofen's
own Jasta 11 that enabled the R.A.F. to study the finer
points of the Fokker triplane. Stapenhorst had set out on
a balloon strafe on the afternoon of January 13th and
had shot one down flaming. Before he could reach his
lines he was pounced upon by three Spads who shot up
his machine so badly that he was forced to land and was
made a prisoner of war. To put aside the pressing back-
log of work at any repair depot to rebuild even the

famed *Red Devil* would, during those critical days, have called for extraordinary justification.

From the comments of pilots and mechanics who made a close inspection of the wreckage, it was clear that the quality of workmanship in the Fokker was previously underrated. One report describes the fabric as "of rather better quality than usual" and the "finish of the engine of better quality than those captured in previous machines of this type." A squadron pilot who took a close interest in the remains marveled at the fine engineering. "We had not known previously how well made the Fokker triplane was, with three-ply box spars, ply leading edges and a steel tube fuselage."

After a week at Poulainville, the wreckage was removed to the nearest salvage yard and unceremoniously scrapped. Much of it was burned.

There is no clue today as to who made the written request through channels for the engine to be given to Roy Brown, which was denied. The rotary, along with the machine guns, was shipped to England on May 26th, but while the engine can be accounted for today, all trace of the Baron's lethal guns are lost. This much is known: Both guns were with the wreckage at Poulainville on the evening of April 22nd; the following morning they had vanished.

Other parts of the plane are widely dispersed. Thanks to those nimble-fingered memento-seekers of the nearby Aussie Divisions, every man eager to take home some part of the circus master's aircraft as a keepsake of his downfall, the war museums of two Commonwealth nations as well as Mother England can display fragments donated by returned servicemen.

One of the black cross insignias (all were straight designs which were then replacing the early cross patee markings on German aircraft) found its way to the Australian War Memorial through the generosity of ex-Lieutenant George Travers. In a letter to *Smith's Weekly* 15 years afterward, Travers wrote:

I don't suppose one can be shot down after 15 years or more for admitting to going souvenir hunting. I got one of the big black crosses, about four feet by four feet ... I wrapped it up and put it in my valise.

A few days later, at Villiers-Brettoneaux, I was severely wounded and eventually arrived at Wandsworth Hospital in England. A Sergeant from the Records Section in London came down to see me and said he had been sent by Major Treloar, O.C. of Records. They said they had heard that I had one of Richthofen's crosses and asked if I would let them have it for the Australian War Museum.[2] Eventually I gave it to them.

In one case at the Canberra Memorial is the triplane's control stick, complete with coupé button,[3] and the individual machine-gun trips which permitted the Dr.I pilots to fire either or both of the Spandau guns. Another display is the plane's compass and the handmade gunsight used on Robert Buie's machine gun, and one of Richthofen's fur flying boots. The title card to the latter reads:

> This flying boot was worn by the German ace when he was killed by machine-gun fire, and bears evidence of the conflict.

The "evidence" is a bullet hole near the top—mute testimony that Richthofen was struck by more than one bullet. The control stick and boot were presented by Lieutenant Warneford.

One memento that was given to Roy Brown was the triplane's aluminum seat, which he in turn donated to the Royal Canadian Military Institute in Toronto. They also have a large piece of the plane's fabric and a walking stick carved from the propeller.

---

[2] This particular cross and a fragment of the propeller are not on public display.

[3] A small, spring-loaded button on the control stick handle of most aircraft equipped with rotary engines. It was used to short out the magneto system and reduce engine power when needed, without repositioning the fuel-and air-control valves.

The Imperial War Museum in London claims the largest single component of the downed war machine—its Oberursel engine, a copy of the French LeRhone 110-horsepower model.

In 1944 and 1945, the relentless Allied air raids on Berlin hammered at the old city's famed *Zeughaus*—War Museum. Along with historical documents of J.G.I, irreplaceable photographs and war records, two airplanes flown by Richthofen—an Albatros Scout and a Fokker triplane—were destroyed.

Surprisingly, a number of the Baron's personal possessions that were taken from his body at the crash site and at Number 3 Squadron found their way into the hands of American collectors of Richthofania. These include his flying scarf, monogrammed handkerchief, swatches from his coveralls, and his flying goggles.

By late evening of the 21st, six British officers, all medics, had received orders from the headquarters of Generals Rawlinson or Monash that they were to examine the corpse of a German airman now being held at an Australian Flying Squadron near Poulainville. With ground casualties still running high along the touchy Amiens front, hospitals overcrowded and medical facilities taxed, each physician wondered what was so unusual about the corpse of a German pilot that could demand their absence from post. *Richthofen?* The R.A.F. medics knew the name of course, but to the Army men the name was perhaps not so familiar. For the two medics stationed at nearby Bertangles, the assignment would only take an hour or so, but for four hard-pressed officers —three full Colonels and a Major—it would mean the better part of the next morning.

At that moment—approximately 10:30 P.M.—medical orderly E. J. "Ted" McCarty entered the hangar. He was under orders from the squadron medical officer to prepare the corpse for a post-mortem examination. With the help of the guards, McCarty stripped the clothing, jacket, coveralls, pajamas, to the waist. In the light of the oil lanterns, and using a cloth dipped in a solution of

alcohol and warm water, the orderly bathed Richthofen's face and did what he could to make the
features presentable. With a guard, he turned the body
as he cleaned the upper trunk and area of the wounds.
Corporal Porter apparently assisted McCarty, for 13
years later he wrote in a letter to the dead man's
mother:

> I washed his face and hands, then powdered the parts
> of his face that were injured. He looked very well then;
> and there was such a peaceful smile on his lips . . .

With the features cleaned of the dried blood and
earth, it was at last evident for those who wished to see,
that there were no bullet wounds in the face. The facial
injuries that Manfred's brother, Lothar, suffered a month
earlier were more serious. They altered his appearance
permanently, but Manfred's injuries in no way disfig-
ured him; and even in death he retained his handsome,
clean-cut appearance.

McCarty saw that several of the dead man's upper
teeth were missing; others had been forced inward by
his impact with the gun butts. These, McCarty straightened. He replaced the clothing, gathered his utensils and
left. It was almost 11 P.M.

Several flying officers entered silently, looked at Richthofen's body in the eerie, wavering lantern glow, then
left.

Shortly before midnight two Royal Army Medical
Corps officers attached to the Air Force, entered the
tent with Number 3 Squadron officers and spent 20
minutes examining the body. Porter gathered they must
have been ordered out at this late hour by Division
Headquarters and were to make their report without
delay. When they left, he settled himself and remained
throughout the night near the body, in a sort of wake,
though he dozed occasionally.

Although the accoutrements of this hostile camp
would have been unfamiliar to a living Richthofen, in

these last hours before the final honors, the Rittmeister was among the men and machines of his element—enemy though they were. The wire and wood and fabric would have been familiar, recognizable*things, and in a few hours, along the rim of dawn the machines would be silhouetted against the sky in the same manner as those at mourning Cappy. The snarling, roaring, R.E.8 engines would sound much like the blattering rotaries in the predawn shadows. Across the damp, dark earth, along the row of sagging hangars wet with dew, there would drift the same provocative scent of petrol and oil, and polished leather and pungent lacquer. Here on alien soil were the same casual lures to which the young Uhlan—and scores like him on both sides of the Western front—had succumbed.

A few days earlier, when given the clear-cut opportunity to retire from active flying he revealed, in a letter to high command, his inner, compelling reason for remaining at the front:

> I should indeed feel myself a despicable person if, now that I have achieved fame and wear many decorations, I should consent to exist as a pensioner of my dignity and to preserve my life for the nation, while every poor fellow in the trenches—who is doing his duty equally as much as I—has to stick it out.

THE 22nd OF APRIL

CHAPTER SIXTEEN
Post Mortem

The "several messages" that passed between Lieutenant-General Sir J. Monash and General Henry Rawlinson during the afternoon of the 21st, are evidence of conflicting official views—and of Rawlinson's personal hand in the matter.

Rawlinson, promoted to full General in January 1917, was a man known to think for himself. A soldier highly respected and admired by his contemporaries, this Commander of the British Fourth Army was a long-standing personal friend of Winston Churchill. With long experience in staff work, he was capable of questioning orders—and subordinates. Thus, when three conflicting claims on Richthofen's death reached his notice that Sunday afternoon—209 Squadron's, the 53rd Battery's, and Number 3 Squadron, A.F.C.—he assumed the responsibility for resolving the growing dissention between the Services. At his express request, arrangements were made for the corpse of von Richthofen to be medically examined and an expert opinion formed as to the source of the fatal bullet. A four-man Anglo-Australian board of inquiry was named by his staff officers that afternoon.

Two post mortems were made—on separate days. On the night of the 21st, about 11:30, the two-man team representing the Royal Air Force arrived at the tent hangar by motor car. One of the medical officers was Captain Norman Clotworthy Graham, Royal Army Medical Corps, assigned as medical officer in charge of the 22nd Wing, the wing under which 209 Squadron was directly assigned. Accompanying the Captain was Lieutenant G. E. Downs, R.A.M.C., also attached to the R.A.F. Downs was to succeed Graham who would be posted back to England in three days. The medics, escorted by Major Blake with Number 3's Medical Officer and medical orderly Ted McCarty as assistants, entered the spare marquee. A small group of squadron officers had gathered to stand in the fringe of light given off by several lamps around and over the still form.

In this eerie glow the medics set briskly to work. Downs saw the blood-stained entrance and exit tears in the flying gear and scraps of clothing and buttons snipped by the scissors fell to the souvenir-minded spectators. Lieutenant E. C. Banks, one of the R.E.8 observers in the morning's encounter, later commented: "About 20 officers attended the final examination when Richthofen's uniform was carefully cut from his body."

From the size and nature of the perforations the medics were in immediate agreement as to the point of entrance. The wound under the right armpit was smooth and clean; the wound in the left breast was larger and jagged. Downs deliberated only a moment as to the possibility that the bullet might have struck the spine and was thus altered in its path. He asked his colleague to comment on this, and Graham reflected only a moment before shaking his head in the negative.

Shortly before midnight noises and loud voices were heard outside the tent as the Crosley tender rolled to a stop. Warneford and the remainder of the crew had returned with the dismantled Fokker and the men set to unloading it on the spot. A raucous gathering of squadron members converged on the scene and the souveniring resumed.

The examination, surprisingly brief, ended shortly after midnight. It was obvious to Graham and Downs that they need search no further than the chest wound for the cause of death. McCarty rearranged the cut clothing. The medical officers left the tent to return to Wing Headquarters where they filed this report, dated the 22nd of April:

We examined the body of Captain Baron von Richthofen on the evening of the 21st instant. We found that he had one entrance and one exit wound caused by the same bullet.

The entrance wound was situated on the right side of the chest in the posterior fold of the armpit; the exit wound was situated at a slightly higher level nearer the front of the chest, the point of exit being about half an inch below the left nipple and about three quarters of an inch external to it. From the nature of the exit wound, we think that the bullet passed straight through the chest from right to left, and also slightly forward. Had the bullet been deflected from the spine, the exit wound would have been much larger. The gun firing this bullet must have been situated in roughly the same plane as the long axis of the German machine, and fired from the right and slightly behind the right of Captain Richthofen.

We are agreed that the situation of the entrance and exit wounds are such that they could not have been caused by fire from the ground.

The final paragraph of the report was gravely in error. So much so in fact, as to invalidate their medical examination as a basis for giving credit in the death of the ace. Neither Graham nor Downs were aware of the red Fokker's position in space, relative to the ground, at the time the fatal bullet found its mark. They could only assume that Richthofen was in level flight, which, in fact, he was not. Too, this finding of the junior medicos has been touted as the unanimous opinion of the four-man board of inquiry. It was not.

Totally ignorant of the details of the air battle, the chase, and the gunnery action during the final moments of the pursuit, Air Force medics Graham and Downs logically assumed their testimony would support the air claim. Instead, it confirmed precisely the firing angles of the 53 Battery's Lewis gunners when Richthofen banked sharply over the artillery line.

The following morning, muffled sounds of sawing and tapping came from the squadron's woodworking shop; Sergeant E. S. Kitto and Flight-Carpenter Fred Lienert were finishing a coffin. It was made from packing cases.

Air Mechanic Robert Barker was shaping a cross for a grave. From the metal shop there were ringing sounds; Coppersmith A. G. McIntosh and Instrument Fitter Harold Edward were fashioning and engraving a plate to be nailed to the hub of the cross, and a small zinc plate for the coffin lid.

It had been a busy night and Major Blake felt the loss of sleep. Inasmuch as Corps Headquarters had given their approval to proceed with the funeral following the second medical examination, the necessary paperwork remained for him to prepare.

Squadron activities went on as usual, except for a slight lag due to the steady stream of pilots, mechanics and administrative officers from neighboring outfits who came to view the "Red Dragon's" remains. Here and there was the uniform of a curious ground trooper.

Before mid-morning, the second group of medical examiners arrived by motor car. There were four physicians, and they were ushered into the tent by Major Blake, Captain Knox and the Squadron Disciplinary Sergeant-Major, W. O. Crawford, all of whom witnessed the post mortem at close quarters. A squadron pilot recalled that just prior to the examination, "one of the Camels from 209 Squadron, a red-nosed one with a 110 Le Rhône, skimmed low over the tent hangars."

The day was bright and balmy, and with the front of the marquee open, the inside was well lighted. A crowd of enlisted personnel and officers loitering around the makeshift dais parted on the approach of the senior officers and dispersed to the background. With little delay the medics bared the upper half of the pale form and began their work.

President of the hastily constituted medical board, and a nonvoting member, was Colonel G. W. Barber. He was Director-General of the Australian Army and Air Force Medical Services. To his right was Colonel Thomas Sinclair, Consulting Surgeon of the British Fourth Army, 61 years old, gruff and businesslike. He was a native Irishman with a crisp, confident manner born of long medical practice. Of late he had not been called

upon to examine the corpse of a flier that was as unmu-
tilated by shot, flame and impact as the one now
stretched before him. This was a clean death. At Sinclair's side was Colonel J. A. Nixon, the Fourth Army's
consulting physician.

To Barber's left was another observer in unofficial
status, Major C. L. Chapman, an Australian medical
officer. Like the R.A.F. medics, these men had not witnessed the gunnery action, and to this moment, had only
hearsay knowledge of what transpired on the Morlancourt ridge to cause this dead airman to be brought
here. They entered into the examination with as little
evidence as had Graham and Downs in regard to the
pilot's position in space at the fatal instant. But from this
point onward, their actions varied markedly from those
of the R.A.F. medics.

From a small musette bag surgical gloves appeared
and were snapped crisply over skilled hands. A metal
probe materialized and Colonels Nixon and Sinclair bent
over the body. The examination proceeded solely under
the flash of the probe. The airman's chest was not
opened and no incisions were contemplated. In the light
of a standard medical autopsy, this serious omission cast
a valid suspicion on the accuracy of the findings. A hasty
medical inquiry is open to doubt in any case, but facilities were lacking and time was valuable to every physician at the front.

Sinclair, assisted by Nixon who braced the body on its
left side, worked steadily, prodding here, probing there.
He noted carefully the puncture; his eyes narrowed
briefly at the angle of tear in the left breast. If anyone
saw other wounds lower on the body, they paid them
little heed.

The physicians consulted in low tones, nodded in
agreement, and stepped back. It is not known what
specific instructions, if any, were given to the officers
before the post mortems were made—or before they
filed their separate reports—but Colonels Nixon and
Sinclair, unlike the junior medics who had examined the
body the night before presented only their findings, with

no opinion as to the source of the fatal bullet. Their report, also dated the 22nd, was submitted to Army Headquarters at Flixecourt.

> We have made a surface examination of the body of Captain BARON VON RICHTHOFEN and find that there are only the entrance and exit wounds of one rifle[1] bullet on the trunk. The entrance wound is on the right side about the level of the ninth rib, which is fractured, just in front of the posterior axillary line. The bullet appears to have passed obliquely backwards through the chest striking the spinal column, from which it glanced in a forward direction and issued on the left side of the chest, at a level about two inches higher than its entrance on the right and about in the anterior axillary line.
>
> There was also a compound fracture of the lower jaw on the left side, apparently not caused by a missile ... also some minor bruises of the head and face.
>
> The body was not opened ... these facts were ascertained by probing the surface wounds.

The bullet that killed the German ace, according to Sinclair and Nixon, came from the right and slightly to the front of Richthofen (as he was sitting in his plane) and glanced off his spine. They described a semifrontal wound.

Colonel Barber and Major Chapman made separate examinations. They disagreed on the spot with the R.A.F. opinion that claimed the missile could not have come from the ground. Barber, in a separate report to General Birdwood, vehemently insisted that the wound was "just as would be sustained as a result of a bullet from the ground whilst the machine was banking." He must have either examined the machine outside the tent, or had first-hand knowledge of its condition, for writing of the findings in 1935, he said: "A bullet hole in the side of the plane coincided with the wound in the

---

[1] Possibly an error for "rifled" bullet, or, it may have been written in this manner to describe the .303 calibre cartridge used in the regulation Lee-Enfield rifle as well as the light Lewis machine gun and the Vickers machine gun.

chest and I am sure he was shot from below while banking."

But the question of the course of the bullet—air or ground—continued as late as 1962, when Captain D. H. R. White, writing in the *Sydney Morning Herald*, declared that the Fokker would have to have been banked at an "impossible angle" for a ground gunner to have inflicted the wound. As impossible as the bank may have been; the bullet did come from the ground—and at a surprisingly short distance—as R. L. C. Hunt vividly testified.

The examining officers withdrew. Now rumors, supplemented by snatches of the conversation overheard from the medics, began to make their way among the troops. They heard there were a few polite, but at times strained, discussions among the physicians about theoretical gunnery angles. To the men of Number 3 Squadron it appeared as though the question was no nearer solution. Sinclair and Nixon were firm in their assertion that the bullet struck the backbone, but Graham and Downs had earlier rejected this and insisted if this were so, the bullet's exit would have been larger. As Corporal deBomford commented later, "There were all sorts of opinions as to how Richthofen was shot down . . ."

One point the six investigating physicians agreed upon was the cause of death—circulatory failure. The soft lead bullet pierced several large blood vessels near the heart, and may have traversed the organ itself, with an immediate and massive loss of blood to the vital organs. The lungs, flooded with blood and responding through the nervous system, sent the body into immediate irreversible shock accompanied by severe spasmodic contractions. It was agreed by all that death from such a wound would be practically instantaneous.

Practically instantaneous. Yet the stricken triplane glided for several hundred yards, turning, with a powerless engine, to make a crash landing without overturning or cartwheeling. Just how instantaneously death came to the famed airman is open to question. Richthofen, the Geschwader Kommandeur who bore his troubles quietly and bravely. Who never yielded to sorrow nor winced at pain. A man who was, if we are to put credence in the war records, absolutely fearless.

Sounds almost superhuman?

When an inspection was made of the triplane's engine, the cylinder heads were found to be undamaged, but the push rods, intake pipes and cooling fins were slightly bent. There were no signs of rotative shearing, indicating that the engine had not been turning at the time of impact. Unfortunately no one thought—until long after the crash when Boxall-Chapman took notice— to check whether Richthofen turned off the Oberursel's ignition switch just after he was struck. It is possible he did, for there is no evidence that the engine and its fuel and oil system, were damaged by gunfire. (The tanks burst in the crash). Is there a connection with Richthofen's first act over Lens in September of 1917 when his fuel tank was punctured and he was forced to glide to a landing without power?

"Instinctively I switched off the engine . . ."

And later, when he fell tumbling under Lieutenant Woodbridge's gun; though seriously wounded in the head and totally blinded . . .

"Mechanically, I cut off the motor . . ."

Was this Richthofen's first thought when struck over the 53rd Battery? Did his fingers move "instinctively" toward the switch to "mechanically" cut off the engine? Here was, after all, the same leader who told his men: "A true chaser pilot never takes his hand from the controls until he drops dead!" Did Richthofen descend in a state of fading semiconsciousness?

That there were multiple bullet wounds on Richthofen's body is indisputable; why this obvious fact was not acknowledged until the appearance of the Rawlinson Report[2] some weeks later is something of a puzzle.

---

[2] Official report on the death of Baron von Richthofen compiled from evidence taken at the enquiry immediately following the event. Source was Headquarters, Fifth Australian Division. See Appendix.

Did the medics mean to imply in their reports that Richthofen was struck by only *one immediately fatal* bullet through his chest? It is strange that none of the six examining medics took note of other bullet wounds. In a newspaper debate in 1928, Major-General Hobbs, who commanded the Fifth Australian Division at the time, and who was a member of Rawlinson's staff, wrote in the *Sydney Morning Herald* that Richthofen sustained multiple wounds in the knees, abdomen and chest. At the crash site, the 53rd Battery, and Number 3 Squadron, Fraser, Hunt, Lovell, Beavis, and deBomford confirmed this.

There remained only the funeral details as Major Blake signed the paperwork to consign the body to the earth. Sergeant Lewis Gyngell was detailed to arrange the funeral party. Ted deBomford recalls that volunteers were called for the burial firing party and that it was made up mainly of squadron mechanics. AM/1C Bob Barker was among the 12 who stepped forward.

It was shortly after 4 P.M. when the coffin was made ready beside the dais by the squadron carpenters. It was plain, simply constructed and finished in a dark color. Warrant Officer Jack Crawford and Corporal Will Scott slid the body carefully from the corrugated metal sheet and lowered it gently into the box which was still pungent with the smell of fresh paint.

The clothing that remained was rearranged as neatly as possible. One man straightened the legs and arranged the arms comfortably. At the last moment someone reached inside the coffin and impulsively ripped off a small swatch of material, already made ragged by souvenir hunters. Another onlooker snipped a button for a final memento. There was a short, heavy pause during which the conversation faded and the men gazed silently—and for the last time—on the pale features of their fallen foe.

"He must have been a scrapper," someone said. A corporal nodded without looking up.

"The Red Devil . . ." another Aussie mused absently.

Two squadron carpenters placed the lid over the wooden box and aligned it carefully as a third man nailed it in place.

Six Officers of Number 3 Squadron, all flying personnel and former foemen, patiently waited around the coffin, bareheaded. A zinc plate, inscribed in English and in German was nailed to the coffin lid with a few quick, hollow taps. Lieutenant Barrow, the observer who flew with Garrett the day before, leaned forward to read the inscription before several floral wreaths from neighboring units were heaped upon it. It said:

CAVALRY CAPTAIN
MANFRED VON RICHTHOFEN
Age 22 years, killed in action near
SAILLY-LE-SEC, SOMME, FRANCE
21 April, 1918

There was a slight error in the inscription. The dead airman was 25, and in eleven days, on May 2nd, he would have been 26.

CHAPTER SEVENTEEN

Full Military Honors

On a less somber occasion, the light glow of spring in the air would not have been lessened by the pall of death. But outside the tent in which Baron von Richthofen lay, men gathered quietly to pay their respects to a fallen leader. Among them was Bob Barker:

> When volunteers were called for the burial party, I offered to serve. Richthofen was buried on the afternoon of the 22nd just inside the gate of a small churchyard not far from the aerodrome.

While it was customary for the pallbearers to be six peers of the deceased, captains, this formality was not observed. Through necessity, several of the bearers were junior grade officers, among them Lieutenants Warneford, E. C. Banks, George Pickering, and M. Sheehan. On signal, they hoisted the flower-covered coffin to their shoulders and stepped reverently from the tent, through facing ranks of the firing party which stood at attention, their Enfields at present arms. The bearers passed slowly among the silent, assembled men of Number 3 Squadron. Visiting dignitaries representing neighboring units came smartly to attention and held their hands at salute. There were no representatives from the 53rd Battery.

A hundred feet from the tent the cortege waited, where the hearse, a Crosley tender, idled beside the red administration building, with Corporal R. E. waiting behind the wheel. Several brilliant wreaths were at its side and when the coffin was placed on the tender's bed, they were heaped over and around it.

Billings remembers that:

> The funeral went from our squadron to the local civilian cemetery—a firing party leading and quite a number of us marching behind (including me).

The cortege formed. The firing party, in two files, rifles reversed, smartly took position ten paces before the tender. Behind the hearse walked the pallbearers, then came a platoon of infantry and finally came the individuals who wished to follow. A second vehicle trailed the procession.

The senior British officer, who wore a mourning armband of black, gave a command and the cortege moved off. At slow march Richthofen was carried almost a mile along a narrow sunlit roadway lined with trees breaking into fresh spring foliage. There was only the sound of the measured tread and the muffled exhaust of the Crosley's engine. To an airman overhead, climbing out on a lone patrol, the day was faultless, and the earth below the stunning indigo sky and warming sun was a gigantic tableau of pleasant greens and brown and bluish purples—except for the pock marks that bordered the ugly scars to the east.

The party neared the small village of Bertangles, which was, in Sergeant Alexander's mind, "such a dirty, foresaken hole in which to be buried," with its ancient churchyard cemetery surrounded by a hedge and tall poplars. Outside the open iron gate the cortege halted, and a Corporal ordered the firing party at open ranks. The bearers formed again, lifted the coffin to their shoulders and passed through the files of Australians who held their rifles at "the present." A chaplain in surplice led the procession. Directly inside the gate a freshly opened grave awaited, across which a ɾ hemlock cast its shadow.

The firing party, rifles reversed, moved i·

beside the open grave as the coffin was placed on the mound of damp, turned earth. The Anglican chaplain began the service for the departed Lutheran with the opening prayer for the Burial of the Dead. Over the simple coffin he asked Heaven's mercy for "our Brother, Manfred" and intoned across the hushed gathering:

I am the resurrection and the life, saith the Lord; he that believeth in me, though he were dead, yet shall he live, and whosoever liveth and believeth in me shall never die.

A pause, then . . .

I know that my Redeemer liveth, and that He shall stand at the latter day upon the earth . . .

Air and infantry officers, diggers in mud-spattered tunics, tommies, mechanics—French civilians; women, children in arms—all attired in their Sunday finery—and old men beyond the age of soldiering, stood inside the brick gate posts and lined the hedgerow opposite the open grave. Roy Brown did not attend; it was not customary for one recognized as the victor, to do so. As the chaplain read the simple burial prayers of the Church of England, another warplane droned overhead, flying toward the front and the distant drumming of artillery ten miles to the east.

A handful of French soil spattered on the coffin. Then the chaplain stepped back and spoke the concluding words of prayer.

The grace of our Lord Jesus Christ, and the love of God, and the fellowship of the Holy Ghost, be with us all evermore. Amen.

A sharp command broke the silence and a dozen rifle bolts rattled crisp and loud. At the order "load—present—fire!", the blunt muzzles were brought smartly to the 45, and the regulation three volleys thundered over the coffin.

Every uniformed man stood at rigid attention as the farewell tribute—the Last Post—was sounded. The slow, plaintive notes of the bugle lingered over the rows of markers and crosses until the last echo faded. The squad closed ranks and moved off—now at the quick step.

Officially, the ceremony was ended, but after the coffin was lowered into the grave, and before it was covered, officers and men walked slowly past, paused as they came abreast of the now-stilled air soldier, and saluted. Billings was one of those who lingered behind with a few of his squadron mates.

> After the burial, I noticed that the coffin had accidently been placed in the reverse position to usual custom—i.e., the body was placed with the feet at the head of the grave—where a cross ... was later placed. We remarked on it at the time and wondered if it was ever thought to have a deliberate meaning which of course it did not.

While a few sullen Frenchmen and boys looked on, the grave was filled. Then the wreaths were placed over the mound. One, from the Fifth Australian Division read: "To our worthy and gallant foe."

Among the onlookers was Private Work. He had just left a nearby clearing station where he finally had his troublesome molar extracted, when he was attracted by a funeral cortege and decided to pause for the final tribute.

More wreaths of immortelles—treated flowers that retained their shape and colors—were heaped on the moist mound of earth when the propeller cross was erected. Until the light faded in the late afternoon, the grave was a favorite subject for soldiers with cameras, and dozens of men posed beside the cross with their comrades. Photographs of the flower-covered grave were later dropped by British fliers at several places over German-held positions.

The escort had scarcely departed and the last soldier

Headquarters. In due course, Major-General John Salmond, Commander of the R.A.F. in France, replied. He said the Royal Air Force could not renounce its claim regarding Richthofen, because three of their scouts were close enough to fire on the red machine. Also, the report of the red triplane having been shot down in aerial combat was made before it was known who flew it. This last comment was interpreted by some as casting aspersion on the honesty of the Australian claim, by suggesting that when the identity of the pilot was learned, the ground troops demanded the credit. Salmond concluded his remarks by saying he was perfectly willing for the R.A.F. to share the claim with the Australians—if they (the Australians) wished it. He had in fact, taken the liberty of redrafting Bean's cable to say that the honors were divided! It was fortunate for the morale of the Aussie troops that the result of this exchange did not become generally known.

Private Weston, who was involved in the gunnery action, came to strongly suspect that the credit was being compromised. About that same time he wrote in his diary:

> Major Hinton was asked to report on the matter—this he did. We believe that he received information to the effect that they could not give credit to anyone in particular as another claim had been submitted and that they feared international complications.

Weston's assumption was very close to the truth, and because the credit was not—or could not—be given to the proper service, there was born the most bitter controversy of air war history.

It was from Bertangles that Lanoe Hawker had flown to meet death at Richthofen's hands. To Bertangles Cemetery Richthofen came to rest. The wheel of Fate had turned full circle.

THE CONTROVERSY

CHAPTER EIGHTEEN

"I Shot Richthofen!"

It would seem an impossible task, almost half a century later, to confirm the details on the finish of the famous "Red Devil." Within a few days the Aussie Troopers would be fighting again at fever pitch to roll back the German tide.

But the unforgettable experience so vividly related by Robert Buie literally demands that every book and article about the most discussed kill of the first air war be rewritten.

Forty-three years after the now-famous action, with his health failing, the frail, asthmatic ex-gunner of the 53rd Battery patiently exchanged detailed correspondence over a ten-month period, writing exhaustive replies to questions, verifying the facts or casting out the fallacies as he knew them. The spark of interest rekindled, it grew into a determined effort to provide every detail his memory could muster. This is Robert Buie's story.

In October of 1916 I enlisted in the Australian Army and three months later sailed for France. On the 21st of April, 1918, I was with the 53rd Battery of the 14th Australian Field Artillery Brigade as an anti-aircraft gunner. We were positioned on the crest of the Morlancourt ridge overlooking the Somme valley, roughly two miles behind the lines. Hamel was out in front of our position. I remember it pretty well because the Germans had a big naval gun in a church steeple there. It was doing tremendous damage well behind our lines until it was located and blown up.

Vaux-sur-Somme was just a little away on our left, Corbie and Villiers-Brettoneaux away on our right, Corbie being the nearest. I was never there, but it looked like a small shopping center in the distance. Behind our position on the western side of the hollow were two little villages, Bonnay and Heilly.

The battle of the Ancre had slackened. We had held this position about 15 days, manning our two anti-aircraft machine guns 24 hours a day by shifts. The big guns had been quiet the night before and I got fair sleep, arising from my dugout at 6:00 A.M. to prepare for my duty beginning at 8:00. My dugout mate, Bombardier Seccull, also arose and together we ate our customary breakfast of bread and marmalade with hot tea. Snowy Evans, our other gunner, was also stirring about, noisy, talking a blue streak and joking with us as usual. We stood and sat in small groups, for the most part young boys dressed in khaki tunics, riding breeches and putties. We wore our helmets constantly for our position was fairly hot most of the time, and we took a good share of shelling by German artillery.

Although it was a beautiful spring morning with a cloudless sky and little or no wind on the surface, the usual early air activity was delayed until mid-morning when, at 10:40, a sizable dogfight between British and German fighter planes centered on our front directly over the lines. The German machines were brightly painted Fokker triplanes and Albatross Scouts and the British squadron was composed of about 15 Sopwith Camels. A moderate east wind high overhead—unfavorable for the Germans—slowly drifted the engagement toward us. The German Red Circus—or *Red Devil Squadron* as we called it—was in the melee. Their red machines were known to most of us and were led by Baron von Richthofen, Germany's crack ace, who had only the day before brought down his 80th plane. To single him out overhead amid the 25 or 30 circling planes however, would have been almost impossible.

I was standing by my Lewis gun, watching the air battle drift closer. Our guns were post mounted, especially fitted for anti-aircraft use. They could hold a pannier of 45 .303-caliber bullets, four of which were tracers equally spaced every tenth round. They were to help us judge where our fire was going so we could correct our aim on the target. As yet we hadn't received the newly designed gunsight to be used on our Lewis mounts, but Fitter Bartlett of our battery had already studied a picture of one in a new ordnance manual and had made one to scale from a discarded 18-pounder shell case. It was installed on my Lewis gun, and although it looked rather ungainly it was supposed to be effective against low-flying aircraft.

Two German machines had fallen from the fight when I noticed one of our machines corkscrewing from the melee and falling toward the ground in the vicinity of Vaux-sur-Somme. It straightened out at a low level and darted across our lines for safety. The all-red Fokker triplane immediately gave chase and although our airman had a fair lead, the German rapidly gained on him. By this time our C.O., Major Beavis, had received a telephone message from our forward observing post at the stone windmill near Vaux, informing us that these two machines had separated from the fight and were flying directly down the Somme valley toward our battery. I had already cleared my gun and made ready for action. The pilot in the Sopwith was twisting and turning to escape the short, erratic maching-gun bursts fired by the German airman, but he continued to be forced lower and lower toward our position. I was not then aware that the Camel was flown by Lieutenant Wilfred May of 209 Squadron, and the pursuing red triplane by the famous Baron von Richthofen.

We were free to fire at any time without command, but as the planes neared us, barely 50 feet off the brow of the ridge, I was prevented from firing immediately, as the two machines were almost in line, with Lieutenant May's blocking my line of fire. Major Beavis and Lieutenant Doyle were on my left, near Evans's gun position, about 30 yards away. Lieutenant Ellis, on slightly lower ground at my center, observed the oncoming planes from the flank and shouted, *"Fire on that plane, Buie!"* But I still could not, owing to Lieutenant May's position.

I was swiveling my gun to follow the red machine, and Snowy Evans, manning the other gun on the opposite flank, got first clearance. He opened up at a range of slightly more than 300 yards. The triplane flew steadily on, still firing short bursts at the Camel. It was barely 20 yards behind and ten feet above May. Very close indeed. I was at the ready with my finger on the trigger, awaiting the clearance.

It came.

I can still remember seeing Richthofen clearly. His helmet covered most of his head and face and he was hunched in the cockpit aiming over his guns at the lead plane. It seemed that with every burst he leaned forward in the cockpit as though he were concentrating very intently on his firing. Certainly he was not aware of his dangerous position or the close range of our guns. His position was much as a strafing attack would appear, and had he not been so intent upon shooting down Lieutenant May, he could easily have maneuvered his machine and fired upon us, had he been so inclined. Richthofen and his men frequently strafed our trenches to the east.

At 200 yards, with my peep sight directly on Richthofen's body, I began firing in steady bursts. His plane was bearing frontal and just a little to the right of me, and after 20 rounds I knew the bullets were striking the right side and front of the machine, for I clearly saw fragments flying.

Still Richthofen came on, firing at Lieutenant May with both guns blazing. Then, just before my last shots finished at a range of 40 yards, Richthofen's guns stopped abruptly. The thought flashed through my mind—*I've hit him!*—and immediately I noticed a sharp change in engine sounds as the red triplane passed over our gun position at less than 50 feet and still a little to my right. It slackened speed considerably. The propeller slowed down and the engine sound disappeared, although the machine still appeared to be under control. Then it veered a bit to the right and then back to the left and lost height gradually, coming down near an abandoned brick kiln, 400 yards away on the Bray-Corbie Road.

I looked to my gun. It was empty. I had fired a full pannier.

Richthofen's plane did not come to earth in a spin, or vertically with full power as some writers have stated. It was far from demolished. Rather, it came down as though the pilot was bringing it down, although on landing parts of the wing and the forward section of the fuselage were damaged quite badly. I remember looking up briefly to see the Camel that had flown on a little way turn back for a quick clockwise circle once around our battery before flying into the west, toward, I presume, his base.

I remained near my gun post, for there was a standing order that no men were to show themselves in the open ground. The plane had landed in full view of the German batteries, Despite the order, souvenir hunters streamed from all directions. I understand that Lieutenant Fraser, Intelligence Officer of the 11th Brigade, was among the first to reach the plane. He released Richthofen's safety belt and lowered him to the ground. Upon examining the airman's papers, he found his name. The rush for souvenirs then began in earnest and I later learned that a padre of the 8th Field Artillery Brigade recovered many of Richthofen's personal effects from the "souvenir kings."

As I watched the activity at the plane, I remarked to some of the diggers from the other positions, "He flew so low over us that we couldn't miss him."

In a short while the word came back. "It's Richthofen, the German ace!" My digger mates slapped me on the back and congratulated me. At first I thought they were carrying on with me, but others came up and confirmed it. I felt very proud. It was the most thrilling experience of my life.

A guard was placed over the body and after awhile it was brought to our position. Major Beavis claimed the body for the 53rd and it was placed on a nearby stretcher. There I saw it. In the crash Richthofen's face was thrown against the gun butts and suffered minor injuries. Blood had come from his mouth which indicated at first glance that a fatal bullet had pierced a lung. According to the popular version, death came from a single bullet which had entered his back and passed forward through the chest.

This is not true.

Richthofen was struck in the left breast, abdomen and right knee. I examined these wounds as his body lay on the stretcher. His fur-lined boots were missing, as were his helmet and goggles and other personal effects, these having been taken before his body arrived at the battery. He was wearing silk pajamas under his flying clothes.

The wounds were all frontal. Their entrances were small and clean and the exit points were slightly larger and irregular in the back. Later, Colonel Barber of the Australian Corps and Colonel Sinclair of the Fourth Army, both medical officers, made separate examinations of the body and their reports agreed that the chest wound was definitely caused by ground fire.

Early that afternoon, there arrived at our station the Wing Commander over 209 Squadron, Lieutenant-Colonel Cairnes, accompanied by another officer and Captain Roy Brown who, to everyone's amazement, claimed to have brought the Baron down. He appeared very sincere in his claim, but Major Beavis and our other officers would have none of it. By then I had learned that a third plane piloted by Captain Brown was supposed to have followed Richthofen from the fight, but while still two miles distant, it had broken away and made a wide curve to the right of our battery, being, at the moment of my firing, well south of us over Corbie, a mile and a half distant. Brown's machine was definitely not in the action at all. No plane pursued Richthofen. There was only May pursued by Richthofen. *Two planes only!*[1]

I have a vivid recollection of Captain Brown. He appeared to me quite well and fresh, hardly the sick and exhausted man described by some writers. He got a glimpse of Richthofen's body on the stretcher. I shook hands with him, after which Major Beavis, Lieutenant Ellis and I reviewed the action and showed the air officers where Richthofen fell. When confronted with the facts—

---

[1] Writing in 1960, 42 years after the incident, Major Beavis (now Major-General on the retired list) had this to say: "I have tried hard to be factual and to avoid any statement of what might have been. I am as sure now as I was then that only two aircraft were in the picture, that Richthofen was deviating right and left trying to keep dead on the tail of the Camel (which was flying a weaving course directly toward our position), that Richthofen turned to the N.W. and then round to the N.E. immediately after our guns opened fire, that he crashed some seconds later and, of course, that the body in the plane was that of Richthofen."

that scores of men and officers had seen his plane on our right and two thousand yards away when Richthofen went down—they went away with Brown apparently satisfied, for he said that he had "brought one down, but it must have been in another sector."

The Germans refrained from shelling the downed plane itself, as they wanted to allow time for our diggers to remove the body. Then too, they may have thought their pilot was only wounded. Later however, they opened fire with a barrage intended to destroy the plane and the troops moving it, but they were too late as it had already been dismantled and was on its way to the Royal Air Force in accordance with the general existing orders governing captured aircraft.

We all knew that the R.A.F. was contesting the action, but as all claims and evidence had gone to British Army Headquarters for evaluation we could only await the official decision we knew would be in our favor. It came one month later, while I was still in the line.[2] The despatch that came from General Rawlinson, Commander of the British Fourth Army in France, was directed to the 53rd Battery and to me. The findings of the inquiry clearly indicated that after very careful consideration and the weighing up of all the evidence, it had been proven beyond all doubt that Number 3801, Gunner Robert Buie, 53rd Battery, was responsible for the destruction of Baron von Richthofen.[3]

During the past 43 years I have read many strange accounts of what was supposed to have taken place during this action, and each has been more fantastic than the pre-

---

[2] Of the investigation, Major-General Beavis wrote in May of 1960: "I was never called upon to give evidence at any inquiry and kept out of what had the appearance of an undignified wrangle."

[3] General Hobbs was directed by General Rawlinson to forward his personal thanks and congratulations to the gunner responsible for shooting down the German ace. During the official inquiry, the facts pointed to Gunner Buie as this man. His assertion therefore, was simply based on the official nature of the dispatch addressed to him by name, rank, serial number and organization. In 1931, the ex-gunner donated the telegram to the Australian War Memorial.

ceding one. But by far the most incorrect versions were those in Gibbons's *The Red Knight of Germany* and Quentin Reynolds's *They Fought for the Sky.*

Gibbons said ". . . *one bullet traversed May's right arm.*" May landed back at base without a scratch. "*There was a bullet hole in both the right and left breast.*"

Apparently Gibbons did not read the medical reports, of which were a total of four. All agreed there was only one bullet *through the chest.*

"*Richthofen crashed in no man's land, on the outskirts of Sailly-le-Sec, not far from Corbie.*"

Actually, his machine came to rest beside the Bray-Corbie Road, well behind the front, two and one-half miles from Corbie and two miles from Sailly-le-Sec. These are measured air distances.

"*Directly in front and beneath the pair* [describing Richthofen's pursuit of May] *are the trench positions of the 33rd Australian Field Battery.*"

Our battery was the 53rd.

"*Lieutenant Mellersh* (of 209 Squadron) *made a forced landing . . . within his own lines*" and: Richthofen's plane "*came to a stop right side up in a shell hole not 50 yards from where Mellersh was standing . . . Under Lieutenant Mellersh's instructions the body was carried to the closest underground shelter.*"

The young flying officer whom Gibbons somehow placed in charge of the situation later became Air Vice Marshal of the Royal Air Force. Letters which he wrote after Richthofen's death, as well as records of 209 Squadron, disprove Gibbons's account. Actually, Lieutenant Mellersh returned to base with Captain Brown, Lieutenant May and other survivors of the dogfight.

Quentin Reynolds drew heavily from Gibbons's faulty material and completely ignored the ground action. Their information is all wrong, as is Captain Brown's personal account that appeared in several American and Canadian newspapers under the title: *My Fight with Richthofen.*[4]

---

[4] A series of dramatized and highly inaccurate articles which appeared during 1927 and 1928 in *Liberty* and the *Chicago Sunday Tribune*. They were ghost-written and published without the consent or knowledge of Roy Brown. In 1935, Australian historian Charles E. Bean queried Brown on the accuracy of these articles. Brown replied that he "was unable to confirm it or otherwise, not having read the paper at the time."

Brown was definitely not there. His narrative, as well as those of Gibbons and Reynolds, are untruths—so intended or not. They are nothing but fabrications and fallacies—and I emphasize this strongly. I have always been hostile about this over the years and never has anyone come to my assistance, although quite a lot of people out here knew the rights and wrongs of it all.

It has been said that the controversy over who shot down Richthofen will never be settled because even granting that he was fired upon from below, the simultaneous firing by Brown from the air complicates matters beyond all hope of solution. This is utter nonsense! There was never a controversy in the first place, but rather, an attempt by the R.A.F. to distort the truth in their reluctance to accept the fact that Richthofen, the greatest ace of World War I was downed by a mere gunner instead of one of their own pilots. It's no secret that the Air Services needed morale bolstering during those critical days.

On May 9, following the results of the inquiry, General Sir William Birdwood and Brigadier-General Bessel-Brown made a special visit to our battery to congratulate me for my work. General Birdwood was the first to approach my gun. He was a small man, very smart, and spoke quickly. He wore a slouch hat the same as we did and was known to all of us as "The Little Digger." He shook hands vigorously with me and remarked that it would have been more fitting had Richthofen been brought down in the air engagement and a great pity also, that he wasn't just wounded and taken prisoner. "Richthofen," he said, "was a very gallant man but, nevertheless, he is better out of the way. He was very destructive toward our men. What do you think of it, Buie?"

"I'm proud to have been the one who brought him down, sir," I replied. "I'll never forget it."

General Birdwood nodded and touched my arm. As he took his leave his last words to me were, "Good Luck and goodbye. Keep on bringing them down, Buie."

I saluted smartly and said, "Goodbye, sir. I'll do my best."

A little more than a week later, Major-General John

Talbot Hobbs visited the battery. He chatted with Seccull and Evans and then greeted me in much the same manner as had General Birdwood. He examined my gunsight carefully and was quite impressed with it. I explained that it was a makeshift sight as our new ones had not yet arrived from Ordnance. He asked me if he could have it as a souvenir when it was replaced and I readily agreed. Later it was sent to him, and after his death it was handed over to the Australian War Memorial at Canberra where it is on display today, along with other items recovered from the crashed plane.

During the night of August 8th—my 26th birthday—after spending eight months in the line, while large-scale operations were in progress along the Amiens front, I suddenly lost consciousness and was carried out of the line to the rear. When I came to in a field hospital I realized the war was over for me. I never understood what happened. For a week I was not allowed to stand on my feet and when I was well enough, I was sent to a convalescent camp on the coast of France—a place called Le Treport. After a short time, I was sent across the channel to Lewisham Hospital in England. A few weeks later I was invalided home aboard the hospital ship *Somali*. On my tunic was a tag which listed my illness. It said *Myocarditis*.

Before my enlistment I was a professional fisherman out of Brooklyn on the Hawkesbury River, where my parents settled from Scotland in the early 1800s. I went back to work as best I could, but my heart condition became critical and I developed chronic bronchial asthma. In 1938 I was readmitted to Randwick Hospital, but after three months was discharged with the usual verdict—*not due to war service*. I've never been able to understand their reasoning on this, for I was marked physically fit when I enlisted.

I often think of the war years and of the day I downed Richthofen. Although I officially received credit, I must include my old digger mate, William John Evans, who passed away in 1928, and who manned our battery's other gun.

Yes, the evidence has been twisted and distorted over the years, but the facts cannot be erased. Many people in America, England, and Canada have not acknowledged Australia's victory. Documentary evidence is what counts however—and I have it.

The honor of destroying Germany's greatest ace belongs only to Australia.

A day or so after the crash, Staff Captain Basil Morris of the Fifth Australian Divisional Artillery, was instructed to assemble at his headquarters those personnel of the 53rd Battery who took part in the action. Morris was informed that C. E. W. Bean, the Australian war correspondent, had been deputed by the London Press to ascertain the truth about the rival claims.

Major Beavis and his section commanders, Lieutenants Ellis and Doyle, with the Lewis Gunners Buie and Evans, together with Bombardier Seccull, were present and waiting when Bean arrived at the large two-story house in Bussy-les-Daours. In the presence of Captain Morris, Bean took statements from each man in turn, all plain statements of fact without claims to have done anything out of the ordinary. Each told of the dogfight overhead; how the German plane followed the Camel down into the Somme valley; how it appeared as though the British plane could not clear the hill as it tried to shake Richthofen who was hard on his tail; how both machines barely made altitude to clear the ridge and flew directly over the battery's flank; how Evans fired a burst and sent splinters flying from the German plane, and how the plane swerved along the battery line to allow a clear target for Buie who sent more splinters flying from the Boche plane which curved around and crashed. All attested to the fact that there was no third plane in the fight at that low altitude and at that time. Major Beavis indicated strongly then and later, that there "was no third plane in the vicinity, certainly not within a radius of 2,000 yards. In fact, there was none to be seen nearer than the fight still going on over Sailly-Laurette."

Recalling the meeting years later as a retired Major-

General, Basil Morris said, "I well remember how, when the story was told, Bean threw down his pen and said, 'That settles it; there's no further doubt about it!' "

But apparently Bean did have some further doubt about it, for in his official report he discounted the 53rd's gunnery claim, to the surprise and disappointment of its personnel, and leaned toward Popkin as the responsible gunner. His opinion is included in the war history published in 1937 and remains the stand of the Australian War Memorial, although it can hardly be justified in the light of overwhelming evidence to the contrary.

Von Richthofen was fatally struck *after* he left the range of Popkin's gun and *before* he again became the Sergeant's target. Between these times the red plane was the object of a simultaneous hail of bullets from Buie and Evans. Buie, in all candor, based his claim solely on the despatch from Generals Rawlinson and Hobbs, but neither Buie nor Evans are known to have claimed categorically that either was solely responsible for killing Richthofen. Obviously, from the nature of the wounds, both shot him, though neither was certain which one inflicted the chest wound and which one inflicted the leg and abdominal wounds.

Does the answer lie in Richthofen's sudden, violent bank? What caused it? Did he roll the Fokker deliberately? Was he breaking off the chase?

As he came from the east, Richthofen flew almost directly over Evan's gun. Then, in utter violence, the plane was wrenched on its side and almost "upset." Was the sudden maneuver the result of Buie's fire striking Richthofen's leg and abdomen—despite the fact that he opened fire after Evans?

A powerful, uncontrollable reflex gripped the German aviator and now, almost midway between the two gunners, the plane's wild swerve with its accompanying slip and skid exposed the pilot's right side and front. Either gunner could have sent a bullet transversely through Richthofen's chest as he came onto the battery, but at no other time was his right side more vulnerable to Evans than at that moment. He fired a final burst directly into the cockpit to inflict the trunk wound.[5]

Logically, the first strikes by Buie caused the clear, open target for Evans. In a manner that would be difficult to dispute, Robert Buie "set up" the target.

Popkin, in his second firing, following the curving and descending plane with his Vickers, fired on a pilot already dead or fast dying, and who, true to his own doctrine in the fast-fading seconds of life, would not take his hand from the control stick until he was dead.

On the day Captain Brown's decoration was gazetted, June 18, 1918, the senior staff officer of the British Fourth Army, Sir Archibald Montgomery-Massingberd, visited with Major Beavis. The Allied offensive was rolling well and the big guns thundering nearby punctuated their conversation. Over a cracked porcelain cup steaming with strong tea, Montgomery-Massingberd informed the battery commander that Army Headquarters had forwarded the reports of Evans's and Buie's actions to General Headquarters. In his diary that evening, Major Beavis wrote " . . . so I think we will ultimately get the credit."

Because the gunnery action was simultaneous, both men were recognized and their actions made known by a citation in an official dispatch. They were not decorated. On discharge, each man received the usual cash gratuity of twenty Pounds.

It is an ironic twist that despite Richthofen's own warning to his men never to be pulled down and be-

---

[5] Long before the details of Buie and Evans's gunfire came to light, an article in the April 1938 issue of *Flying* contained a statement to the effect that a member of Number 3 Squadron's salvage detail, A. A. Boxall-Chapman, saw a bullet hole in the right side of the triplane's cockpit (looking forward toward the propeller), but none on the left side. Visually, he traced the path of the bullet. It entered halfway down the pilot's right side and passed upward and outward. The angle coincided with Evans's line of fire.

come trapped behind enemy lines, he met death by violating his own tactical concept. Somehow, being shot down by ground fire seems too ignominious an ending for the World War I airman who had gained the highest pedestal of the German *Luftstreitkräfte*. But the thirst for legend was better satisfied by the groundless claims and inaccuracies that followed—almost half a century the facts were to lie buried.

CHAPTER NINETEEN

Sergeant Hart

The 50-50 column of the *Sydney Daily Telegraph* is read faithfully by the newspaper's long-time subscribers. On February 11, 1959, it contained this brief request:

BARON

    As a World War I Digger, I would like to hear from any other Diggers who witnessed the bringing down of Baron von Richthofen, Germany's air ace. Please write to Robert Buie, Calga via Gosford, N.S.W.

And here is the reply:

> Concord West
> Sydney-February 12, 1959

Dear Robert,

    Only very occasionally do I glance in the 50-50 column. Most of the items in my opinion are silly. So you can regard my noticing your request as a fluke.

    Not since Les McEvoy of the 53rd—who worked for the *Evening Sun*—started a controversy about Richthofen because the paper was short of sensations, have I heard the name.

    You who manned the Lewis guns with Evans I remember very well. You were a smooth-faced boy, just as quiet as Evans was noisy. I saw Evans in George Street in front of the Lyric Theatre just after my return.

    I wrote the official account of the Baron's death and gave full credit to you and Evans who undoubtedly brought him down. I saw my report in the War Records after the war. I don't know why you are anxious now to hear from an eyewitness of the tragic death of a gallant airman, but here I am in possession of all the facts.

I hope, Robert, that you are in good health. Let me know what is troubling you; I shall be glad to assist.

> With kind regards,
> Sincerely yours,
> H.E. Hart

Horrie Hart
Late Sgt. 53rd Battery, A.I.F.
One time Battery Clerk

When he read Hart's letter, Buie chuckled to his wife Laurel, "You can see by their letters that they think I've gone crazy asking about Richthofen after so many years."

The ex-gunner's request for authentication led him to Sydney and to the man he had not seen in 43 years. Hart remembers: "Buie still had the same nice eyes and fine features that I remembered, but he was thin."

Hart had resurrected the manuscript of the *History of the 53rd Battery, Australian Field Artillery, Australian Imperial Force*, that he had laboriously compiled in London in 1919 and it recalled to them many memories long forgotten. "I really don't know how I performed the task," he commented. "I'm sure it would be beyond me today."

Trained in Egypt as a gun layer when the Fifth Division was formed, Hart narrowly missed Gallipoli. In France he saw heavy action and suffered a partial loss of hearing from gun concussion. Major Beavis took advantage of Corporal Hart's impairment to press him into duty as Battery Clerk, but later, at Hart's insistence, he returned to artillery duty as a sergeant.

From 1960, we corresponded often and in August of 1967, while he and Mrs. Hart were visiting their daughter's family in Texas, we arranged a meeting.

Horrie Hart was surprisingly robust and agile for his 78 years. "I'm able to play ball with my grandchildren," he

boasted as we sat in a Monroe, Louisiana, motel with
Ray Strickland, his son-in-law, and became warmly acquainted over a drink. The old soldier's faculty for plac-
ing names and dates is remarkable. The keen power of
observation that was his in 1918 served him well and he
spoke unhaltingly, with vigor and with color in recounting the dramatic events of that historic morning. As the
hours passed, I took the story down as he told it. Here it
is; how he came to record the most famous anti-aircraft
action of all time:

"Major Hely, who was the last O.C. of the Battery,
placed me in charge of the demobilization after the Armistice. I spent some months in Froid Chapelle, Belgium,
attending to the evacuation of personnel until the last. The
Major was keen to have a history compiled and he obtained the necessary authority for me to repair to A.I.F.
Headquarters at Horseferry Roads in London to gain ac-
cess to the war records. I left Belgium with the remnants
of the old battery and on arrival at Étaples, where the
troops were allotted ships for England, was delayed for
three weeks because one of the sergeants in my hut
developed measles and the rest of us who had occupied it
were placed in Contact Camp. Accordingly, when I arrived in London, Major Hely could not be located. Un-
daunted, and with permission of Headquarters authorities,
I set myself to the task conscientiously. For four and a
half months I worked long and arduous hours tracing
every movement and event that affected each operation
from the battery's formation until its disbandment, sand-
wiching items of interest or humor that I held in my own
memory, here and there. Major Hely turned up when I
was nearing the end of the job and promised to get in
touch with me later. Forty-nine years have passed and I
have not heard from him since.

It is to be expected after the lapse of these many years
that memories—however retentive—fade, at least as far as
details are concerned. But there are some outstanding
experiences that remain vivid. In my case, the tragic death
of Germany's greatest airman stands out as though it
happened yesterday. Maybe because I was called upon to
describe that last flight shortly thereafter, and that later,
in the War Records, I saw my own words taken as the

official account of the incident. There is tangible evidence
to assist my recollection, but without these adjuncts I
would still remember.

I was stampeded into writing the description of the
death of Richthofen, *hors-de-combat* with a sprained ankle
at Pont Noyelles whither the battery had moved from
Bonnay. A messenger came from Major Beavis, armed
with an Army memo pad and orders for me to write the
account forthwith and return the pad with the messenger.
With my bad ankle stretched in front of me, I sat on the
grass and wrote furiously. It transpired that the Major had
been instructed to supply the document urgently—the
same day. Then, as now, I am convinced that Buie and
Evans were wholly responsible for the downfall of Germany's famous son and that any other claim cannot be
substantiated. So, I can only set down as nearly as possible
the original description. Here it is, baldly, and without
literary flourishes:

The morning of April 21st, 1918, broke clear and still
and at 10:30 A.M. was bright, with the sun that has given
the country the title "Sunny France." Nowhere have I
seen the same sunny stillness.

Suddenly, breaking through the quietness, came the
staccato *rat-tat-tat* of machine-gun fire overhead. The men
for whom aerial combat held fascination above all else
rushed from their dugouts. Above the valley of the Somme
many planes were engaged in fierce fighting. One red
plane was particularly active and dodged and maneuvered
at terrific speed. Suddenly one British plane detached
itself from the main fighting body and sped away toward
our lines with the red plane in hot pursuit. Thus began
the chase that will never be forgotten by those who
witnessed it.

Across the valley of the Somme the planes approached
the ridge that rises sharply and upon which our battery's
guns were mounted. As they passed over the infantry lines
in the distance, the German triplane fired on the plane in
front and I heard a single machine gun fire from the
ground. Both planes were only 150 feet above the ground
and by this time the red plane had so gained upon the
British pilot that it was only a matter of moments before
the German pilot would be victorious. The watchers, and
I was one, held their breaths as the two planes flew

directly toward the two Lewis guns of Buie and Evans, which were mounted close to each other on high ground behind the battery of 18-pounders. I was standing with the others below the ridge at Bonnay, on lower ground and forward of the two machine guns, against a protective ridge under which the dugouts were built. Buie and Evans were less than 50 yards away.

The planes were so close together that the gunners had to hold their fire until the British plane passed. Evans's gun, more at an angle, opened fire first. Buie held his fire momentarily because Evans appeared to be in his line of sight. The German plane was then so near that the body of the pilot was clearly visible. The plane bore frontally, practically into the muzzle of Buie's gun and after the first burst of fire the plane shook, splinters flew from it and it veered—drifted in an arc northward out of control—and gradually reached the ground. It crashed about 500 yards from the battery position.

As soon as the plane struck, a shell from a German gun exploded near it, probably to discourage the rush made toward it by neighboring troops. But the airman was dead, his body riddled in front from his chest to his knees. Our watching gunners were not allowed to go to the crash. Only Bombardier Seccull, who was in charge of the Lewis gun personnel, was permitted. Seccull collected the airman's papers and when he returned he handed them to Major Beavis and I heard the Major say: "Seccull, you've done the best day's work in your life. These papers belong to Richthofen, the greatest German airman!"

When Major Beavis made his report, there was tremendous excitement at Headquarters, Throughout the afternoon many red-capped military officers visited the battery and spoke to Buie and Evans. They were Brigade and Corps officers whose red-banded ornate caps and red tabs distinguished them from the common herd.

Thus ended the career of Germany's famous son—"The Red Devil" who had brought to earth 80 enemy planes and whose name to this day is perpetuated in many ways in Germany and other parts of the world. It was said at the time that Baron von Richthofen was a chivalrous foe who preferred to drive to earth a helpless opponent rather than ruthlessly destroy him. How true this statement is, I don't know. But at the time, papers publishing his death said just that.

Following the crash the German artillery ringed the plane with fire and souvenir collectors were in danger of flying shrapnel. It was not until later in the afternoon that the body was brought to the line of battery dugouts. Among others I saw the extensive nature of the wounds, that they were frontal, in the chest, abdomen and legs—all in the front of the body. I had the impression that, owing to his sitting position in the plane, the knee and abdomen wounds could possibly have been caused by the same bullets. It was easy to identify the body from a picture in a magazine I had been reading the same day. It was in a sense tragic, if the airman had to die, that it could not have happened in the course of air combat at the hands of another airman. I remember my father relating to me the story of the mortal injury of a famous whaler who was injured by a small whale. While his life was ebbing he said: "I wouldn't mind dying if a decent-sized whale had got me—not a miserable squid like this!"

The viewing of the dead airman was brief. I remember how sad I felt to see his mutilated youthful body, below a singularly handsome face.

Robert Buie at the time was a quiet, well-behaved boy. He was retiring in disposition and I cannot recall him having hit the high spots at any time. A boy from the Australian bush, he was a good shot, hence his selection as machine gunner. Evans was a good soldier and a capable gunner. He was a typical Australian "rough and ready." Seccull was a good chap, and popular.

One Anzac Day a few years ago I was seated in a suite of the Hotel Australia—Sydney's largest and most modern hotel. I was the guest of Stan Leech—one-time driver of the 53rd—along with ten or so of our old battery. It was Stan's pleasure on Anzac Day to entertain as many of his old mates who are willing. It was, he told me, his one big day every year. He flew from his grazing property at Narrabri, 350 miles northwest, to meet the boys and fight the war again. Being a prosperous grazier he could afford to be generous, and playing host to his old Digger friends was his greatest pleasure.

When the drinks were flowing freely I was able to divert the conversation to Richthofen. Vic Howard, a prosperous printer in the city (who has also passed on) was there and reminded me that he stood alongside me when the two planes appeared over the hill at Bonnay.

"Buie's gun was on our left about 30 yards up the hill. The planes appeared to be bearing down on us. Somebody yelled '*Shoot, Buie!*' But Buie, calm lad that he was, bided his own time and held his fire because of his fear of hitting the British pilot." Vic was entirely in agreement with my remembrance, but I'd forgotten that he stood alongside me. His being there wasn't strange because his habit was to stay with me whenever possible. He had the idea that if he stayed with me he would be perfectly safe.

No recollection of the Richthofen matter would be complete without the evidence of Joe Punch, who passed away this year. Joseph J. R. Punch was a lieutenant in the battery and easily the most capable and popular of our officers. No history of the battery could be concluded without strong references to the part he played in the successes the unit enjoyed in our operations in France and Belgium. Originally, Joe Punch was a sergeant in the 49th Battery. He was sent to St. John's Wood in England and obtained a commission. He was posted to the 53rd and joined us at Wytschaete Ridge near Ypres, early in 1918. My first encounter with him occurred one morning when I was doing a job in a dugout for Major Beavis. Someone was on the roof pulling something about and making clatter that was disturbing my concentration. I was about to make an investigation when part of the roof was lifted and a face I hadn't seen before appeared at the opening. Its owner said, "Hope I'm not a nuisance, Digger," at once disarming me and checking the flow of Australian abuse I had ready to shoot.

"Who are you?" was all I said.

"Just a new arrival," he replied. It was then I saw the star on his shoulder pinned to an ordinary soldier's tunic. "I'm Joe Punch," he said. "Who are you?" Thus began a friendship that's lasted all these long years.

Though doubly decorated (Military Cross and Bar), Joe Punch appeared without medals on Anzac Day. In the battery he proved to be the most fearless and enterprising officer we had. A small man, alert, energetic and conscientious, he was the idol of the men, who would have followed him anywhere. Captain C. E. W. Bean, the Australian war historian, knew Joe Punch took the forward guns into action on August 8, 1918, the day that really decided the war. Although pestered by Bean to provide information concerning his part in the action of that momentous day, Joe to use his own words, "wouldn't be in it. I didn't want my name in print," he told me later. Here is what he had to say on Anzac Day in 1960 about the morning Richthofen was killed:

(His observation post was the stone windmill on a cliff at Vaux-sur-Somme commanding a view of the German lines and the Somme River. His telephonist was Fred Rhodes who lives in Sydney today. Both men were watching the air fight and particularly the antics of a red triplane. Suddenly a smaller craft detached itself from the main body of fighting planes and headed toward the British lines, closely pursued by the red machine.)

"The small plane had no chance," Joe said, "coming out of the valley of the Somme and heading for higher ground. The leading plane stood on its tail, and the red plane did likewise right alongside our position on the cliff. They were so close I believe that if I'd aimed at the leading pilot with my revolver I'd probably have hit the pursuer. The thought occurred to me that the pilot of the red plane must be a good bloke because he could easily have shot the other down. I told Fred Rhodes to phone the battery that two planes were heading for the guns and to alert the machine gunners who might get a shot at the chaser. Of course I didn't know then that the pursuer was Richthofen."

The significant part of Joe's narrative was his reply to my question about the Canadian, Roy Brown.

"Brown?" Joe replied. "He 'squibbed it'—cleared out when the fight was on and didn't reappear until it was well and truly over. As for his 'claim,' that was the greatest piece of colossal nerve that I ever heard of. He was nowhere near Richthofen on that day!"[2]

Let me say this in conclusion: Brown, the Canadian, admitted to Robert Buie that he was mistaken when he claimed Richthofen. He had a colossal nerve to do this; the hide of a rhino to make this claim. Buie, I think, told him so. Brown was nowhere near the scene at the vital

[2] Brown pulled away from the chase before May and Richthofen passed the stone windmill. Somehow Punch, at his position near Vaux-sur-Somme, took note of the machine later identified as Brown's. From its flight path he surmised the Canadian had "cleared out."

time. Only two planes were involved. No plane pursued Richthofen.

The Sydney *Daily Mirror* recently had an article about Richthofen. It mentioned that many claims had been made regarding the manner of his death, but said that it had been finally medically proved by the nature of his wounds that the airman was shot from behind by another pilot. This is a foolish claim because no plane followed Richthofen when he came over our battery. If you saw a man led before a firing squad, heard the order *"Fire!"* and saw the man fall lifeless, would you say the bullets from the squad killed him or somebody who was not there?

Richthofen died at the hands of the machine gunners as surely as the man before the firing squad. I was there, I saw it, and I had good eyesight.

The next afternoon I said a reluctant goodbye to the artilleryman late of the 53rd Battery. He stood straight and proud, as Australian soldiers have a way of standing; and I suddenly realized how greatly their ranks have thinned since 1918.

In that brief moment of parting I could see in Horrie Hart the diggers of Gallipoli, Egypt, Palestine and Flanders. And I thought, perhaps, I could hear them answering roll.

(H.E. Hart included this extract from the War Records:)

Citation

No. 598 William John Evans   Mentioned in despatch
No. 3801 Robert Buie   as under . . .

These gunners were on duty with Lewis guns of the 53rd Battery on hills north of *Corbie*. At about 11 A.M. two aeroplanes flying low approached the battery position. Discerned to be a British Sopwith Camel closely pursued by a single-seater red triplane. As soon as the British plane had passed the line of fire both these gunners opened fire at close range at the hostile plane. Splinters were immediately observed to fly from the latter which crashed about 800 yards from the guns. It was then discovered that the enemy pilot was dead and identified as Richthofen. This action undoubtedly saved the British airman and is worthy of recognition.

CHAPTER TWENTY
At Bertangles

Despite his outward concurrence with the digger's victory claim, Roy Brown remained unconvinced. He was certain it was his quick burst of fire as he closed on May's pursuer between Sailly-le-Sec and Vaux-sur-Somme that forced the red triplane to crash. Until light could be shed on the reason for the Canadian's quiet persistence in this belief, his counterclaim would remain forever a riddle.

The number of men who flew against Richthofen is fast diminishing. Today there are barely enough to man an average Camel squadron. Most of the one-time war pilots now living are in retirement, but one, former flight leader LeBoutillier remains an active businessman in Las Vegas.

It was in 1958 that I first heard of Oliver Colin LeBoutillier, an American volunteer who joined the (then) Royal Naval Air Service and rose to the rank of Captain and B Flight Leader in 209 Squadron. After months of inquiries I located the former war bird. My letter brought this reply:

> So far, I have never released to anyone the information in my possession pertaining to Baron von Richthofen, but maybe this is the time to tell the complete story. In my old scrapbook I have photographs of Bertangles Aerodrome showing most of the officers who were engaged in this particular battle; also a photograph of a piece of fabric off Richthofen's aircraft with signatures of pilots participating
> . . .

I have not been in contact for many years with Roy Brown or Wilfred May ...

"*. . . never released to anyone the information in my possession pertaining to Baron von Richthofen . . .*" It was the most intriguing phrase I had come across in years of study in the Richthofen matter. I knew that in the air Brown and May had been the nearest Allied pilots to the Red Ace, but LeBoutillier, close behind and above, had witnessed the entire chase. What did he see over the Somme half a century ago that other pilots missed? Could he unravel the riddle of Roy Brown's claim? I flew to Las Vegas for the answer.

"Boots" stands erect and tall. His appearance reminds one of an unassuming, distinguished statesman. He is lean and muscular with the sharp, tanned features of an outdoorsman. He is ever casual and relaxed and can put one immediately at ease.

For some reason over the years, LeBoutillier chose to remain silent on the matter. As we talked, I sensed that his decision to reveal candid impressions on the underlying reason for Brown's puzzling claim came only after much soul-searching. His long-time respect for a war comrade and fellow flight leader was very much in evidence. Over Scotch and sodas—LeBoutillier's favorite holdover from the war years—the final story unfolded as we were seated comfortably in his spacious home.

"Boots," I began, "how did you get into the big fracas?"

He ran his slender fingers through his curly, graying hair and reflected for a moment before answering.

"I was just a punk kid at the time, always dying to get into whatever was going on. I guess you might say I ran away from home. Mother and Dad were dead set against my enlisting of course, so I left New Jersey, crossed into Canada and joined the Royal Naval Air Service in Ottawa. I was trained to fly in England." A thin smile played on his face. "Now that was really something."

"We flew in just about anything and everything before we soloed. First a Farman, then a Caudron. Then a

Curtis or an Avro—we never remained in one machine long enough to master it before we were moved to another type. To add to the muddle the engine controls on the French machines operated backwards from the British machines, so if a green student on his solo flight took too long to remember which way to move the throttle lever, he usually ended up by smashing the plane. There were fatalities of course, and I'm amazed that so many of us survived. How I soloed in a little over seven hours I'll never know.

"When I reached France I flew Sopwith Pups and old B.E.s. Later I was posted to Number 9 Squadron, R.N.A.S. at Bray-Dunes, one of the two squadrons equipped with the Sopwith triplane. Now that was a real fighting aeroplane—more than a match for anything else at the time. High rate of climb, superb maneuverability and performance. But it wouldn't stand up in a dive and was replaced with Camels; first Clerget, then Bentley powered ones.

"Some people have the wrong idea as to why we flew dawn patrols. They were simply to catch the German night bombers returning home in the early light of daybreak when they would be silhouetted against the sky. A number of us got our victories that way, taking off 15 or 20 minutes before dawn to catch the cripples coming back and the recons setting out."

"Then German planes did cross the lines into Allied ground for offensive operations?"

"Oh yes," LeBoutillier replied. "But they were bombers—not fighters. Our aerodrome was bombed a number of times and the enemy aeroplanes frequently went well behind us. But the pursuit squadrons rarely crossed over. The Germans had orders to remain on their side of the lines and play it safe. This was the main reason our losses were so high. They knew we were coming over so they waited to pick us off over their own ground. And even though our rotary engines were fairly reliable, they sometimes conked out over German-held territory. By today's standards all of our aircraft were very frail. We had no safety devices whatsoever—no parachutes, no self-sealing fuel tanks, no radio. We communicated by hand signals. Our gas was limited and often, when a pilot became confused and got lost after breaking away from a dogfight, he couldn't make it home because the prevailing wind was rarely in our favor. All these things gave the German Air Service a decided advantage but nevertheless the Air Ministry ordered flights across the German lines and our patrols frequently carried us well into their territory."

"I understand that Brown had known May earlier and took him under his wing—made some practice flights with him."

LeBoutillier frowned. "Well . . . he knew Wop before the kid joined 209, but I don't think Brown did any extra flying with him. They were friends, yes, but this is one of those things that's been carried along and dramatized out of proportion."

"Like the old story of Brown going to bat for May when he arrived from a party two days late in reporting to the C.O.?"

LeBoutillier nodded. "I don't recall that May reported late. There's been much misunderstanding about what went on in those hurried, hectic days. Take this last thing you mentioned. The fact is that Roy Brown was far too tired and sick to take on anything but his regular duties. Physically, he was in bad shape; he'd been driving himself for a long time."

"His stomach?"

"Yes, a gastric condition caused him considerable suffering. Then too, he may have been having trouble from an old training crash injury he received in England. These were trying days; the situation at the front was still uncertain and we could all have done with a good rest.

"When the big push started, Brown had additional responsibilities as senior flight leader. The strain was beginning to show. It would be impossible to describe the emotions and confusion we experienced during a single day's fighting. The things I saw and felt have often made me wonder about the limits of human endurance.

"And then came that unforgettable dogfight on the morning of April 21st.

"Somehow, we all made it back to base. A few straggled in late; Aird had engine trouble and landed at Camblain; Brock made a forced landing at Vert Galand Farm. Drake and Redgate were forced out of the patrol before the scrap started. Mackenzie was slightly wounded in the back. A few of our pilots barely made the field; two Camels were shot up so badly the pilots couldn't taxi them after they landed. They simply left them where they stopped rolling and walked back to the hangars. We were all dazed and shaken up.

"Brown's flight—with the exception of Lomas who was trailing—arrived at base before me and the remainder of my flight. The first thing I heard Brown say after he got out of his Camel was, 'Well, I got a red triplane.' Mellersh, who had been a bit to the north of me when the red machine hit the ground, agreed with him. May said, 'Yes, I saw him crash.' Everything seemed to point to Brown's kill. Even I told him later, 'You must have hit him, because I saw him pull up and back,' and I knew the trailing Camel was Brownie's because I recognized the two white stripes on his fuselage. I even indicated this in my combat report.

"After we had completed our combat reports—all of which are now a matter of record in the War Ministry—we gathered for the noon mess. During the meal our squadron received a telephone message from Wing Headquarters, and our Engineering Officer, Simpson, relayed the news that Baron von Richthofen had been shot down and killed in the morning's fighting. We were excited by the news of course, but if Roy Brown had any inkling that Richthofen was in the red machine he dived on—and which he just claimed in his combat report—he gave no indication. I don't think it crossed his mind.

"A short time later, Lieutenant-Colonel W. J. Cairnes, the 22nd Wing Commander, arrived and asked to see

Brown in the Squadron Commander's office.[1] It now became apparent that there was more to the downing of the red triplane than met the eye, and another picture began to take shape. Cairnes asked Brown if he claimed to have shot down von Richthofen. Brown replied in the negative, and said that he'd only claimed a red triplane. Then Cairnes told Brown that the pilot of the red machine had been Richthofen but that Australian ground gunners and an R.E.8 Squadron—Number 3 Australian Flying Corps at Poulainville—had put in claims. Brown was dumbfounded. After a short discussion with his superiors, he agreed to accompany Cairnes to the crash site. The reports say another man accompanied them. This was probably our C.O., Major Butler, for he was not at the squadron while Cairnes and Brown were absent.

"I imagine that most of us would have been scared to death had we known Richthofen himself was in that melee—for we all knew what a great fighter he was and he certainly had our respect. But we rarely knew the Jastas we engaged or who led them.

"While the officers were gone, 209 hummed. Rumors and speculations flew, but of course we knew nothing. Now I'm coming to something that hasn't been made known. I hope it will clear up some of the misunderstanding of Roy Brown's actions. Let's examine his 'unjust' claim in the light of it.

"When Brown returned to 209 later that afternoon, he was quiet. It seems—as we later found out—that he had received orders from the Air Ministry that he was not to discuss the fight with anyone. As an officer, and he was a good one, he complied without question, though it hardly requires any stretch of the imagination to realize that by now he was thoroughly confused. And to add to the disorder he was transferred that very afternoon to England! He left almost immediately and his gear was sent after him.

---

[1] According to official records, Colonel H. V. Holt was still the Wing Commander. Possibly Cairnes, who officially succeeded Holt on the 24th, was already carrying out some of his duties.

"Now let's pause and look at the whole picture. Brown returned from the flight absolutely convinced he'd shot down a red triplane. Squadron pilots agreed. Then he was taken aside and told it was Richthofen and that two other claims had been made for the same machine. Still convinced he'd shot down the triplane in question, and while he was returning to 209 from the Australian battery, he was given orders to say nothing about the matter to anyone and was immediately transferred! The man had only performed his duty and now it appeared to be taking on the aspects of some sort of crime. And whether or not Brown actually got Richthofen, with this puzzling hush-hush treatment added to his already ragged physical condition, the mental strain was hard to take.

"We never questioned the decisions of the Air Ministry. They had their reasons for the action. It should be obvious at this stage that they had suddenly found themselves in the middle of a somewhat embarrassing situation—one they couldn't withdraw from gracefully. They weren't prepared to retract an official combat report that was already on record. And so, for that matter was the claim of the 14th Australian Field Artillery Brigade.

"If the ground claim was completely untenable there would never have been a question. The unfortunate fact is simply this: Roy Brown, unaware of gunfire from the ground, was obliged to suffer in silence. Later, in England, when I saw him at the Savoy in London and casually brought up the subject, he made it clear he didn't care to discuss it. By now he was under fire from many sides. Some believed him, some didn't and, to add injury to insult, he was not permitted to defend his position. It was a closed matter. If ever a man had reason to be bitter, it was Roy Brown, although this wasn't his attitude when I saw him. It's no mystery to me why he refrained from discussing the details of the controversy, even after the war when he was relieved of military restriction. He was so tired of the contention that he didn't feel anything he could say would help matters.

"During the postwar years I occasionally heard of the controversy, but I decided to remain silent. I didn't feel that anything I could add would help the situation. I felt a certain obligation to respect Brown's feelings in the matter. For the past 15 years I've been out of touch with many of my old flying buddies—in fact I hadn't heard of the deaths of Brown and May, although I learned of Sir Francis Mellersh's fatal helicopter accident several years back. Until your inquiry came to me as a bolt out of the blue so to speak, I'd almost forgotten about the great stir Richthofen's death once created—and still seems to be creating. I was the only American in the squadron, so I hesitated to comment. However, as probably the last survivor of 209's pilots who took part in that particular air battle, I believe it's time to look at the facts. At one time this question was well on its way toward becoming an international ruckus between the very nations of the British Empire, and I still didn't think, even then, that it needed any help from a lone Yank volunteer whose two cent's worth probably wouldn't have been considered seriously anyway.

"Naturally, there was always that element of doubt among some of us, despite our strong loyalty to the Royal Air Force. Having brooded over the statements—and misstatements—that were made, I'm still of the opinion that Brown, Mellersh, May and myself had *pretty close* to the right answer at the time. After giving all due credit to the ground personnel there's no question in my mind that the men of 209 were a contributing factor to Richthofen's downfall."

"Then you believe that Richthofen was killed by ground fire?" I ventured.

"I believe," said LeBoutillier soberly, "that we can now reach certain conclusions." He settled back in his chair, stretched his long legs and took a deep breath.

CHAPTER TWENTY-ONE
Brown Was There!

Why did Brown turn away from the chase at the moment a victory seemed assured? Why was he convinced he shot down the red triplane?

LeBoutillier would not answer directly; he paused thoughtfully before he remarked, "Dale, I don't know how far you've delved into this matter or what conclusions you've already drawn about Richthofen's finish, but I assume you intend to reach a conclusion—one way or the other—on this controversy."

"That's the general idea. Certainly there's concrete evidence to prove the manner of death. I've been on the track of this riddle since age 13. A few years ago I started to collect eyewitness accounts and discovered they all said the same thing—substantially." I outlined my correspondence with former Diggers who were on the Morlancourt ridge when Richthofen died.

"And they say Brown wasn't there?"

"Yes and no. Some Australian reports from the vicinity of Vaux and Sailly-le-Sec claim a second Camel was there—at least for a few seconds. Others claim there was no other Camel in sight."

LeBoutillier nodded. "Roy Brown was there. I saw the entire action from overhead and nothing will make me change my mind about it." He said this firmly and without hesitation. "But I believe there's a lot more to the issue than whether or not Brown was present. I'll tell you what I saw—you can draw your own conclusions."

Evidently the former war bird gave considerable

thought to the Richthofen matter. His narrative coincided closely with the main points at issue, but his approach was unlike anything I had encountered before. He had an astonishing ability to pinpoint altitudes, distances and time. His memory rarely failed him and he repeatedly pulled details from the past. As he talked, the parts of the puzzle began to drop into place.

"The Somme River, especially where it makes its sharp bend to the south, was the best landmark in the sector. By the time I reached the vicinity of Vaux, I'd dropped down to eight hundred or a thousand feet and was flying parallel to the Somme and a little on the northeast side of the village. I happened to look off to my left, forward and down, and saw a Camel zigzagging low toward the west and almost over the Somme. Directly behind and slightly above it by not more than three or four plane lengths a red triplane followed doggedly, maneuvering for a burst now and again. I got the impression this was the same triplane I had fired a burst into earlier and which had slipped into a cloud, but I could be mistaken about this with so many red-decorated planes in the air. The Camel was fairly hard pressed; it was wobbling its wings and rocking from side to side in violent maneuvers to shake off the triplane.

"Then, almost immediately, I saw coming in from the right in a steep 45-degree dive at an angle of about 15 or 20 degrees to their flight paths, another Camel with two white stripes around its fuselage. It dropped from about 3,000 feet in a roaring drag as the red triplane kept up its fire on the lead Camel. The second Camel was Brown's—no mistaking it.

"Brown's speed was terrific—at least half again the speed of the two hedgehopping planes over the Somme. In fact, his speed was so great that when he pulled out above and behind the German plane, he had only a very few seconds for firing. I clearly saw his tracers strike the red triplane, and I'd judge he had only time to fire about 40 rounds from both guns. The red triplane immediately pulled up and to the right. In his dive, Brown came as close as two plane lengths, but he overshot quickly and pulled up into a climbing turn to the left. I continued to watch the German aeroplane which, after appearing to falter for a few seconds, leveled out and went back to its original position behind the Camel."

"Still firing?"

LeBoutillier shook his head. "I can't say for certain that he was, although I continued to watch them both. I can't say I saw tracers coming from the triplane after it made its sudden lurch, but this of course doesn't mean the pilot was not firing. It's possible that the remaining bullets in his belts weren't tracers. I simply can't be sure."

"What about head or body movements in the Fokker after Brown's burst. Could you make out anything?"

"I didn't notice activity in the cockpit after Brown fired," LeBoutillier replied, "but of course this doesn't mean the pilot was struck. He may have been concentrating on the Camel."

"What would you estimate their altitude to be?"

"Very low. I'd say under 150 feet."

"Then what happened?"

"I knew the German was now well behind our lines, so I kept my eye on him to see how he was going to escape. I knew I was in an ideal position to go after him if he turned for home. After Brown's burst he must have flown on about a half to three-quarters of a mile. Then he suddenly curved to the northwest and after a few moments, swerved in a north-northeasterly direction and crashed into the ground beside the Bray-Corbie Road. He didn't roll far after he hit."

"At that moment, what was Brown's position?"

"The best I can tell you is that he was south, but exactly how far I don't know. I can assure you though, that at no time was he very far south of the river— probably not more than a few hundred yards at the time of the triplane's impact."

"Didn't it seem a little unusual that there was such a long time and distance between Brown's firing and the crash?" I asked.

"In a dogfight," LeBoutillier explained, "trying to estimate time in the battle excitement is a difficult thing. Seconds are stretched into minutes and minutes jammed into seconds. Things tend to get out of proportion. In studying the map later, you can get a better perspective. After Brownie pulled out, I'd estimate that it was about 20 to 25 seconds before the triplane turned in a northeasterly direction and another 15 to 20 seconds before it crashed. Certainly it wasn't more than a minute from the time Brownie fired and the impact occurred. I'd say about 45 seconds."

"What about the theory that Brown may have been in a position to fire on the Fokker a second time?"

"That's definitely out," LeBoutillier ruled emphatically. "In the first place Brown never said he fired a second time, and in the second place his climbing turn put him too far away from the Fokker for another pass. At the time of the crash I saw Mellersh ahead and slightly to the north of me. He hadn't as yet overshot the crash site and his Camel was nearest. I was now down to 500 feet, and as I came over the crash I made a 180-degree turn to the right and then a 90-degree turn to the left and headed for base."

"Do you recall whether the triplane's propeller was turning when it hit the ground?" I asked.

"I can't say for certain, but I have the impression that the triplane had slowed considerably after its curve to the northeast and northwest, so apparently it was in a glide before it struck. No one can say whether the engine was damaged seriously or the pilot had time to cut the ignition before landing, though the propeller could have been turning over because of inertia and the plane's forward speed. I'm afraid there are many questions to which we'll never have the answers."

"So that's how it happened. Pretty much as earlier reports indicated. Still . . . it doesn't make sense. You say that Brown *did* dive on the red triplane; the Australians on the ridge swear there was no third plane following. There's still a contradiction."

"No," LeBoutillier smiled, "there really isn't. Brown was there all right, but the Australians also have a point.

It may sound confusing, but actually it hinges on something else. There's an explanation."

"But what about the weather question? The Australians said it was good and the air reports indicate it was bad."

"Actually, both reports were substantially correct—as far as they go. Visibility to the ground observer isn't the same visibility to the airman. As a pilot, you've no doubt had the experience of taking off from a field with apparently good visibility only to find it reduced to almost nothing at a few hundred feet of altitude. Weather is a funny thing."

"Then what's the answer?"

"Let's continue in sequence," LeBoutillier suggested. "There's more to this story."

CHAPTER TWENTY-TWO

The Missing Moment

"The exact set of conditions under which Richthofen was killed would be impossible to duplicate, Dale. And it was these very conditions that caused the misunderstandings. Without compromising the situation, let me say that I've always regarded Richthofen's death as a joint Allied effort, and personally I don't believe any one person can claim the sole credit for putting him out of action. If it wasn't for 209 Squadron and some member of that squadron whose maneuvering somehow worked the German ace into an outside position where he saw May as a sitting duck, Richthofen would not have been lured low behind our lines, and the Australian gunners would not have had the opportunity to get a crack at him. Normally, Richthofen would not have allowed himself to become caught in such a trap.

"The question of visibility? I believe under the circumstances that an airman was in the best position to see the entire flying picture, even with the haze. This must be so, for I saw Brown dive on Richthofen near Vaux and pull away, while the diggers on the Morlancourt Ridge over a mile away apparently did not. Either the full attention of the waiting gunners was entirely narrowed to Richthofen and May as they came through the haze, or Brown's high-speed dive across, behind and away from Richthofen, simply wasn't considered to be part of the chase. You remember that several Australians near Vaux and the front lines *did* report Brown's dive on the Fokker. So when the Australians say no third plane

263

followed Richthofen, they're absolutely correct. Of course Brown couldn't have 'followed' Richthofen in the manner that the triplane was pursuing May—the speed of Brown's dive didn't permit it. He only had time to make a quick pass, fire briefly, then curve off. It would have been impossible for him to have stayed on the Baron's tail at that time.

"Another thing. There were *four* Camels nearby when Richthofen crashed. Brown, May, Mellersh and myself. But the ground troops said there weren't any other planes nearby. In the haze at the levels through which we were flying, and at the slant angle at which they would have had to look to see us, they simply overlooked us. I recall that one newspaper report said May turned back over the crash site and the gun battery[1] to observe the wreck before flying to base. So did I, and any intermittent observer might easily have mistaken my Camel for May's, which was by now flying directly for Bertangles. While Richthofen was swerving and gliding down for the crash, May pulled out of the picture and I came into it—while most eyes were fixed on the crippled triplane. Shortly after the crash I made a 180- and a 90-degree turn over the spot and then flew for base. So when the Australians say their horizontal visibility was good, it probably was. Obviously it was good enough for their needs that morning. Under these circumstances, then, both air and ground versions were correct. Even in perfectly clear weather there were times when we returned home in such a way as to be hidden from the German and Allied troops in that hilly area. We simply flew below the dikes of the Somme. It was dangerously low of course, but it served our purpose.

"When Brown dived, fired his quick burst and overshot, Richthofen was said to have turned in his cockpit and looked back. I saw Brown's tracers hit the triplane so naturally Richthofen glanced around to see where they were coming from. His sudden pull-up to the right

---

[1] There is no evidence that May did this.

was probably no more than an evasive maneuver to escape Brown's line of fire. And considering Richthofen's remarkable ability to make a snap judgment in a pressing situation, he reasoned that Brown's high speed would quickly carry the Camel out of range and remove the threat until he could finish off May.

"The crux of the matter is this. As soon as Brownie made his pass and saw the tracers enter the triplane, he began his climbing turn to the left. His right wing blanketed out what followed. He didn't see Richthofen settle back down on May's tail. Unaware of the deceptive time element, Roy Brown held his Camel in the turn during those critical 20 or 25 seconds of the chase—as May led Richthofen over the Australian battery. When he leveled out, turned to the right and looked down, it was in time to witness Richthofen's stagger and crash. Naturally he assumed his bullets had got him."

"The possibility of ground fire never entered his mind," I suggested.

"Pilots rarely looked for ground fire," LeBoutillier said. "Had I been in Brown's position I would have arrived at the same conclusion. As it was, Brownie made a simple mistake by his last maneuver. He lost sight of his target. I've sometimes thought of it as the 'Missing Moment.'" If he hadn't turned so that his wing obstructed his view, he would have realized the German pilot was still very much in the fight."

"So Brown didn't see the triplane until it was in its death glide."

"Apparently not," LeBoutillier agreed. "My impression was that he held his climbing turn that long."

"But what about Brown's combat report—that the red triplane 'went down vertical?'" I asked. "Then there's his statement that he 'fired on two more but didn't get them.'"

"I have no idea why he said the aeroplane went straight in unless it appeared that way as he zoomed up. As to the other two machines he said he fired on, well, no doubt he did and this could have occurred at any time during the scrap, even before he dived on Richthofen. I assume that's what happened, because he came in shortly after the crash."

"That covers the air action, Boots, but what are your thoughts on the ground action. What do you think happened on the ridge?"

"As I understand the ground reports, the gunners saw splinters flying from the aeroplane. In the air we rarely saw this when firing on an enemy, unless some large part of the plane separated, such as a wing or tail surface. But if splinters flew, the gunners must have been concentrating very intently on the machine or firing point-blank. Then there are the reports that Richthofen was still firing past Vaux and right up until the gunners opened up on him. If this is so, the gunners must have got him. It's true that Brown's tracers entered the red machine, but whether they damaged the plane's controls isn't for me to say.

"The medical reports were in disagreement. Some said Richthofen was killed by a bullet fired from the air; some said ground fire was responsible. The fatal bullet through his chest entered behind the right armpit and made its exit *slightly higher* and below the left nipple. I'm positive Brown did not drop below Richthofen and fire up into the cockpit or even level with it, nor was his fire at such an angle as the fatal bullet's path. No, the combined actions of May and Brown, as well as other members of 209, put the great man into the position to receive the fatal blow from elsewhere."

Boots dipped his hand into an open briefcase beside his chair and withdrew a photograph of a piece of autographed fabric. "Here's something few people have seen. Shortly after Richthofen was killed, this piece of fabric was torn from his machine and brought to 209 Squadron where it was signed by those who took part in the fight. As you can see by the writing across the top, there was no doubt by the squadron pilots as to how Richthofen was put out of action."

It read: '*Fabric from triplane which was used by B. von Richthofen when shot down by*'—then followed the signature *A.R. Brown* and those of ten other squadron pilots. It was dated 21. 4. 18.

"As you can see," LeBoutillier pointed out, "this is documentary evidence that only 11 pilots of 209 tangled with the Circus that morning—instead of the 15 often claimed. Through no fault of their own, four did not take part."

The signatures of Redgate and Drake, the two who were forced out of the engagement, as well as those of Edwards and Lomas, were absent.

"Neither the R.A.F. nor the Australian ground forces were able to comprehend the whole picture at the time. It's unfortunate, because they could have saved these many years of argument. I see no reason for making an issue of it now, for in his own mind Roy Brown had reason for his claim and I or any other pilot would have believed as he did under the circumstances. Conditions developed in such a way as to make the young Canadian appear foolish, but there was never cause to doubt his sincerity.

"The next day several of us got into lorries and went to Bertangles to represent 209 at the funeral. We weren't able to view the remains. While the services were conducted we stood outside the cemetery and watched over the tall hedge directly opposite the open grave. Richthofen was buried with full military honors and the service ended with several rifle volleys over the grave by a squad of Australian Flying Corps men from Number 3 Squadron."

There it was—the complete story. Having delivered the much-needed parts to the puzzle, LeBoutillier leaned back in his chair.

Late in the afternoon, Boots saw me aboard my plane. As I turned for a parting handshake with the striking figure, I sensed the heroic spirit of that glorious corps of five decades ago, and of one man in particular—a daring youth with bushy hair and a cocky grin who mounted the war-torn skies on shaky wings. I think it was the same spirit that tells a fighter pilot to seek out and destroy the enemy, not wait for the enemy to come to him. The men of World War One have left a proud heritage—the heritage of fighting men down the long corridors of time.

"Boots, for more than 20 years I've waited to hear this story. I've often wondered if I'd find the answers."

A short time later, as I was seated comfortably in an eastbound airliner at 21,000 feet, my thoughts wandered over the past three days with Boots. There came to mind a striking similiarity between something he said and the words Roy Brown wrote to the editor of Australia's *Reveille* magazine in November of 1930. I thumbed through my case and found it.

> As far as I am concerned, I know in my own mind what happened, and the war being over, the job being done, there is nothing to be gained by arguing back and forth as to who did this and who did that. The main point is that, from the standpoint of the troops in the war, we gained our objective.

POSTSCRIPTS

CHAPTER TWENTY-THREE

Postscripts

Still ahead for J.G.I were the days that would decide the war; despairing weeks of gray skies, wet earth, gloom and more empty places at the squadron mess. Under Reinhard, Richthofen's successor, the predominently red scheme of the planes was toned down for more subdued colors.

On April 25, German infantry made its final attempt to attack in the direction of Amiens. The Australian line held firm. By July 1, Rawlinson's Army had grown to 512,000 men, and a hundred thousand of these went over the top in the first assault. With their capture of Hamel on July 4th the tide was turned.

The weeks passed with violence. The summer of 1918 was the most brutal, the most terrible, the most bloody. It ended—as the German General Staff was long convinced it would end—in total defeat. The Air Service drew little comfort in the knowledge that the months between April and the Armistice failed to produce an Allied aviator to equal Richthofen's score.

Perhaps you wonder, as I did, about the long-delayed homage the mourning Fatherland paid its young Siegfried of the Air, and what became of those men who took part in the events of April 21, 1918. Here is what I have been able to record:

Twice in the postwar years, the remains of Germany's wartime hero were exhumed and reinterred. Soon after the Armistice Manfred's body was taken from the

French cemetery at Bertangles and with small ceremony was reburied 20 miles to the east. Samuel B. Eckert, an American who served with the 80th and 84th Squadrons, RAF, was an honorary pallbearer.[1] Here, at Fricourt, in the midst of thousands of his fallen countrymen, he found temporary rest.

During the early Twenties the Baroness Freifrau von Richthofen negotiated with French officials for the return of her son's body to his beloved country home in Silesia. There, in a churchyard cemetery of Schweidnitz rested Father Richthofen who died soon after the war, and Lothar, who had survived the war with 40 victories only to become the victim of a 1922 air crash.

In November of 1925, Karl Bolko, Manfred's youngest brother, made the cheerless journey to France with the necessary authorization to exhume his brother's body and return with it to Germany. Word of his coming had been sent ahead, but when he arrived at the cemetery under a darkening, gloomy sky he was greeted with the distressing news that the officials were not prepared for the exhumation. Herr Richthofen queried the caretaker, an elderly Frenchman retired from the noncommissioned ranks, but was answered with a shrug. Of the 18,000 men buried there, 6,000 were identified soldiers in individual graves; the remainder rested in a great common grave. To the caretaker, the remains of the soldier in question were simply one among the thousands; the ace's former glory was of little importance now.

After a frustrating delay, Karl Bolko walked with the caretaker and an official of the War Graves Commission to find his brother's plot. They trudged back and forth along the endless rows of white crosses, pausing here and there to examine more closely those inscriptions that were faded and weather-worn. Somewhere in this very earth over which the great flier had fought during his last days, he rested in a grave marked with a plain

---

[1] Mr. Eckert is a resident of Philadelphia, Pennsylvania, today.

wooden cross. An overcast, gray-leaden sky and a chill wind added discomfort to the dismal search.

At last they found a cross to which was nailed a zinc plate—the identification plaque that was nailed to Manfred's coffin by the men of Number 3 Squadron. Grave diggers set to work as a steady drizzle began to fall.

The coffin was uncovered within the hour and found to be in an advanced state of deterioration. Extreme care was needed in raising it. Despite the seven intervening years, however, identification of the body from the clothing and features, was positive.

In this sad moment Karl Bolko did not tarry. He instructed that the remains be wrapped in the appropriate burial raiment and placed in the new zinc casket he had brought. Partly as an afterthought, Bolko picked up the cross and placed it beside the casket.

The remains were taken to Albert on a motor vehicle and, with the final papers cleared, transferred to a goods wagon for the rail journey to Strasbourg.

At midnight, November 16, Manfred von Richthofen returned to his homeland. The train rumbled slowly over the great Rhine bridge and coasted quietly into Kehl station. Rumors preceded the train's arrival and had reached the ears of the few railway workers on duty at that hour. Solemnly they removed their hats as they gathered on the platform, for this was not an ordinary train. In hushed silence they transferred the casket to a German wagon and gently cushioned it on a bed of fir branches. Over and around it the attendants heaped floral wreaths held in readiness for this moment.

From the beginning, the required clearance at the government level attracted the attention of German officialdom. When von Hindenburg learned that his nation's famous son was returning at last he respectfully claimed the remains in the name of the German nation and ordered that a place of honor be prepared in Berlin as the airman's final resting place.

All day of the 16th the casket remained in Kehl. That evening there began a low and mournful tolling of church bells as a torchlight procession wound its way through the town. Here, former war pilots of J.G.I assembled to escort the casket to Berlin.

Wherever the train paused along the route—Karlsruhe, Darmstadt, Frankfurt—crowds of reverent citizens, war veterans among them, thronged the station platforms to pay homage. The train steamed slowly through other towns between groups of bareheaded patriots and everywhere along the way the German flag hung at half staff. In Potsdam the car doors were opened to reveal the dull metal casket heaped high with floral tributes and attended by its honor guard. Another torchlight procession escorted the gun carriage that carried the remains to the Gnadenkirche of Berlin, where the body lay in state.

Banks of flowers over black bunting draped the bier and against the foot of the casket rested the simple wooden Cross of Fricourt. Before this, on a black satin pillow, were the Rittmeister's decorations—25 in all—including the *Ordre Pour le merite* and the First and Second Order of the Iron Cross. Atop the casket lay his cavalry sword and Uhlan helmet.

For two days reverent countrymen filed slowly past the bier. Princes and Princesses of the Old Empire walked with citizens of the German Republic. Britons and Americans attended the state service on the 20th.

Two honor guards surrounded the flower-banked catafalque—18 silent men who were once the young nobleman's flying comrades. Former Allied pilots who exchanged gunfire with the famed ace over the Western front were among those who paid their solemn respects. The sea of mourners overflowed into the streets.

When the solemn church services ended, the casket was lighted by eight officers of the *Order Pour le merite*, carried from the church and placed on the waiting gun carriage. The Baroness was guided from the church by Karl Bolko. They took their place behind a horse-drawn gun carriage of the Ninth Prussian Infantry Regiment and walked a step ahead of former Field Marshal von Hindenburg who was now the President of the unstable German Republic. Behind him, in sober measured steps, followed other members of the Richthofen family and state dignitaries. After these came the survivors of Jagdgeschwader I and Eskadron Nr. 3, First Uhlan Regiment.

To the slow beat of muffled drums the procession moved through the Berlin gate, led by a steel-helmeted soldier carrying the deceased's glittering decorations. It was the most widely attended service in the history of the German capital.

At Invaliden Cemetery the carriage halted and the casket was borne to an open grave. Amid the glorious presence of other national heroes, sons and soldiers, Manfred von Richthofen was given final rest. The casket was slowly lowered and at the close of the graveside rites von Hindenburg cast a handful of German earth onto the casket.

The following October the Baroness stood quietly again at her son's grave, surrounded with heads of state. She unveiled a flat stone placed there and with the accompaniment of a military band hundreds of German voices rose in *Deutschland über Alles*. A sharp volley of rifle fire echoed over the stone rows.

In 1938 the flat marker was replaced with a larger, more imposing monument. It was unveiled by the last commander of J.G.I, the man who was now *Generalfeldmarschall* of the Luftwaffe—Hermann Goering.

It was on April 21, 1933, the 15th anniversary of Manfred's death, that the big house at Schweidnitz became the Richthofen Museum, a shrine for the nation's air-minded youth and future flying officers. Here the Baroness displayed the medals, letters, pictures and souvenirs of both her warrior sons; scraps of fabric, airplane numbers, captured machine guns, instruments, Major Hawker's engine—and the 60 silver victory cups.

In the closing days of World War II, the Russian advance threatened to engulf the Silesian manor house. On a January midnight in 1945 the aged noblewoman quickly gathered some clothes and food by the light of a candle and awakened Ilse and some children who were in their care. Outside a heavy snow was falling and the temperature dropped to four degrees below zero. With each passing hour the Russian artillery grew louder. The Richthofens had the remarkably good fortune to obtain a car and all crowded into the small vehicle for the dash to safety. In recalling the escape she wrote in 1959:

> The Russians had crossed the Oder and we were forced to stop and wait with every car we encountered for fear it might be a Russian one!
> Now you ask me whether I have saved my son's chandelier fashioned from an aircraft engine, Major Hawker's machine-gun and other souvenirs! We saved nothing but our lives—and we heard the Russian machine-guns firing behind us!

The contents of the museum were seized by the advancing Russian infantry. They ransacked the rooms, packed the relics and shipped them into the Russian interior where all record of their whereabouts has been lost. Attempts by the West German Government to recover them have failed.

The Baroness found haven in Weisbaden where she remained until her death in the early 1960s. Manfred's only sister, Ilse, is also dead, but Karl Bolko, a successful businessman, still lives in West Germany.

On November 6, 1918, J.G.I, under Goering, fought its last battle in the skies and three Spads were downed. Five days later as Adjutant Karl Bodenschatz was moving to the rear with his ground crews, the pilots surrendered their D.VII's to a French Commission.

Bodenschatz remained in the service. In 1933, as a Major, he was transferred to Goering's command and became his Chief Minister. Bodenschatz's book, *Jagd in Flanderns Himmel*, was published in 1935 and served to inspire many German youths to join the newly revived Richthofen Geschwader that served the Luftwaffe so dramatically during World War II. Promoted to Major-General in 1938, he helped build the Luftwaffe for the coming war, during which he was Verbindungsoffizier for Goering in Hitler's headquarters.

On July 20, 1944, when the attempted assassination of the Fuhrer occurred, he was next to the bomb and was badly wounded. In 1940 Bodenschatz became General of the Air Force. He resides today in West Germany.

Hauptmann Reinhard, Richthofen's choice as J.G.I Commander in the event of his death, soon went the way of his leader. It happened at the Second Fighter Competition at Adlershof in July. Competing manufacturers periodically assembled their latest designs, and it was standard practice for front-line fighter pilots to test them under simulated combat conditions and approve the better ones.

Reinhard drew a rakish-looking biplane of revolutionary design—a Dornier D.I. It had no interplane struts and was largely constructed of aluminum—a radical departure in aircraft construction. At 3,000 feet the wings suddenly sheared away and the fuselage plummeted to earth, killing the pilot.

Ernst Udet ended the war as the Fatherland's second-ranking ace. He barnstormed, built airplanes, flew camera planes for film companies in Africa, Europe and Greenland. In America during the 1930s he flew at the Cleveland National Air Races and in Hollywood he thrilled thousands in his tiny *Flamingo* stunt plane. While in the film capital he heard from Fox Films.

One of their agents asked me to attend an interview. We went at once to the point. "We want to shoot a Richthofen film and we need a technical adviser," he said, and mentioned a fantastic fee.

I thought for a few moments. Richthofen? No! It was too big a theme for Hollywood.

"Sorry, can't be done," I said.

The agent shrugged his shoulders. "A pity," he said. But he did not press me to reconsider my decision, nor did he ask my reasons for refusing. He was completely objective and unsentimental. Typical American.

"Have a drink," he said.

This time I did not refuse.

Friction and serious political intrigue developed between Udet and Manfred von Richthofen's cousin. Wolfram von Richthofen, who saw the end of the war with eight victories, left the service in 1920, returned within five years and served as a cavalry and artillery officer. In 1933 the Luftwaffe beckoned and within four years he was in Spain as Chief of Staff of the Legion Condor. He was a Colonel at its deactivation in 1939.

When the Polish war broke out, Wolfram was promoted to Major-General in command of the *Nahkampf-Flieger-Division* (Stukas). His Luftarmee very nearly annihilated the defenders of Warsaw for which he gained the nickname *Puma 1* (Puma First). After campaigns in the Balkans, France and the Russian front, he became a Colonel-General and from June of 1942 to June of 1943 commanded *Luftflotte 4* on the southern sector of the Eastern front. He held his command during the siege of Stalingrad when his Junkers Ju 88s pummeled the city nearly to ashes. Hitler promoted him to *Generalfeldmarschall*, and von Richthofen commanded *Luftflotte 2* in Italy until October of 1944. His last assignments were with the Supreme Command Group of the Luftwaffe.

Wolfram's life was filled with political and military intrigue. He was described as a fanatical Nazi, a worshiper of Hitler and the Führer's pet. He had many enemies, among them his former flying comrade, Ernst Udet, who was not a party member and who could not stomach the cruelties of the Nazi regime.

In 1936, after several drinks, Udet confided to a house guest: "After the 'Night of the Long Knives' in July of 1934, when many of my friends were assassinated, Hitler appointed Wolfram as the Gestapo's representative to the Air Ministry and Luftwaffe. He was directly responsible to the Führer. Although Baron von Richthofen (Wolfram) was my friend in J.G.I, he is my malicious enemy now."

Udet's dislike for Wolfram von Richthofen, Goering, State Secretary Milch and other top Nazis preyed on his sensitive nature. Udet had allowed himself to be pushed into high position—*Generalluftkriegmeister*—and he knew he had permitted many decisions to be made for him. When it was clear that the Luftwaffe had failed in its avowed boast to level England, Milch and Goering (with Wolfram's assistance no doubt), sought a scapegoat in Udet. Under their pressure and growing intrigues he became so frustrated that he ended his life in November of 1941.

Of Wolfram's death, there are conflicting reports. One says he shot himself to death with a Walther in May of 1945 when he learned of his Führer's suicide. But another report lists his death on July 7, 1945, in Bad Ischl, Austria, following an unsuccessful brain tumor operation.

Sunday, April 21, 1968, was *Richthofen Tag* in West Germany. At Wittmundhaffen Air Base, West German Fighter Squadron 71—today's counterpart of J.G.I—was host to the remaining members of Richthofen's band. Colonel Horst Dieter Kallerhoff spoke the words that have been repeated to three generations and thousands of young German fliers; that they may be called upon to fight in the shadow of Richthofen and should, for their country's survival, be ready to follow his example. He praised his nation's hero as a great soldier, a great comrade and a chivalrous flier. "This Richthofen spirit has set an example for fliers of all nations, and to us it spells the obligation to be as ready for battle as possible in order to help prevent another terrible war."

Present at the roll-call ceremony were the distinguished men of J.G.I, that ever-dwindling group of fearless, once-dashing airmen who, 50 years earlier were, like Richthofen, the pride of Imperial Germany with their leather jackets, goggles and streaming scarves. On this day they wore sunglasses and suits of military cut. Some wore beards and a few carried canes. General der Flieger Karl Bodenschatz, now 77, was present. At his side was Air Chief Marshal Sir Robert Foster, 71. Overhead in a dazzling air display were jets of nations allied with West Germany.

D. G. Lewis returned to Rhodesia and took a position with the Department of Native Affairs. In the years that followed the war he kept in touch with former members of the Royal Air Force.

In 1938 he was invited to Germany for the dedication of the new Richthofen Geschwader. On arrival at the Döberitz Aerodrome he was greeted by the commander, Colonel von Massow, who escorted Richthofen's 80th victory through the hangars to inspect the new machines—the famous Messerschmitt 109s. A representative of the Air Ministry told Lewis that if Reichmarschal Goering and Chancellor Hitler were not in Czechoslovakia at that time, one or the other would have greeted him.

After the inspection von Massow escorted Lewis to the officer's mess, crowded with squadron pilots. Recalling this moment 39 years later, Lewis said:

> I had no idea there was anything special about my visit and I naturally fell back from my host to join Group Captain Coope, who was the British Air Attaché in Berlin. He suggested that I rejoin the Colonel but before I could do so, I heard the Colonel call out for "Herr Leutnant Lewis!" I joined him at his table at which were gathered some of the squadron officers. A short time afterward he rose and called upon those at his table to drink to my health and he clinked glasses with me two or three times after saying something in German.

Lewis corresponded with Roy Brown on one occasion to inquire if the Canadian intended to take part in the impending war. Brown replied in the negative, and mentioned nothing of his encounter with Richthofen.

Later Under-Secretary, Administration, for the Department of Native Affairs, Lewis retired in 1958 at age 60 and resides with his wife in Salisbury.

The old 1918 Poulainville and Bertangles Aerodromes that once resounded with spinning, popping rotary engines and swarms of gawky reconnaissance machines is now one large, silent farm. Atop the Morlancourt spur, the old brickyards, rebuilt, enlarged, and with a more imposing brick stack, is again in operation on the same site.

Major-General Leslie Beavis, now 71 and retired in Victoria, retains a vivid recollection of the spectacular fall of Richthofen. He continued his command of the 53rd during the Allied counteroffensive, carried the battery through Hamel and Chuignes and took part in the capture of Peronne.

A career officer, Beavis returned to Australia to serve as an artillery instructor, then went to England for advanced studies and to serve in Intelligence. During the two decades between wars, when the Richthofen controversy flared forth in the press, Beavis was prompted to reiterate his impressions from the ridge for that morning. He has steadfastly maintained that the responsible gunners were Buie and Evans.

When World War II broke out he was a Colonel and a year later was made Brigadier-General. Early in the war he served in Egypt and the Middle East and later, in Australia, he was Master-General of Army Ordnance. In 1947 Beavis was instrumental in planning the Woomera Rocket Test Range in Central Australia. One of the most brilliant technical and administrative officers of the Australian Military Forces, he remains active as a tireless writer on military affairs.

"Horrie" Hart was one of the Battery's two sergeants who saw 28 months of war service, uninterrupted by illness or wounds. He took part in the battles at Ypres, the Somme and Villiers-Brettoneaux. He holds the Military Medal. Partial deafness from gun concussion was his only disability.

The Sergeant's talent for expression led to his selection as the battery's official war historian. The task completed in 1919, he returned to Australia to his former job on the Railways.

In full possession of the facts, Hart could not keep still

when the rash of newspaper articles sparked arguments about Richthofen's death. Gradually the ex-digger's patience wore thin.

"When former Sergeant Les McEvoy of our Battery originated the controversy in the *Evening Sun* in the late 20s, I held my fire," Hart says today. "Some of the claims put forth were simply ridiculous. Finally I decided to enter the fray. I wrote to the *Sun* but my letter, which would have put the issue beyond doubt, was not published. I saw Les McEvoy and complained. Sensations were in short supply at the time and McEvoy told me himself that he originated the controversy for this reason. He said, 'Things were slack, Horrie, so I started the brawl.'

"Les knew as well as I did how the airman met his end."

Hart retired from the Railways in 1959 at the age of 70, and he and his wife reside in Sydney.

Gunner Buie watched the final futile attempt of the German infantry in its frontal assult on Amiens. From his perch on the ridge he saw the waves of soldiers stopped cold with Australian bayonets and machine-gun fire, and felt the ground shocks as round after round of H.E. arced from the 18-pounders. Buie saw the growing Allied build-up that was soon to hurl the British armies across the Somme trenches and into Germany and victory. But he was not to become a part of the victorious force.

At 3:00 A.M. on July 4th, the 5th Australian Infantry Division went "over the top" in the long-awaited push. Hamel was among the first of the villages to fall as the 53rd backed up the advancing diggers. The Prussian military situation deteriorated rapidly and Ludendorf called August 8th the "black day of the German Army ..." It was also a black day for Robert Buie, for that night he was carried, unconscious, to the rear. When he regained consciousness in a field hospital he realized that for him the war was over. At his request he was discharged in 1919—but without compensation for his infirmity.

The Australian press kept the "Who killed Richthofen?" controversy raging from 1925 to 1929. One Saturday in January of 1928 a small, wiry, sunburned ex-gunner stalked into the editorial office of the *Sydney Daily Mirror* and slapped a copy of a telegram on the desk.

"I'm Gunner Buie," he said, "and I've been reading the letters and articles in the papers—all about who shot Richthofen, and who didn't. I'm fed up with this argument and now I'm going to have a word myself."

Buie's document was convincing. It was an official copy of the telegram sent to Hobbs from Rawlinson. The editor was impressed, but the journalists decided there was still a well of sensationalism to be tapped and the controversy continued.

When Buie was readmitted to Randwick Military Hospital for further examinations in 1938 the verdict was unchanged: *not due to war service*. The former gunner could not understand the reasoning of the authorities for he was declared physically fit when he enlisted. His bitterness grew, especially when doctors warned him not to do any kind of work. But now, with a wife and children to fend for, Robert Buie put his family foremost and continued to work as best he could. He had a small piece of land near Calga and from there he doggedly struggled to provide for his wife, two sons and five daughters.

In 1952 Buie made a final attempt to obtain a soldier's pension and was again refused. When he reached the age of 60 he was granted an old-age pension which was supplemented a few years later with an invalid pension. At 66 he went into full retirement at his "humble old place in the Bush."

Those who knew Bob Buie took him to have a quiet and unassuming disposition. In a crowd the slight, bespectacled man could have passed for a bank clerk, but a close look at his hands would have marked him as a man of the outdoors. Thousands of tiny scars covered his leathery palms and fingers, the result of 53 years of constant cuts from needle-sharp fish fins.

In 1956 and 1957 he entered the Richthofen controversy again to answer other claimants and try to set the record straight. He never dwelled on his war deed, calmly confident that he was the only one with the official document—and he was.

Early on the morning of April 25, 1964—Anzac Day in Australia—while thousands of ex-diggers from three wars marched in the Dawn Services to commemorate the invasion of Gallipoli by the Anzacs, Robert Buie lay dead, adrift in his small dinghy. The 70-year old veteran suffered a heart attack hours earlier while fishing alone in Mooney Mooney Creek just north of White Mount. He was found by his son, Douglas, who became concerned when his father failed to return from a fishing trip down river. Thus, 46 years later, very nearly to the day of the death of the German ace whom he was instrumental in taking from the skies, Robert Buie was laid to rest at Brooklyn on the Hawkesbury. Gordon Allen, of Calga, had this to say of his small, suntanned friend: "He was always a quiet sort of chap. It was generally considered around these parts that he could have shot down Richthofen . . . but he never boasted about it."

Of William John Evans little is known after his return to Australia. He was seen occasionally on the streets of Sydney by former soldiers, but in all likelihood he became an itinerant. The Australian war historian, Bean, notes simply that he died in April of 1925 at age 34.

Sergeant Popkin was wounded during heavy action at Buscourt on June 18th. He lost one leg and after being fitted with an artificial limb was discharged. He retired as postmaster of Tyalgum after World War II and passed away at Tweed River in June of 1968.

Interviewed by the press during one of the Richthofen revivals, the late ex-Vickers gunner politely and patiently referred newsmen to the *Official History of the A.I.F.* In 1966, at age 75, Popkin said, "I saw red on the publication of Gibbon's book: *The Red Knight of Germany*, which set out to prove that Captain Brown shot Richthofen down, when in fact he was not within a mile of the place!"

Rupert Weston, Popkin's Number 2 man on the gun that day, lives in Campbellton, New South Wales. George Ridgway lives in Lang Lang, New South Wales, and recalls vividly today: "There's no doubt Richthofen was alive and not wounded until the last second when his head fell sideways." Ex-gunner Ray McDiarmid lives in Moruya, New South Wales. Donald L. Fraser returned to Australia to become a colliery owner, assayer and metallurgist. Writing on the 42nd anniversary of Richthofen's death he said, "In the past I have written frequent letters to many parts of the world in an effort to correct the report claimed by the Canadian Roy Brown." Fraser died in Queensland in 1963.

In July of 1969, in a ceremony sponsored by the local Royal Canadian Legion in Carleton Place, Roy Brown's memory was assured a niche in the annals of Canadian history. A plaque, recognizing him as "Victor in aerial combat over Baron Manfred von Richthofen—was unveiled in Memorial Park by his widow and brother. It marked a stubbornly persistent belief that has survived 51 years, through the storm of controversy laced with international reverberations.

Within a few days of Richthofen's death, Brown, frustrated and distraught with the vagaries of military politics, found his troubles multiplied. To the strain of a stomach perpetually knotted against a battle-weary determination to hang on to his convictions, was added a serious case of influenza. The young man finally collapsed under the nervous and physical pressure. He was placed on the critical list and for three weeks was semidelirious. He remained in hospital until late June of 1918 and when physicians declared him fit for duty he was posted—not to France—but to the RAF Number 2 School of Fighting as a combat instructor. It was there the Prince of Wales pinned an additional Bar on his Distinguished Service Cross.

But Roy Brown was not fit for duty of any nature. A few weeks later, while flying alone at 500 feet, his airplane was seen to power-dive into the English countryside. When an ambulance arrived at the wreckage the medics found a totally smashed machine with the huddled form of the pilot still in the wreckage. They lowered the badly mangled body to the grass and a medical officer bent over it. He shook his head slowly. Brown's neck was broken in three places and seven vertabrae were cracked. Both lungs were punctured, there were severe lacerations on his head and face. His skull was fractured. If the examination was hasty it was because his pitifully broken body was obviously lifeless.

The medic closed his bag and stood up. "This chap's gone, I'm afraid." He stepped back and closed his bag as attendants lifted Brown's body onto a stretcher and pushed it into the back of the ambulance. Before the medic mounted the cab he glanced back at the heap of twisted metal, fabric and wood. "Odd," he mused, "that it didn't burn ... or explode." Then he waved the driver on to the base morgue.

As the body awaited preparations for burial, a close friend of Brown, a fellow pilot from his home town, entered the morgue. He stood quietly over the still form and then noticed a faint coloring in Brown's face. He touched the airman's hand. It was neither cold nor deathlike. Then he saw that blood was still seeping, pulselike, from the wounds. This meant heart action— and he hurriedly summoned a doctor. Medics bent over the body and worked quickly to fan the faint spark of life, and instead of a short ride to the cemetery in a stained pine box, Roy Brown spent the next 18 months in hospital.

He could not recall the Armistice, nor did he have any recollection of the plunge and crash in his training plane. On occasion, when asked about it, he would simply shrug and reply vaguely "I don't really know ... I suppose I just blacked out ..."

With D.S.C. and Bar, he was placed on the Retired List of the Royal Air Force on April 9, 1919. When he returned to Canada, thin and weak, he quietly took a position with a chartered accountancy. He married Edith Moneypenny and settled in Toronto where they raised two daughters and a son.

As long as he lived, the ghost of the Richthofen affair lingered. He suffered unreasonable abuse at the hands of a sensation-seeking press and ill-informed war veterans. Letters of inquiry about the war's most famous kill came to his mailbox regularly. Most were cordial and held warm praise—but there was a surprising number of abusive missiles from Germans who accused him of murdering the Fatherland's hero. Against his wishes Brown became the center of a renewed controversy. After Richthofen's reburial in 1925, threats against the former war pilot increased, due largely to an irresponsible report published in the German *Lauber Neuste Nachrichten* that Brown had merely forced the ace to land unharmed, but before he could leave his plane Canadian infantrymen mercilessly gunned him down. Close friends in Toronto cautioned Brown about a plot that was growing among German groups in Detroit and he was advised to keep a revolver within ready reach. Brown scoffed at the idea.

Whenever he could do so, Brown tried to clarify the story through the same press that mercilessly exploited the incident at the expense of the veteran's integrity. He soon came to realize that his repeated defenses were of no avail; they only stirred the dust for the war of words that was yet to come in 1927 and 1928. The wrangle became full blown with the publication of a sensationalized ghost-written series that appeared in American and Canadian newspapers under the titles: *My Fight with Richthofen* and *The Death of Richthofen.* They were allegedly written with Brown's knowledge and cooperation, but he later denied this and said he never read the papers. When LeBoutillier saw copies for the first time in 1960, he shook his head. "This doesn't sound like something Roy would write. He wasn't inclined to dramatize things."

The hassle kept Brown on the defensive and grew worse with Floyd Gibbons's imaginative account of the fight in his book, *The Red Knight of Germany*. Everything published thus far gave the credit to Brown—and Australians were hopping mad. The Canadian corresponded with former members of the Australian Corps and the editor of the veteran's publication, *Reveille*, but nothing was settled. The clamor wearied Brown, who wanted to forget the entire matter. His nervous stomach returned to harrass him.

In the late 1920s Brown became a director and sales manager of a Toronto paint and varnish firm. He resigned in 1934 to organize General Airways Limited, a small mail service. He did not become active in the flying part of the venture and the business folded just before the outbreak of World War II. Brown, now 45, gave his ill health as one reason for its failure.

With another war beginning in Europe, the controversy that once split the ranks waned at last for the man who had been maligned as a liar and a murderer. The bespectacled and now-graying businessman welcomed this respite to become even more reticent about the matter. Even when asked to comment on rare occasions he seldom elaborated on his wartime flying—and sidestepped questions on Richthofen's death. His family, who knew and loved him as a thoughtful, sensitive father and husband, never heard him discuss his victory score with anyone.

Late in 1939, when Hitler's *Panzers* rolled across Europe and Goering's shrieking *Stukas* dropped death on the beleaguered French and British, Brown's friends were surprised when this normally taciturn man journeyed to Ottawa to lobby vigorously for a position with the Royal Canadian Air Force. He was unsuccessful and on his return to Toronto had little to say about his cool reception from the Department of Defence. On radio and to reporters he made bitter comments on the attitude of the MacKenzie King administration toward the

Canadian war effort and former war pilots in particular. Brown believed his government could find a place in the defense effort for former combat pilots; some type of activity whereby they could enlighten the young airmen of this war on what to avoid and what to expect, and thereby save lives. "The tools are different," he readily acknowledged, "but the rules are the same." A year later he denounced Canada's snail-like progress in pilot training.

In 1943 Brown again astounded his friends when he announced he would run as a provincial Liberal candidate for Woodbine. But his scathing attacks on the King government and his fame as the recognized victor of Richthofen had scant effect on the voters. He was soundly defeated.

Thus passed Roy Brown's final bid for public service. Soon after the election he retired quietly to a farm he had bought near Stouffville. His name appeared in print once again, on March 9, 1944, when Canadian newspapers recorded his death due to a sudden heart attack. He was 50.

Wilfred Reid May remained with 209 Squadron for the duration of the war, and became a Captain and flight leader. When he was awarded the Distinguished Flying Cross his victories totaled 13 official and five unconfirmed. Upon his return to Edmonton the young man became active in Canadian bush flying. Unlike Brown, May spent much time in the cockpit to pioneer the burgeoning commercial aviation in the barren North.

Paradoxically, May regarded his narrow brush with the deadly Red Baron as secondary to the unforgettable hunt for the "Mad Trapper" in 1923. He tracked the killer by air through the frozen Yukon and directed the Mounties to the trapper's lair. As he circled overhead he watched the hot gun battle that followed. When one officer was wounded May landed and rushed him to the hospital at Aklavik, Northwest Territory, in time to save his life from a bullet imbedded near his heart.

In 1929 May became the third winner of the coveted

McKee Trophy awarded for the advancement of Canadian aviation. That year, in midwinter subzero weather, he took part in a mercy flight from Edmonton to Northwest Alberta. In a small open-cockpit Avian biplane he and Vic Horner flew to Fort Vermilion to deliver the serum that checked a diptheria epidemic. During one leg of the flight the temperature dropped to 40 degrees below zero.

In 1936 May retired from the active part of flying and, suffering from the effects of a steel splinter that had been imbedded in his left eye many years earlier, his eye was surgically removed in 1937 and replaced with a glass one.

The man who very nearly became Richthofen's 81st victory became involved only indirectly in the postwar Richthofen issue. Whenever the controversy flared he came several times to the defense of his former flight leader and told his version of the chase for several newspapers. He assured the public that it was Roy Brown, and no other, who plucked Richthofen from his tail on that memorable spring morning in 1918. To other claims he paid scant attention and remained particularly unconvinced of ground action. In 1944 he was present with a group in Edmonton when the Australian polar air explorer Sir George Hubert Wilkins recounted in detail how in traveling toward the front in a car, he had watched the low-flying triplane shot from the air by Australian machine gunners as the famous ace chased a Sopwith Camel. Wilkens, a Captain in 1918, was the official photographer for the Australian Forces. May strode forward to identify himself as the pilot of that Camel—and insisted that it was his flight leader, Roy Brown, who did in the Red Baron.

During World War II, May directed air-observer schools for the British Commonwealth Air Training Plan. George VI bestowed on him the Order of the British Empire. Later he became the western chief of Canadian Pacific Airlines, Limited.

In 1952, the man who unwittingly lured von Richthofen to tree-top level behind the Somme was quietly vacationing in Provo, Utah. There, at 56, while accompanying his son, Danny, on a hiking trip, he died of a sudden heart attack. The remains were returned to Edmonton.

Francis John Williamson Mellersh saw the end of the air fighting with nine victories. He returned to England and in 1919 was granted a permanent commission as a pilot with the Royal Air Force. After a tour of duty in Iraq and the Middle East, Mellersh instructed pilots in England. During World War II he commanded an Air Group, then an Air Force in Ceylon and Southeast Asia. He returned to England as Commandant of the RAF Staff College, then held command positions in the Far East and Malaya and upon his return to the homeland was made Commandant-General of the Royal Air Force Regiment, which he held until his retirement in 1954 at the age of 56. In May of 1955, he and Lieutenant-Commander M. Barry of the Royal Navy were killed in a helicopter crash at Itchenor, England.

William J. Mackenzie, who was born in Tennessee and raised in Port Robinson, Ontario, attained the rank of Captain with 209 Squadron. It was he who souvenired the scrap of fabric from the red triplane at Poulainville and encouraged the 11 participants to autograph it. It is now on display in the National Aviation Museum in Ottawa. In 1925 Mackenzie graduated from the University of Toronto as a civil engineer. He never married. He died in New York City in September of 1959.

Robert Mordaunt Foster, who joined the Royal Flying Corps in 1916, shot down nine enemy machines, scored three possibles and earned the D.F.C. He chose to remain in military service, served in India until 1923, then at the RAF Staff College. After six years in Iraq he was a Group-Captain in the Bomber Command from 1939 to 1941, during Britain's darkest hours. Later in the war he served in the Near East, North Africa and Italy. From

1952 to 1953 he commanded the Second Allied Tactical Air Force. Heavily decorated, knighted, Sir Robert Foster retired in 1954. Today, at 72, he resides in London.

Sammy Taylor, of LeBoutillier's flight, who sent down his first plane over the Amiens-Roye road 20 minutes before the famous dogfight began, continued to serve with 209 Squadron. On the regular noon patrol of May 2nd, the day Richthofen would have been 26, he approached to within 20 yards of an all-white triplane and shot down Leutnant Hans Weiss who now led Richthofen's own Jasta 11. Shortly after the Richthofen affair Taylor wrote in a letter: "It makes me feel proud to think that I took part in the scrap, although I had nothing to do with the bringing down of the Baron. I hope to tell you about the whole scrap some day . . ." The day never came, for on July 7th, Taylor joined Weiss and Richthofen in death.

Redgate gained seven victories and the D.F.C. He was promoted to temporary Captain on May 3rd and given command of Brown's old flight. He also inherited Brown's famed Camel, B7270.

Aird fell exactly three weeks after Taylor shot Weiss to earth. The day after the Armistice, Aird's former flight leader, S. T. Edwards, was fatally injured in a flying accident. Edwards, with D.S.C. and Bar, had five victories.

In commemoration of the combat in which Roy Brown gained his measure of notoriety, the badge that was later officially adopted by 209 Squadron depicts a falling red eagle. The squadron is presently based at Singapore and is equipped with short-range transports, a far cry from its beginning on a muddy field in France. In 1967 a cousin of the war ace—another Baron von Richthofen—now the West German ambassador to the Republic of Singapore, was an honored guest at a dinner celebration held by the pilot officers of the squadron in commemoration of the Red Knight.

The nearest air observer to the May-Richthofen-Brown chase, Oliver C. LeBoutillier, also remained with 209 Squadron for the duration of the war. With 600 flying hours at the Armistice, he was credited with six official victories and a number of probables. Later, in England, in recognition of his services to the Crown, he was awarded a citation by Winston Churchill.

Back in the United States LeBoutillier was so impressed with the thought of "flying an airplane without having to dodge bullets" that he decided to find another flying job. The first paying proposition came in the newly devised "skywriting," and the former war pilot was at home in the cockpit of a converted S.E.5 Scout. He became one of the pioneers and officials of the Skywriting Corporation of America.

Aerial advertising took him to Hollywood where he joined the daredevil stunt pilots. During the late Twenties and the early Thirties he flew for 18 films including *The Eagle and the Hawk* and the air war classic, *Hell's Angels*.

When newspapers resurrected the Richthofen controversy from time to time, LeBoutillier remained quietly in the background. The one-time American volunteer for the 'suicide squadrons' considered himself "something of an outsider" and in respect for the man who was the target of an unpleasant debate, he could not see where his "two cents worth would help the matter."

In 1928 LeBoutillier was selected as Mabel Boll's pilot for her transocean attempt to become the first woman to fly across the Atlantic. Headed for Newfoundland, their Bellanca *Columbia* was swallowed up in bad weather and they turned back, relinquishing the race to Earhart and Stultz.

After motion pictures, LeBoutillier flew in the National Air Races and later, gave Amelia Earhart her first dual instruction in a twin-engine airplane. In 1937 he joined the Civil Aeronautics Administration and during

World War II was Inspector-in-Charge over Colorado and Wyoming. After the war he flew flight checks in B-25s to qualify military pilots for their commercial instrument rating. When he retired from the CAA post in 1948 he settled in Nevada where he founded Associated Researchers Incorporated, a pharmaceutical firm. With 19,000 hours in planes ranging from the Wright Model B to multi-engine bombers, LeBoutillier retired from active flying a year later.

Today the tall, distinguished gentleman who was impatient for action in 1916, still puts in a busy day as company President. He lives quietly with his wife in Las Vegas and many of his long-time business associates are unaware of his role on the day the Red Baron died.

APPENDIX 1

Official Report of the death of Baron v. Richthofen compiled from evidence that was taken at the enquiry immediately following the event.

(The original source of this document is thought to be HQ 5th Australian Division)

From the Australian War Memorial Records.

SECRET

REPORT OF THE DEATH OF CAPTAIN BARON VON RICHTHOFEN AT 62D.J.19.b.5.2. ABOUT 11 a.m. 21st April, 1918.

The following report is based on the evidence of eye witnesses, written down immediately after the events.

Captain Baron von RICHTHOFEN was flying a single seater triplane painted red and reported to be of a new pattern. When first engaged he was pursuing one of our own machines, reported to be a SOPWITH CAMEL, in a WNW. direction, flying towards the wood in J.19.c. HERE, according to a reliable witness, he was fired at by an A.A. gun of the 24th Machine Gun Company. RICHTHOFEN'S machine seemed to move unsteadily for a moment, but still continued in pursuit of the British plane.

He had now left the SOMME Valley and come over the high ground north of CORBIE. Both machines were flying very low, being not more than 150 feet up. They were coming swiftly towards the A.A. Lewis guns of the 53rd Battery, 14th Australian Field Artillery Brigade, situated at 1.24.b.9.5. and 1.24.b.6.5. respectively. RICHTHOFEN was firing into the plane before him but it was difficult for the Lewis gunners to shoot owing to the British plane being directly in the line of fire. They accordingly waited their time till the British plane had passed. RICHTHOFEN'S plane was not more than 100 yards from each when they opened fire. The plane was coming frontally towards them so that they were able to fire directly on to the person of the aviator. Almost immediately the plane turned N.E. being still under fire from the Lewis guns. It was now staggering as though out of control. Further effective bursts were fired; the plane veered to the north, and crashed on the plateau near the brickworks in J.19.b.5.2.

The aviator was already dead. There were bullet wounds in the knees, abdomen and chest. The plane was badly smashed. It was a triplane painted dull red, and was armed with two air cooled machine guns. It had only been assembled in March 1918.

The British plane was undoubtedly saved by the action of the Lewis gunners. It altered its course and circled back over the spot where the enemy plane had crashed.

The papers of the aviator were taken to the Headquarters of the 11th Australian Infantry Brigade. They established his identity as Captain BARON MANNHEIM VON RICHTHOFEN, born 2nd March 1892 in BRESLAU, province of SILESIA, PRUSSIA. The machine was numbered D.R. 425.

Captain Baron von RICHTHOFEN was a great adversary. The German official wireless for the 21st April, 1918, the very day of his death, contains the notice "Captain Baron von RICHTHOFEN, at the head of Pursuit Flight 11, attained his 79th and 80th air victories." It was fitting that he should have fallen, in old Roman fashion, "with all his wounds in front."

After the machine crashed, a troupe of German Planes flew over and circled above the spot until driven off by the A.A. guns. An infantry guard was posted over the body and the plane, but they were relieved of their duty shortly after by the German Artillery, which placed a ring of shells bursting with instantaneous fuzes, around the plane.

The Lewis gunners who brought down the machine were: No. 598 Gunner W.J. Evans and No. 3801 Gunner R. Buie, of the 53 Battery, 14th Australian Field Artillery Brigade, 5th Australian Divisional Artillery.

Telegram sent by General Rawlinson to the 5th Australian Division asking that the 53rd Battery be congratulated for having shot down the red triplane.
From the Australian War Memorial Records

To — 5th AUST. DIV.

- - - - - - - - - - - -

Sender's Number — G.808.
Day of the Month — 21.

Following from General RAWLINSON beings AAA Please convey to the 53rd Battery 5th Div my best thanks and congratulations on having brought down the celebrated German aviator RICHTHOFEN AAA Ends.

From — AUST. CORPS.

- - - - - - - - - - - -

Extract from the war diary of No. 3 Squadron, Australian Flying Corps 21st April, 1918) which describes the fight, salvage of the body and plane, and the burial of Richthofen).

From the Australian War Memorial Records

Poulainville 21/4/18
  Another enemy machine was accounted for on this day by Captain E.J. JONES, Pilot, and Lieut. A.L.D. TAYLOR, Observer. This Pilot and Observer were engaged on an early morning Artillery Patrol when they encountered a formation of six single-seater enemy aircraft at 4000 feet patrolling North and South over ALBERT. Two of these scouts separated from the formation and Captain JONES decided to engage them. Giving his Observer an opportunity of getting in several good bursts the Pilot outmanoeuvred one of the E.A. which went down hopelessly out of control. On hitting the ground it burst into flames. The other E.A. followed the first one down to the ground and then withdrew East. The same day saw the celebrated Baron von RICHTHOFEN brought down near SAILLY-LE-SEC. This celebrated German air-

man was at the time flying a FOKKER triplane painted all red which had earned for him the name of "The Red Falcon". He invariably flew in what was known as "the Richthofen Circus," a formation of German airmen renowned for the number of air victories. Two machines of this Squadron encountered the Circus about the same time as the Baron was shot down although they were not concerned in the actual shooting down of the celebrated enemy. Lieuts. GARRETT and BARROW, and Lieuts. SIMPSON and BANKS were proceeding to the line for the purpose of photographing the Corps front when they saw the enemy triplanes approaching. Lieuts. Simpson and Banks were the first to be attacked by four of the triplanes. The Observer fired 100 rounds at point blank range at the E.A., one of which was seen to separate and go down. The others withdrew and attacked Lieuts. Garrett and Barrow. The Observer in this case got in 120 rounds Lewis, in bursts and another of the E.A. was seen to go down out of control. Both pilots then proceeded over the line and carried out their task of photographing the whole Corps front. On returning from the line, Lieuts. Simpson and Banks were again attacked by a Big formation of Albatross scouts. By skilful manoeuvring, the Pilot enabled his Observer to make a running fight and finally succeeded in evading the E.A. and returning safely to the aerodrome with the results of his photographic reconnaissance.

In the meantime reports had come from the Infantry that one of the triplanes shot down in the general combat which had ensued between our scouts and the enemy circus after they had been driven off by the RE8's of this Squadron, was that of Baron von RICHTHOFEN. The Lewis gunners of the 5th Divisional Artillery, A.I.F. claimed the honor of firing the shot which brought him down, but after the matter had been carefully investigated, the award was made to Captain BROWN, of No. 209 Squadron, R.A.F.

The recovery of the body of the German airman and the remains of his machine was carried out by a party of mechanics of this Squadron under Lieut. W.J. WARNEFORD, Equipment Officer. The point at which the machine had crashed was under observation of the enemy lines and he consistently shelled the position by day.

Despite this 1/AM Collins, C.C., crept out to the machine and succeeded in moving Baron von RICHTHOFEN'S body. The remnants of the machine were collected after dark and, with the body, brought back to this Squadron's aerodrome at POULAINVILLE. The following afternoon the remains were accorded burial with full military honours, a firing party being supplied by the mechanics of this Squadron. The coffin which was made in the Squadron workshops was inscribed in English and German as follows:—

CAVALRY CAPTAIN
MANNFRED BARON VON RICHTHOFEN,
Age 22 years,   killed in action,
aerial combat, near SAILLY LE SEC,
SOMME, FRANCE, 21st April, 1918.

Statement made by Sergeant Cedric B. Popkin, Nr. 424, of the 24th Australian Machine Gun Company, 4 April, 1918.

From the Australian War Memorial Records.

I was the Sergeant in charge of a Machine Gun Detachment at J-19 d.

About 10:45 a.m. on the 21st April, 1918, one of our Aeroplanes was being engaged by a German Aeroplane and was being driven down. The Planes came from an Easterly direction and when within the range of my gun were flying very low, just above the tree tops. I immediately got my gun into action and waited for our own plane to pass me, as the planes were close together, and there was a risk of hitting both. As soon as this risk was over, I opened fire on the German Plane. The Plane at once gave up the chase, our own escaped, and the German Plane banked, turned round and came back towards my gun. As it came towards me, I opened fire a second time and observed at once that my fire took effect. The machine swerved, attempted to bank and make for the ground and immediately crashed. The distance from the spot where the Plane crashed and my gun was about 600 yards. I handed my gun over to the No. 1 gunner and proceeded to where the Plane fell. The pilot (whom I was subsequently told was Captain Baron Von Richthoven) I saw had at least three machine gun bullets through his body, one in his ribs at the side, and a couple through his chest, and I consider he died as a result of these wounds from the time he was hit till he hit the ground, a matter of 2 or 3 seconds. He bled freely after he hit the ground from the wounds in his chest.

The British Plane which was being chased, did not fire at

the German Plane when they were both low down and within range of any gun.

I am quite satisfied that the Plane was brought down as the result of the fire from my gun.

C.B. Popkin, Sgt.

4 April 1918

Statement made by Lieutenant George M. Travers, 52nd Battalion.

From the Australian War Memorial Records

J.O. 52nd Battalion A.I.F.   April 23, 1918   No. 8

Herewith report on Captain Von RICHTHOFEN's plane which was brought down on the 21st April 1918, at about 11:45 a.m. and landed at (Map Reference, Sheet 62.D.) J.19.b.3.4. and was hit directly over J.19.c.8.5.

On the 21st April I was instructed to report to 11th Brigade Headquarters as liaison Officer, situated at J.19.c.8.5. At about 11:45 a.m. I was lying on the ground accompanied by my runner, about 50 yards from Brigade Headquarters, setting my map and having a general look round with my glasses. I heard a plane "or planes" coming at a tremendous pace from the direction of 26 Central, a Vickers gun was firing from a spot situated at J.25.a.8.9. The first plane which came into view was one of our own and less than 20 paces behind was an enemy plane painted "RED." The red plane was overhauling our plane fast and both were flying so low that they almost crashed into the trees at top of hill. Almost directly over the spot where I was laying, the enemy plane swerved to the right so suddenly that it seemed almost to turn over. Our plane went straight on from that moment. The enemy plane was quite out of control and did a wild circle and dashed toward J.19.b.3.4. where it crashed. I went over with other Officers and had a look at the plane and also the driver who was dead, a machine gun bullet had passed from the left side of his face and near bottom of jaw and came out just behind his right eye. His description would be:

> Height about 6 feet.
> Age 26 or 28 years.
> Eyes very light blue.
> Closely cropped fair hair.
> Clear complexion, clean shaven.

The Vickers gun mentioned was the only gun firing at the time the driver first lost control of his machine.

I made enquiries and found the gun was handled by No. 424 Sgt. POPKIN CEDRIC BASSETT, 24th Aust. M.G. Company.

Date 23-4-1918   Geo. M. Travers Lieut.
Time 2:10 p.m.   52nd Battalion A.I.F.

HQrs. 13th A.I. Bde.

Above report is submitted for your information.

Statement made by Lieutenant Donald L. Fraser, Brigade Intelligence Officer, 11th Australian Infantry Brigade.

From the Australian War Memorial Records
11TH AUSTRALIAN INFANTRY BRIGADE.
Reference Sheet 62D.N.E. 1/20,000.

Description of the shooting down of Cavalry Captain Baron Von RICHTHOFEN, the famous German Aviator at 10:45 a.m. on 21st April, 1918.

At about 10:45 a.m. 21st instant I was in the wood at J.19.c.75.65. and saw two aeroplanes approaching flying Westward directly towards the wood, at a height of about 400 feet above level of River SOMME over which they were flying.

I had noticed that the leading Machine had British markings just as it reached edge of wood and immediately afterwards heard a strong burst of M.G. fire coming from direction of South East corner of the wood.

Immediately afterwards the red painted enemy machine appeared overhead flying very low and unsteadily and probably not more than 200 feet from the ground.

I lost sight of the British machine and my attention was concentrated on the enemy plane which was flying as if not under complete control, being wobbly and irregular in flight, it swerved North, then Eastwards rocking a great deal and suddenly dived out of my sight, the engine still running full open.

I ran out of the wood and over to where it had fallen about 200 yards away along side BRAY-CORBIE Road in J.19.b.-40.30. About six men reached the wrecked plane before me.

I immediately undid the airman's safety belt and got assistance to pull him from the wreckage but he was quite dead, and was considerably cut about the face and apparently shot through the chest and body.

As a large number of men were collecting I requested Captain Adams of 44th Battalion A.I.F. to place a guard over the plane to prevent looting and to disperse the crowd, as the spot was open to the enemy observation and I feared we would be shelled.

A guard was duly placed over the machine and the crowd dispersed.

I searched the dead airman taking his papers and personal effects which consisted of a few papers, a silver watch, gold chain with a medallion attached, and a pair of fur lined gloves. I gave them to Captain Hilliary of 11th Brigade Staff who took them down to our German speaker, Corporal Peters, who on investigation gave the identification of the famous German airman Baron von Richthofen.

I at once reported this to General Cannon and Third Australian Division promptly.

On General Cannan's direction I went out to get particulars of the machine gunners who had brought the plane down, and found Sergeant Popkin, of 24th Aust. M.G. Company at his antiaircraft M.G. at 25.b.3.7. (approx) (SOMME Valley)

At this time I was not aware that any other M.G. had been firing at this plane. I congratulated Sergeant Popkin on his successful shoot, but afterwards found out that two A.A. Lewis Guns belonging to the 53rd Battery A.F.A. had also fired at this plane when it was directly over my head, but the noise of engine prevented my hearing the shooting.

The 53rd Battery Lewis Gunners probably assisted in sealing the fate of this airman, as he apparently flew right into their line of fire. However, I am strongly of opinion that he was first hit by Sergeant Popkins' shooting as he was unsteady from the moment of that first burst of fire.

The airman's body was afterwards taken in charge by Officers of the A.F.C. and the wrecked plane salvaged by them after dark.

D.L. Fraser
Brigade Intelligence Officer
11th Australian Infantry Brigade A.I.F.

BONNAY
21st April, 1918.
Map Reference.   Sheet 62D.N.E. 1/20,000.

A.J.M.

Report of the Salvage of Enemy aircraft. Aeroplane salved at 62D, J.19b.4.4 on 21-22 April, 1918.

Report by Lieutenant Warneford, Equipment Officer of Number 3 Squadron, Australian Flying Corps, on the salvage of the aircraft.

From the Australian War Memorial Records

I went to the pin point given, arriving at 2 p.m. The position of the machine was being shelled by H.E. I went up to the areoplane and saw that the Pilot was still among the wreckage. A rope was fastened round his body (he was afterwards identified as Baron Von Richthofen). We drew the body across the road and down a trench and brought it to the aerodrome. Later I returned and brought in the machine.

Description—FOKKER TRIPLANE No. 2009 (painted all red) fitted with two machine guns, Spandau type, 1917 model, air cooled, Nos. 1795 and 650.
RUDDER—balanced type, no fin
ELEVATORS—balanced
WINGS—Three in number. Built up on one spar which is made of 3-ply, box principle. Leading edge also of 3-ply.
FUSELAGE—Steel tubing, square built, braced with piano wire.
INSTRUMENTS—No instruments were on the plane when taken over by Flying Corps.
OIL AND PETROL—Both tanks had burst. A sample of the oil was taken from the crank case and forwarded to the 15th Wing, E.O.

The machine was knocked about by shell splinters, all the planes were salved, the undercarriage was complete but much knocked about by the crash. The propeller could not be found.

ENGINE—Oberursel type, bore 112 stroke 170. The following markings were on the crank case:
No. 2478 A/1567 Model Oberursel bei Frankfurt A/M.
Bosch magneto.

N.J. Warneford

"B" Form.

MESSAGES AND SIGNALS.

Army Form C.2128
(In code of 1218)

No.

Prefix.			Received	Sent
Office of Origin and Service Instructions.	Words		At	At 12
B98F	24	From	To
		By	

TO	Genl GLASGOW

Sender's Number.	Day of Month.	In reply to Number.	AAA
P.M.229	21		

One of your AA Machine
guns brought down
in J 19 B pilot Capt.
VON RICHTHOFEN aaa
Congratulations.

From	
Place	

Message reads: "One of your AA machine
guns brought down in J. 19 B pilot Capt.
VON RICHTHOFEN. Our congratulations."

Lieutenant, Equipment Officer, 3rd Squardon, Aust. Flying Corps

O. C. 15th Wing R.A.F.

Forwarded

David Blake Maj.
24-4-18   O. C. 3rd Squadron A.F.C.

Photocopy of message to General Glasgow from the 11th Brigade informing him of the shooting down of Richthofen "by one of your A.A. machine guns."

From the Australian War Memorial Records

Particulars of the Richthofen relics held by the Australian War Memorial (also indicates those relics not on display.)

RICHTHOFEN RELICS ON DISPLAY IN AUSTRALIAN WAR MEMORIAL

Main title card to exhibit reads:

"Cavalry Captain Baron Manfred von Richthofen, the German ace, was credited with having shot down no fewer than 80 Allied planes before finally falling a victim to an Australian bullet. His well-known "Circus" of which Hermann Goering was a member, flew Albatross Scouts painted a vivid red. There is still a good deal of controversy as to who killed Richthofen and, though the honour was rather hastily given to the Royal Air Force, there is strong evidence that he was shot down by an Australian machine-gunner. About 11 o'clock on the morning of 21st April, 1918, the troops on Somme-Ancre peninsula heard the distant chatter of machine-guns coming from two fleets of British and German planes which had been fighting high above the enemy lines, when a German plane was seen to be diving after a Sopwith Camel. These two, detached from the dog-fight, came so low that they were temporarily hidden by hills. Presently the sound of approaching engines was heard, and low over the west near Vaux-sur-Somme came the British machine closely pursued by a red German triplane. The German was pressing the British plane desperately close and firing short bursts from his machine-gun. The troops on the ground immediately opened fire on the triplane with rifles, and Lewis and Vickers guns; after going for about a mile the German abandoned the chase and suddenly turned eastwards, and, quickly rising several hundred feet swerved northwards and crashed. The pilot who was killed immediately was later identified as Captain von Richthofen. The compass exhibited here (presented by Warrant Officer H.J. Tesch, 41st Battalion) was picked up about 100 yards from where the machine hit the ground. The joy-stick and boot were presented by Lieutenant W.J. Warneford, Equipment Officer, No. 3 Sqn. A.F.C., by whom the plane was salvaged. Richthofen was buried by the Australian Squadron with full military honours at Bertangles"

Individual titles from items on display
1. The joy-stick from Richthofen's machine.
2. The foresight and backsight of the Lewis gun that was brought to bear upon Richthofen's machine by Gunner Robert Buie of the 53rd Battery of Australian Field Artillery, when the German ace was shot down in the Australian lines on 21st April, 1918, (Note: The foresight is inscribed:
   "5th Australian Division Artillery. Foresight and backsight of Lewis gun manned by Gunner Robert Buie of 53rd Battery AFA., which (?) shot down Captain Baron von Richthofen on April 21st, 1918. Presented to Major General Sir J. Talbot Hobbs. . . . . (unreadable) by members of 53rd Bty 14th Australian Field Artillery Brigade, 21st April, 1918")
3. Richthofen's compass.
4. Richthofen's Flying Boot. This flying boot was worn by the German ace when he was killed by machine-gun fire, and bears evidence of the conflict.
Relics not on display:
1. Piece of fabric (linen) from the fuselage of the aeroplane flown by Capt. Richthofen who was brought down at 11.15 am on 21st April, 1918, near Corbie.
   (Donor: Brig. Gen. Grimwade)
2. Portion of propeller from the aeroplane flown by Capt. Richthofen.

APPENDIX 2

The Victory Log
of
Baron Manfred Von Richthofen

From September 1915 to April 1918

As compiled from various sources including personal accounts of the victims and the Rittmeister's own official combat reports as submitted for victory claims.

Date	Aircraft Model and Serial	Victory Number and Location	Squadron Number	Personnel	Notes
Sept. 1915	Farman S.11	Champagne	French (unknown)	Unknown	Unofficial (1)
April 25, 1916	Nieuport II single seater	Fleury, Douaumont	French (unknown)	Unknown	Unofficial (2)
Sept. 17, 1916	English F.E.2b 2 seater 7081	1. Villiers-Plouich	Nr. 11 RFC	2/Lt L.B.F. Morris, Lt. T. Rees	(3)
Sept. 23, 1916	Martinsyde G.100 single seater	2. Beugny	Nr. 27 RFC	Sgt. H. Bellerby	Fate of pilot unknown
Sept. 30, 1916	F.E.2b 2 seater 6973	3. Fremicourt	Nr. 11 RFC	Lt. E.C. Lansdale, Sgt. Clarkson	Both occupants killed
October 7, 1916	B.E.12 6618 single seater	4. Equancourt	Nr. 21 RFC	2/Lt W.C. Fenwick	Killed
October 10, 1916	B.E. 12 single seater	5. Ypres	Nr. 24 RFC	S. Cookerell	No accurate records
October 16, 1916	B.E. 12 6580 single seater	6. Ypres	Nr. 19 RFC	Lt. C.R. Tidsdale	Killed
October 25, 1916	B.E. 12 6629 single seater	Bapaume	Nr. 21 RFC	2/Lt A.J. Fisher	(4)

Date	Aircraft Model and Serial	Victory Number and Location	Squadron Number	Personnel	Notes
November 3, 1916	F.E.2b 7010 2 seater	7. Loupart Wood	Nr. 18 RFC	Sgt. G.C. Baldwin, 2/Lt C. A. Bentham Bentley	Both killed
November 9, 1916	B.E.2c 2506 2 seater	8. Beugny	Nr. 12 RFC	2/Lt J.G. Cameron, obs; Lt G.F. Knight, pilot.	(5)
November 20, 1916	B.E. 12 single seater	9. Gueudecourt	Unknown RFC	Unidentified pilot	(6)
November 20, 1916	F.E. 2b 4848 2 seater	10. Grandecourt	Nr. 18 RFC	Lt G. Doughty, 2/Lt G. Hall	(7)
November 23, 1916	D.H.2 5964 single seater	11. Baupaume–Albert	Nr. 24 RFC	Major L.G. Hawker, V.C. D.S.O.	Killed
December 11, 1916	D.H. 2 5986 single seater	12. Mecatel	Nr. 24 RFC	Lt P.B.G. Hunt	Wounded made P.O.W.
December 20, 1916	D.H. 2 7927 single seater	13. Moncy-le-Preux	Nr. 29 RFC	Lt A.G. Knight	Killed
December 20, 1916	F.E. 2b A5446 2 seater	14. Noreuil	Nr. 18 RFC	Lt A.G. D'Arcy, Sub-Lt. R.C. Whiteside	Both killed

Date	Aircraft Model and Serial	Victory Number and Location	Squadron Number	Personnel	Notes (8)
December 27, 1916	F.E. 2b 6997 2 seater	15. Ficheux	Nr. 11 RFC	Unknown	
January 4, 1917	Sopwith Pup N5193 single seater	16. Metz-en-Couture	Nr. 8 RNAS	Flt/Lt A.S. Todd	Killed
January 23, 1917	F.E.8 6388 single seater	17. Lens	Nr. 40 RFC	2/Lt J. Hay	Killed
January 24, 1917	F.E.2b 6937 single seater	18. Vitry	Nr. 25 RFC	Capt. O. Greig, pilot, Lt J. E. MacLenan, obs.	Both wounded, made P.O.W.
February 1, 1917	B.E. 2e 6742 2 seater	19. Southwest of Thelus	Nr. 16 RFC	Lt P.W. Murray, pilot, Lt T. D. McRae, obs.	Both died of wounds
February 14, 1917	B.E.2d 6231 2 seater	20. West of Loos	Nr. 25 RFC	Lt C.D. Bennet, pilot; 2/Lt H.A. Croft, obs.	Bennet wounded, made P.O.W.; Croft killed
February 14, 1917	F.E. 2 seater	21. Southwest of Mazingarbe	Nr. 20 RFC	Capt. H.E. Hartney, pilot; Lt W.T. Jourden, obs.	Both injured and hospitalized

Date	Aircraft Model and Serial	Victory Number and Location	Squadron Number	Personnel	Notes
March 4, 1917	Sopwith 1½ Strutter A/1108 2 seater	22. Acheville	Nr. 43 RFC	Lt H.J. Green, pilot; Lt W. Reid, obs.	Both killed
March 4, 1917	B.E. 2d 6252 2 seater	23. North of Loos	Nr. 8 RFC	F/Sgt R.J. Moody, pilot; Lt E.E. Horn, obs.	Both killed
March 6, 1917	B.E. 2c 2 seater	24. Area of Souchez	Nr. 16 RFC	C.M.G. Libby; G.J.A. Brichta	(7)
March 9, 1917	D.H. 2 A2571 single seater	25. Between Roclincourt and Bailleul	Nr. 29 RFC	Lt A.W. Pearson, M.C.	Killed
March 11, 1917	B.E. 2d 6232 2 seater	26. South of LaFolie near Vimy	Nr. 2 RFC	2/Lt J. Smith, pilot; Lt E. Byrne, obs.	Both killed
March 17, 1917	F.E. 2b A5439 2 seater	27. Oppy	Nr. 25 RFC	Lt A.E. Boultbee, pilot; Air Mec. F. King	Both killed
March 17, 1917	B.E. 2c 2814 2 seater	28. West of Vimy	Nr. 16 RFC	2/Lt G.M. Watt, pilot; Sgt. F.A. Howlett, obs.	Both killed

Date	Aircraft Model and Serial	Victory Number and Location	Squadron Number	Personnel	Notes
March 21, 1917	B.E. 2c A3154 2 seater	29. North of La Neuville	Nr. 6 RFC	Sgt. S.H. Quicke, pilot; 2/Lt W.J. Lidsey, obs.	Both killed
March 24, 1917	Spad S7 A6706 single seater	30. Givenchy	Nr. 19 RFC	Lt R. P. Baker	Wounded, made P.O.W.
March 25, 1917	Nieuport 17 A6689 single seater	31. Tilloy	Nr. 29 RFC	2/Lt C.G. Gilbert	Pilot made P.O.W.
April 2, 1917	B.E. 2d 5841 2 seater	32. Farbus	Nr. 13 RFC	Lt J.C. Powell, pilot; A/M Bonnet, obs.	Both killed
April 2, 1917	Sopwith 1½ Strutter A2401 2 seater	33. Givenchy	Nr. 43 RFC	2/Lt P. Warren, pilot; Sgt. R. Dunn, obs.	Warren made P.O.W.; Dunn killed
April 3, 1917	F.E. 2d A6382 2 seater	34. Between Lens and Lievin	Nr. 25 RFC	2/Lt D.P. McDonald, pilot; 2/Lt J.I.M. O'Bierne, obs.	McDonald wounded, made P.O.W.; O'Bierne killed

Date	Aircraft Model and Serial	Victory Number and Location	Squadron Number	Personnel	
April 5, 1917	Bristol F2A A-3340 2 seater	35. Lembras	Nr. 48 RFC	Lt A.M. Leckler, pilot; Lt H.D.K. George, obs.	Leckler wounded, made P.O.W.; George died of wounds
April 5, 1917	Bristol F2A A-3343 2 seater	36. Quincy	Nr. 48 RFC	Lt A.T. Adams, pilot; Lt D.J. Stewart, obs.	Adams wounded, both made P.O.W.
April 7, 1917	Nieuport 17 A6645 single seater	37. Mercatel	Nr. 60 RFC	2/Lt G.O. Smart	Killed
April 8, 1917	Sopwith 1½ Strutter 2 seater	38. Farbus	Nr. 43 RFC	Lt J.S. Heagerty, pilot; Lt L.H. Cantle, obs	Heagerty wounded, made P.O.W.; Cantle killed
April 8, 1917	B.E. 2e A2815 2 seater	39. Vimy	Nr. 16 RFC	2/Lt K.I. Mackenzie, pilot; 2/Lt E. Everingham, obs.	Both killed

Date	Aircraft Model and Serial	Victory Number and Location	Squadron Number	Personnel	Notes
April 11, 1917	B.E. 2c 2501 2 seater	40. Willerval	Nr. 13 RFC	Lt E.C.E. Derwin, pilot; Gunner H. Pierson, obs.	(9)
April 13, 1917	R.E.8 A3190 2 seater	41. Between Virty and Brebieres	Nr. 59 RFC	Capt. J. Stuart, pilot; Lt M.H. Wood, obs.	Both killed
April 13, 1917	F.E. 2b	42. Between Monchy and Feuchy	Nr. 25 RFC	Sgt. J. Cunliffe, 2A/M W.J. Bolton	
April 13, 1917	F.E. 2b 4997	43. Henin-Lietard	Nr. 25 RFC	2/Lt A.H. Bates, pilot; Sgt. W.A. Barnes, obs.	Both killed
April 14, 1917	Nieuport 17 A 6796 single seater	44. South of Bois Bernard	Nr. 60 RFC	Lt. W.O. Russell	Pilot made P.O.W.
April 16, 1917	B.E.2c 2 seater	45. Between Bailleul and Cavrelle	Nr. 4 RFC	Lt W. Green, pilot; Lt C.E. Wilson, obs.	(10)
April 22, 1917	F.E. 2b 7029 2 seater	46. Laignicourt	Nr. 11 RFC	Lt W.F. Fletcher, pilot; Lt W. Franklin, obs.	(11)

Date	Aircraft Model and Serial	Victory Number and Location	Squadron Number	Personnel	Notes
April 23, 1917	B.E. 2e A3168 2 seater	47. Mericourt	Nr. 4 RFC	2/Lt E.A. Welch, pilot; Sgt. A. Tollervy, obs.	Both killed
April 28, 1917	B.E. 2e 7221 2 seater	48. East of Pelves	Unknown RFC	Lt R.W. Follit, pilot; 2/Lt F.J. Kirkman, obs.	Follit killed, Kirkham wounded, made P.O.W.
April 29, 1917	Spad S.7 B1573 single seater	49. Lecluse	Nr. 19 RFC	Lt. R. Applin	Killed
April 29, 1917	F.E. 2b 4898 2 seater	50. Southwest of Inchy, near Pariville	Nr. 18 RFC	Sgt Stead, pilot; Cpl A. Beebe, obs.	Both killed
April 29, 1917	B.E. 2d 2 seater	51. Roeux	Nr. 12 RFC	Unknown	D.E. Davis; G.H. Rathbone
April 29, 1917	Nieuport 17 A6745 single seater	52. Between Billy-Montigny and Sellaumines	Nr. 40 RFC	Capt. F.L. Barwell	Killed
June 18, 1917	R.E.8 2 seater	53. Strugwe	Nr. 53 RFC	Lt R.W. Ellis, pilot; Lt H.C. Barlow, obs.	Both killed

Date	Aircraft Model and Serial	Victory Number and Location	Squadron Number	Personnel	Notes
June 23, 1917	Spad S.7	54. North of Ypres	Unknown	Unknown	(11)
June 26, 1917	R.E. 8 2 seater	55. Between Keibergmelen and Lichtensteinlager	Unknown	Unknown	(12)
June 25, 1917	R.E. 8 2 seater	56. Le Bizet	Unknown RFC	Lt L.S. Bowman, pilot; 2/Lt J.E. Power-Clutterbuck, obs.	Both killed
July 2, 1917	R.E. 8 A3538 2 seater	57. Deulemont	Nr. 53 RFC	Sgt H.A. Whatley, pilot; 2/Lt F.J. Pasco, obs.	Both killed
August 16, 1917	Nieuport 17 single seater	58. Houthulster	Unknown	Unknown	
August 26, 1917	Spad S.7 B3492 single seater	59. Between Poelcapelle and Langemarck	Nr. 29 RFC	2/Lt C.P. Williams	Killed
September 2, 1917	R.E. 8 2 seater	60. Zonnebeke	Nr. 6 RFC	2/Lt J.B. Madge, pilot; 2/Lt W. Kember, obs.	Madge wounded, made P.O.W.; Kember killed

Date	Aircraft Model and Serial	Victory Number and Location	Squadron Number	Personnel	Notes
September 3, 1917	Sopwith Pup B1795 single seater	61. South of Bousecque	Nr. 46 RFC	Lt A.F. Bird	Made P.O.W.
November 23, 1917	D.H.5 A9299 single seater	62. Boulon Wood	Nr. 64 RFC	Lt J.A.V. Boddy	(13)
November 30, 1917	S.E.5A B40 single seater	63. Moevres	Nr. 56 RFC	Capt. P.T. Townsend	Killed
March 12, 1918	Bristol F2B B1251 2 seater	64. North of Nauroy	Nr. 62 RFC	Lt C.F. Clutterbuck, pilot; Lt H.J. Sparks, obs.	Sparks wounded, both made P.O.W.
March 13, 1918	Sopwith Camel B5590 single seater	65. Between Gonnelieu and Banteaux	Nr. 73 RFC	2/Lt J.M.L. Millett	Killed
March 18, 1918	Sopwith Camel B5243 single seater	66. Audigny	Nr. 54 RFC	Lt W.G. Ivamy	Made P.O.W.
March 24, 1918	S.E.5A C5389 single seater	67. Combles	Nr. 56 RFC	2/Lt W. Porter	Killed
March 25, 1918	Sopwith Camel C1582 single seater	68. Contalmaison	Nr. 3 RFC	2/Lt D. Cameron	Killed

Date	Aircraft Model and Serial	Victory Number and Location	Squadron Number	Personnel	Notes
March 26, 1918	Sopwith Camel single seater	69. South of Contalmaison	Nr. 54 RFC	2/Lt W. Knox	Pilot killed (14)
March 26, 1918	R.E.8 B742 2 seater	70. Northeast of Albert	Nr. 15 RFC	2/Lt V.J. Reading, pilot; 2/Lt M. Legget, obs.	Both killed
March 27, 1918	Sopwith Camel C8234 single seater	71. Northeast of Aveluy	Nr. 70 RFC	Lt H.W. Ransom	Killed
March 27, 1918	Bristol F2B B1156 2 seater	72. Foucaucourt	Nr. 20 RFC	Capt. K.R. Kirkham, pilot; Capt. J.H. Hedley, obs.	Both made P.O.W.
March 27, 1918	Bristol F2B B1332 2 seater	73. Chuignolles	Nr. 11 RFC	Capt. H.R. Child; Lt. A. Reeve	Both killed
March 28, 1918	A.W.F.K.8 C8444 2 seater	74. Mericourt	Nr. 82 RFC	2/Lt J.B. Taylor, pilot; 2/Lt E. Betley, obs.	Both killed
April 2, 1918	R.E.8 A3868 2 seater	75. Northeast of Moreuil	Nr. 52 RAF	2/Lt E.D. Jones, pilot; 2/Lt R.F. Newton, obs.	Both killed

Date	Aircraft Model and Serial	Victory Number and Location	Squadron Number	Personnel	Notes
April 6, 1918	Sopwith Camel D6491 single seater	76. Northeast of Villiers-Brettoneaux	Nr. 46 RAF	Capt. S.P. Smith	Killed
April 7, 1918	S.E.5A C1083 single seater	77. Hangard	Nr. 24 RAF	P.J. Nolan	Killed
April 7, 1918	Spad S.7 single seater	78. North of Villiers-Brettoneaux	Possibly Nr. 23 RAF	Unknown	
April 20, 1918	Sopwith Camel D6439 single seater	79. Southwest of Bois-de-Hamel	Nr. 3 RAF	Major R. Raymond-Barker, M.C.	Killed
April 20, 1918	Sopwith Camel B7393 single seater	Northeast of Villiers-Brettoneaux	Nr. 3 RAF	2/Lt D.G. Lewis	Pilot injured, made P.O.W.

A tally of von Richthofen's official victory log gives the following breakdown concerning the fates of the personnel who fell under his guns:

Known to have been killed or died of wounds   75
Captured, made prisoners of war   25
Escaped behind British lines   8
Fate unknown due to lost or unavailable records   16

                 Total   124

NOTES

(1) Plane landed three miles behind the lines and no confirmation could be obtained. Shot down by Richthofen while acting as observer.

(2) No confirmation as plane fell behind lines. First plane shot down by Richthofen as a pilot, using crude machine gun mounting on upper wing of two-seater.

(3) Both occupants died of wounds. Richthofen landed at crash site to confirm this.

(4) Pilot seriously wounded. This claim was contested by a pilot from another Jasta and Richthofen did not receive official confirmation although there is little doubt he was the actual victor.

(5) Observer died of wounds; pilot made prisoner of war.

(6) Some reports say: B.E.2c, Nr. 16 Squadron, RFC; T.H. Clark and J.E. Lees, occupants.

(7) Some reports read: Nr. 22 Squadron, RFC.

(8) Certain data indicates occupants H.J.H. Dicksee and Quested.

(9) Both wounded and escaped capture when found by advancing British troops.

(10) Green wounded, escaped behind British lines; Wilson killed.

(11) Both wounded and escaped behind British lines. Aircraft salvaged by RFC crew.

(12) Possibly a machine from a Belgian squadron. No Allied report available but possibly belonged to Nr. 23 Squadron, RFC.

(13) Pilot wounded, escaped behind British lines.

(14) Certain data indicates pilot was A.A. Lindsay.

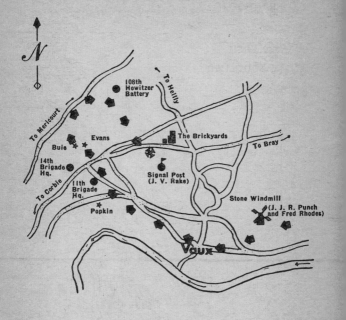

The area of the site showing the path of von Richthofen's Fokker triplane during the final minute of flight.

Ⓐ	RICHTHOFEN
Ⓑ	MAY
Ⓒ	MELLERSH
Ⓓ	LE BOUTILLIER
Ⓔ	BROWN

Heilly

Ancre

Bonnay

la Neuville

Ancre

**51st
Battalion**

CORBIE

Somme

Hamelet

Fouilloy

**5th Australian
Division**

Aubigny

The low-level chase of Lieutenant Wilfred May by Rittmeister von Richthofen as they sped along the floor of
the Somme Valley. Also shown are the flight paths of

A — Gunner Robert Buie
B — Gunner W. J. Evans
C — Sergeant C. B. Popkin
D — 108th Howitzer Battery
E — 11th Brigade Headquarters
F — 14th Brigade Headquarters
G — Stone Windmill
H — Brickyards
I — Richthofen's Crash Site
▲▲▲ Front Lines 21 April 1918

Mericourt

3rd Australian Division

52nd Battalion

Somme

SAILLY le Sec

VAUX s.

Vaire s. Corbie

SAILLY-Laurette

German Army

Hamel

2000   1000   0 yards

Captain Brown, Captain Le Boutillier and Lieutenant Mellersh.

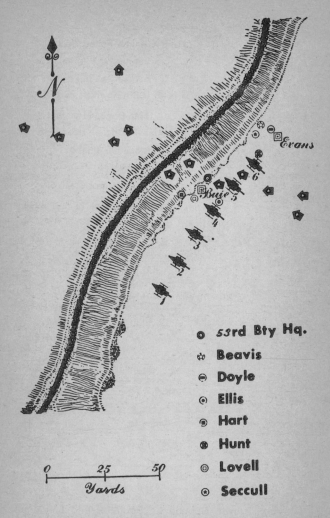

Evans

Buie 5

6

4

3

2

1

◉	**53rd Bty Hq.**
⊛	**Beavis**
⊖	**Doyle**
⊙	**Ellis**
◉	**Hart**
✳	**Hunt**
◙	**Lovell**
⊛	**Seccull**

N

0   25   50

Yards

The flight paths of von Richthofen and Lieutenant May over the 53rd Battery, Australian Field Artillery.

Index

About the Author

DALE M. TITLER was like many air-minded youngsters of the 1930's. He read aviation books, strung model airplanes from his bedroom ceiling, and saw every flying picture that came to his home town of Altoona, Pennsylvania. At 13 he became interested in the combat experiences of Manfred von Richthofen and especially with the intrigue that surrounded the ace's death.

The author learned to fly in the early 1940's at age 16 and within two years was a licensed flight instructor. A part of the fast-waning helmet-and-goggles era, he flew open-cockpit biplanes, served in the Army Air Corps during World War Two, later graduated from the Pittsburg Institute of Aeronautics, taught aircraft engineering to Air Force officer pilot and aviation cadet trainees, and instructed in aircraft crash firefighting and rescue.

A free-lance writer since 1951, Dale Titler's aviation and general interest articles have appeared in numerous national periodicals. His first book, *Wings of Mystery,* was published in 1966.

Mr. Titler resides with his wife and three children in Gulfport, Mississippi.

THE
TWELVE-YEAR
REICH

A Social History of Nazi Germany

Richard Grunberger

How Germans lived, worked, relaxed, and re-garded themselves and others in Hitler's Germany. One of the most devastating portraits ever drawn of a human society.

"A powerful and important study."
—Publishers Weekly

"Grunberger's book is invaluable for every student of the Nazi era."

—The New York Times Book Review

"A fascinating companion piece to George Orwell's fictional 1984."

—Book Week

$1.95

To order by mail send price of book plus 10¢ for handling to Dept. CS, Ballantine Books, 36 West 20th Street, New York, N.Y. 10003.

Japan's Longest Day

Compiled by

the Pacific War Research Society

Japan's struggle to bring herself to face surrender
—or annihilation. The military fanatics' last-ditch
effort to stop the forces for peace. Based on direct
interviews with participants, cross-checked with
official sources.

The book that became an immediate, although controversial, best seller in Japan.

$1.65

For a complete list of Ballantine titles or to
order by mail, write to: Dept. CS, Ballantine
Books, 36 West 20th St., New York, N.Y. 10003